THE WONDERMENT OF

THE WONDERMENT OF

GARY L. HOLLEN

Copyright © 2021 by Gary L. Hollen

All rights reserved. No part of this publication may be reproduced, distributed, or transmitted in any form or by any means, including photocopying, recording, or other electronic or mechanical methods, without the prior written permission of the copyright owner and the publisher, except in the case of brief quotations embodied in critical reviews and certain other noncommercial uses permitted by copyright law. For permission requests, write to the publisher, addressed "Attention: Permissions Coordinator," at the address below.

ARPress
45 Dan Road Suite 5
Canton MA 02021

Hotline: 1(888) 821-0229
Fax: 1(508) 545-7580

Ordering Information:
Quantity sales. Special discounts are available on quantity purchases by corporations, associations, and others. For details, contact the publisher at the address above.

Printed in the United States of America.

ISBN-13:	Paperback	979-8-89389-695-4
	eBook	979-8-89389-696-1

Library of Congress Control Number: 2021923902

Table of Contents

Author's Referral vii

Chapter 1	The Source 1
Chapter 2	Waking Up 10
Chapter 3	Evolving 20
Chapter 4	Who Am I 30
Chapter 5	I Do 48
Chapter 6	Beginning the Honeymoon 54
Chapter 7	Campus Visitations 57
Chapter 8	Classes Begin 67
Chapter 9	Stand in There and Take Your Cuts 74
Chapter 10	The Sound of Music 84
Chapter 11	An Omaha Landing 86
Chapter 12	Moving On 96
Chapter 13	A Summer Place 107
Chapter 14	Aloha 114
Chapter 15	Back to School 121
Chapter 16	Treage and the Sophmore Year 124
Chapter 17	How Do You Stop A Runaway Train? 131
Chapter 18	Another Summer Vacation 141
Chapter 19	Goals and Accomplishments 146
Chapter 20	The Final Quest 154
Chapter 21	Cynthia 158
Chapter 22	Omaha Landing IV 164
Chapter 23	We Are a Family of Three 173
Chapter 24	Life Goes On 177

Chapter 25	Retirement	182
Chapter 26	Good Enough Isn't Enough	187
Chapter 27	Campaigning	197
Chapter 28	Returning	203
Chapter 29	Courting Angelina	206
Chapter 30	Decisions, Decisions, Decisions	217
Chapter 31	Who Are We	234
Chapter 32	Angelina's Story	236
Chapter 33	Wearing Another Hat	246
Chapter 34	Going Home	253
Chapter 35	Another Journey	256

Epilogue 261

Author's Referral

Readers are referred to other novels by this same author for added reading enjoyment.

1. Coriolis as written, compiled and created by Gary L. Hollen
2. The Blackthorn Conspiracy as written, compiled and created by Jerry May, Gary L. Hollen and Dr. John W. Wood under the pseudonym, T.T. Brothers
3. Tributes to Sadness and Happiness as written, compiled and compiled by Gary L. Hollen
4. The Wonderment of Life as written, compiled and created by Gary L. Hollen

Chapter One

The Source

Who am I? Who are you?

Forget what Continent, Country, Island, Territory, Provence, State, County, City, Town, or Village you live or where I live. Throw away the titles and shed the makeup if you wear it, I don't. Shed all clothing and all of assumptions about whom you are or who I am. Let's get down to the bare essentials, where we really exist, and ask that question again. Who am I and who are you?

"Who am I" is a very important question, a question seldom asked by many. If we haven't asked that question perhaps it is because we are afraid to look deeply inside ourselves to discover the real "you", the real "me". If we have asked, how did we feel about what we discovered? Did it disappoint us? Was the answer reasonable? Did the answer make us happy? Did the answer intimidate us or make us sad? Maybe the answer caused us to do something to overcome the disappointment we felt with the answer we discovered?

Perhaps the questions we might have asked or didn't could be or could have been an attempt to resolve the mystery of life. We should never fear exploring the unknown, discovering the truth or at least attempting to do so.

An all-encompassing, commanding, yet soothing, melodic and comforting voice spoke softly to the slumbering form before its magnificence, "I have given you a language, English. When you awaken you will be able to partially understand what I am about to say. Not all that I say will be completely clear to you, but in time you will come to understand." The form then delivered a compelling disruption to the slumbering human form, "Wake up, Gary." The friendly but firm voice continued, "I am The Source. The time has come for you to experience me, and begin your journey to learn to know me."

Gary stretched, yawned, and began to rub his eyes as The Source continued, "Your experience, or as you will call it, time has come to take your first journey. Before I send you off on your first life's excursion, I am going to take you on a tour of discovery. You are going to learn a little about me and how you evolved."

Gary roused and was immediately aware of something quite awesome surrounding him, an indescribable shape, a form, an aura, an entity that seemed to have no dimension, yet it seemed to contain everything. It appeared to be everywhere, possessing all colors and shapes. It presented an awesome spectrum of wondrous intrigue. The something surrounding him emitted an aura of love and peaceful serenity. Its presence was more significant than he could comprehend, even put words to, but oddly he was not afraid. Rather, he was spellbound, completely awed and fixated on the form.

He studied the figure and then looked down to examine his own personal form. Strangely his being, his shape and appearance was so different. The mellow, melodic voice continued, "Before you begin your first life's experience I want to show you something that you will not recall after we are through taking the special discovery journey I have planned for you. In fact, you will not recall this conversation or your encounter with me until you return." The voice paused and then commanded, "Rise and let us begin."

Confused, Gary inquired, "Why do I look so different from you?"

Suddenly the almost indescribable shape appeared as a figure much the same in appearance as his form. "I can be anything I want. I can look like man which I have created, or I can look like what you saw when your first encountered me when I awakened you. I can be male or female. I can be black, brown, or white. Then again, I can seem to be nothing even though I am everything." The voice paused. "I prefer my other form." Immediately the new shape returned to its original state.

Gary was drawn to that which surrounded him. Somehow he felt no fear, only awe. He felt compelled to reach out for and allow the form to guide him as though taking his hand as they began the journey. Looking about he noted they were headed toward a massive black hole in the distance. It was surrounded by twinkling orbs, some far, far away, some nearer. They were of varying sizes. Some appeared to twinkle while others appeared to emit a steady bright light amid surrounding rings of light with smaller orbs contained within. He was quite taken by the panorama of colors and shapes surrounding him that were all configured in an intricate artistic design that was so pleasant to view, so beautiful and so pleasing to his eye.

Entering the dark black hole, the colors, varying shapes and the bright lights disappeared. It appeared as though he was entering a tunnel that seemed to narrow as they proceeded. Only the shadow or whatever description that one might conjure up to describe the form that remained beside him. Behind him as he proceeded was only a bright white light, probably the collective all that he and the form had left behind, blinding if one chose to look at it. Ahead in the complete darkness, nothingness surrounded him except for the form that had seemingly taken his hand. "We are nearing the beginning, Gary. It is from here that all has evolved. You will have trouble understanding this now, but that point ahead that seems to come from nothing is the beginning, me, as I am everything as well as the beginning. The beginning appears to end, but that is an illusion as there is no end. We shall not go any further because if we do, you will not exist nor will all that you have seen except for me. I will always continue to exist. We stop here because there is no need to start over again." The voice paused. "I wanted you to see from whence you came as I have chosen to show everyone that I send on their first life's journey."

Gary stood looking about in awe as the voice continued, "You should know that the totality it has taken us to make this journey cannot be measured as you will come to know it on Earth. Measuring the journey is not in terms of, soon to be your word, time, but in distance. Distance, as opposed to what you will discover on earth is not measured in miles as where we are is part of the infinite all that I have created and yet if I choose it can be seem to be nothing. You will learn more about what distance is all about later.

Time and distance as known on Earth only exist because I have given those ideas to you and all the others that I have sent on their life's journey so that it will be easier to comprehend." The voice paused. "You might say that we began this journey and now we are here as we began and returned to whence we began as though we never left. It is comparable to the blink of an eye, or, better yet, an electron changing orbits inside an atom. Again I want to remind you that time means nothing here. All you need to know is that I am everything so I can give you time to make your first journey easier to understand. Although time is meaningless, the people you will meet when you begin your trip will speak of it often."

Gary shook his head in wonderment as the voice continued, "I want you to think of time up here as distance, and distance is never ending. It is infinite. It really has no beginning or end except in me. Where you are going distance is influenced by time because where you are going people have been taught time is required to travel a distance. Imagine what happens if you are here and then there and no time, as known on earth, elapses. That is a mystery that I am not quite ready to reveal to you now or to those you will meet where you are going." Again the voice paused. "As I am everything, I give you time as it is understood on Earth. I am also distance as known on Earth, but I am so much more because I am everything. Thus time is irrelevant, but I am relevant, everything, so for you time is relevant. Because of me there no such thing as nothing because I am everything and you and all other things are of me."

The voice continued, "Very soon you will belong, become a part of another spectrum. This place where you are going, Earth, can be thought of as being millions of years from the beginning and yet it will not be different than the beginning except that everything has evolved or traveled a great distance. What has evolved is distance and distance is infinite or never ending. On Earth you will experience only a small segment, insignificant in terms of the entirety of everything of which I am. Yet to you, it will appear to be very significant."

Gary was confused, but so in awe that he remained content to listen as the voice continued, "On Earth, time will have meaning and dimension as you will learn about seconds, minutes, hours, days, weeks, years, decades, and centuries, etc. This will happen after you have experienced something called birth. With your birth, you will have a mother and a father, and you will appear, at first, much differently than you do now. You see, Gary, you are about to experience the beginning of life, a beginning on a place called Earth." The voice stopped to allow Gary to catch up. Finally continuing The Source explained, "After you have lived your life on Earth you will return to me to prepare for your next journey. While you are on Earth you will grow and age. You will learn and explore some of the mysteries of life. You will learn to love and hate. You will be told tales about me, but it is only now that you truly know me. You see I am love, wondrous relationships and continuous learning. I am everything and everything evolves from me and everything of me is good."

The Source paused creating silence, eerie silence. After an uncomfortable moment the voice continued, "Again I say, when you leave me you will have no memory of this conversation or having experienced me. You will become human, but you will be of me."

Gary nodded and then asked, "How long will I be gone?"

"For me, it will be as though you never left, but for you and those you will meet, they will know it to be 43 years."

"Is that a long time or a long whatever?"

The Source chuckled. "No, to me, it is less than a blink of an eye, but to some it is significant. To others, it isn't long enough. They will say that you were taken before your time."

"If time doesn't exist and time is you, then why do you bother allowing me and those I will meet to come to know about something that does not exist or only exist in you?"

"That is the concept that you will learn about as your journeys continue. For now it is enough for you to know that I had to make it simpler for you so that you could gradually come to understand the entirety of me. You see, you will soon learn of the creation as explained in something to be known as a book. There is more than one book. There is the Bible, the Koran, Book of Mormon, and many more books that speak of me. In those books there are very simple explanations of how everything you will experience came about. Man is not ready for everything to be revealed at this time.

Man has to evolve to come to understand, but man will eventually come to know me and be completely of me."

"When will we be ready?"

"That is unimportant because that would refer to time and that doesn't exist. Just know that from time to time, a poor choice of words, I will send or have sent special people to those on Earth to help them take another step toward understanding what this is all about and come to truly know me, to become a part of me."

"Will I meet these people?"

"Yes and no as some have already returned to me. To know them or of them will require you to learn and experience something that is called faith and acquiring knowledge. Your challenge is to learn from this concept and go beyond to formulate some ideas of your own. Nothing can be completely wrong because it is from me and everything about me is right and good as I am perfection."

"Is there anything else that you want to tell me, to prepare me for my journey?"

"Yes. You need to know that your journey and the journey of others will never end. You, as they, will have an Earthly father and Mother. Your Earthly father's name will be Fredrick and your Earthly mother's name will be Claudia. You will have a brother, Gregory, and you will be born in a country called the United States, in a state called Oregon and a city called Lake Oswego. It is a city near to a larger city called Portland and many smaller villages too numerous to mention at this time. A lot of things will happen to you as you grow and age that I need not tell you about now other than to say that it is all planned and mapped out for you. Perhaps I should also say that although your life is mapped out, you will be given free will and the ability to think, decide for yourself, plan, achieve, and take what some call a fork in the road. You will experience failure and success and much achievement. However, your final destination has been defined. That is what I mean by saying that your life has been mapped out for you."

"My destination, am I supposed to ask about that?"

"I have already told you that your destination is to return to me. Beyond that, as time, your Earthly word, unfolds more will be revealed to you."

further?" "You speak of a father and a mother. Could you explain this to me "Yes, your mother and father will be involved in something called marriage. They will express their love for each other in a special way that will produce you. That is something that you will also experience. You too will marry. After you marry, you will have two children."

"Wait a minute. You said that my Earthly mother and father will produce me. According to you I already exist."

"That is true, but on Earth you are but a hoped for or anticipated event because to exist on Earth you have to be born."

"Hmm, could you tell me about the person that I will marry?" "Better yet, before you leave I will introduce you to her. Ah, there she is now." The voice paused. "Before I introduce you, you must know that both you and she will pass from this dimension into a new dimension and experience birth on Earth. You might think of Earth existing in a universe parallel to where we are now. After you have met your soul mate, you future wife, you will leave me. Your wife will be someone that you will love very deeply, and she you. You will be born as a baby boy and she as a baby girl."

"That means that my father is a boy and my mother a girl?"

"In a way that is true. You see as people on earth grow and change as they evolve. Eventually a boy becomes a man, a girl a woman. The girl that will eventually become your wife is a very beautiful woman. On Earth you will eventually meet her, get to know her, and then you will marry. As you are now and as she is now that is exactly how you both will appear after you have grown into a man and a woman. Of course further aging will make you appear somewhat different, but when you return to me you will be as you are now."

"This is all very confusing to me."

"That is because this is your first adventure. I have been saving this adventure especially for you. I have great plans for you as I do all that I sent on the journey."

"When I return to you, will I recall all that I experience in my journey into that other place, um, Earth?"

"Yes. That is all according to the plan. When you return I will have another plan for you and send you out on another adventure. You see, you will continue to grow, to learn, but never fail to love as you take journey after journey. That is what I am all about and what the mystery of life is all about."

"Does anyone you send on this journey ever fail to love?"

"Yes and no. That is all I will say about that now as you are not ready for that information, but know that a term you will learn about on Earth, Hell, does not exist because there is only good because everything is of me and I am good."

As the form spoke, Gary seemed to pass through space with many events passing before his eyes, the history he would soon begin to learn about. He studied the form and then asked, "What am I supposed to call you."

"It doesn't matter what you call me. I really don't have a name other than The Source, The Beginning, or The Eternal Entity. On Earth they call me God, Yahweh Buddha, Allah, The Great Spirit, and so forth."

"And here, do I call you The Source, God, or"

"I prefer to be called The Source as all peoples on earth are from me, of me. Although peoples scattered throughout Earth have different names for me, I am the one, the only one, the only God as I am The Source." Again the voice paused as they seemed to near the woman that would become his wife. "Again, let me remind you that you are of me and you are good, but on Earth, you will have those times when you are bad. I prefer to call it misbehaving. Know that I love you and to me you will never be bad. You will have your moments, but you will evolve into something that is good."

Gary diverted his attention to a beautiful woman that appeared to be coming nearer as The Source and his movement through the continuum continued. Suddenly they stopped. The breathtakingly beautiful woman stood before him. She was blond with fair skin and blue eyes. She was of medium height and appeared to be athletic, well-toned. Every contour of her body appeared to be perfect. He was already drawn to her, but it was her smile that sealed the deal. Her smile revealed even white teeth and emitted warmth that seemed to invade his entire being. She was so perfect, possessing wonderfully contoured dimensions and indescribable beauty. She smiled at him.

The Source began, "I want you to meet Angelina. Angelina, this is Gary."

Gary returned Angelina's smile. Almost as you would see in a tennis match, their smiles were given and returned, and given again and returned again. When they looked into each other's eyes something magical occurred. Love was already in the air, the connection had already begun.

Gary continued to look at Angelina as he inquired of The Source, "Do you do this with everyone you send on to Earth?"

"Yes, I already explained that to you."

"How many people do you send on a journey to Earth in a day, um, whatever it is called here?"

"In a day as it is called on Earth I not only send people to Earth, but I also send them elsewhere." The Source paused. "Don't you recall that I told you time has no dimension? It is irrelevant." The voice paused. "The number of people I send is not important for you to know at this moment."

"Why"

"You are not ready to or able to comprehend infinity." The form paused, seemingly turning towards Angelina. "Angelina, your journey is about to begin. Your parents are waiting for you to join them." The voice paused. "Angelina, as you and Gary are of me, it is important for you to realize that you are my daughter, and, Gary, you are my son. All others who have been sent before you have the same distinction. Each of you has a mission and will make significant contributions to what is called life." The form paused. Seemingly emitting a smile, the form said, "Enjoy your journey, Angelina."

No sooner than had Angelina vanished, The Source made a clapping sound and commanded, "And now Gary, your journey will begin as your parents are waiting for you as well. I will see you soon.

Chapter Two

Waking Up

"When is it that a child, you, I can/could first recall events in our lives? What was your first memory, my first memory? When did it occur? No matter, it is different for everyone. It is akin to waking from a long sleep. What happened during the previous moments before waking?"

When Gary first recalled his existence, he and Angelina both had experienced birth and gradual aging and growth. They, as promised, were born to wonderful parents, the Crawford's and Mallon's. Both of Angelina's parents were teachers at Lake Oswego High School. Guy, a physical education teacher also coached football, and Sue, a music teacher, attempted to teach with great success her students the wonderment of and an appreciation of music. Gary's dad was a professional baseball player, playing for the Seattle Mariners, and his mother an English teacher at Lake Oswego High School. She wrestled with her students over issues with grammar and attempting to understand the meanings contained in the literature they read. Getting her students to form complete sentences and write meaningful and interesting prose was also her goal. The families had been friends since the times that both mothers and fathers went through Lamaze classes to prepare for natural birth. First it was Claudia that added support during Sue's birthing of Angelina, and then it was Sue that supported Claudia during her birthing of Gary. The Crawford's other child, a son, was named Lance. Gary's brother was named Greg. When

The Wonderment of Life

Gary awakened to the reality of life it was when he was about five. He was in the Crawford's living room playing with his friend, Angelina. It was her fifth birthday, November 1. Gary was on the cusp of celebrating his birthday also, a Thanksgiving November 23rd event.

Sitting around the dining room table with his next door neighbors and close friends, Guy Crawford smiled and offered, "It is good to have you back home in the neighborhood, Fredrick." Guy continued, adding, "Another long season has finally come to an end." You put up some pretty impressive numbers this year."

The Crawford's and Mallon's had gathered at the Crawford's beautiful home in Lake Oswego on the north side of A Street, a short distance from the lake. Next door neighbors, both families lived comfortably in four bedroom ranch style homes with spacious back yards with covered patios equipped with all the necessary tools for a barbeque gathering when the weather cooperated. When the Crawford's looked across the fence into the Mallon's backyard it was nearly a reflection of theirs, both homes boasting nearly the same floor plan. Only the color of the homes differentiated one from the other to the casual onlooker.

"Thanks Guy, I was very fortunate to stay away from injuries and have the good fortune to have teammates to support and make me look good. As you know team sports such as baseball and football require teammates to support one another and try to make each other better." He paused and looked out into the living room where Gary and Angelina were playing, "Yeah, sometimes I wonder if it's all worth it. Don't get me wrong. I love to play baseball, but I am away from home a lot. Thank goodness I have been blessed with the opportunity to play for the Seattle Mariners. Even so, it still puts a lot of pressure on Claudia to be both the mother and father during the season when I am away. On top of that, even though she doesn't need to, she continues to hold down a full time job because she loves working with kids. Of course both of you know exactly what I mean."

Claudia nodded her head chiming in, "At times it is a bit much, but I am not complaining. I love the fact that Fredrick gets to pursue his dreams while still being a wonderful husband and father. With him playing on a team so close to home, we get to spend a lot of time in Seattle when the Mariners are not playing on the road."

Sue joined the conversation, offering, "We love having you and your children as neighbors in case I haven't mentioned it before."

Guy nodded and continued, "So Fredrick, I see where you're eligible for free agency this year. What are you going to do?"

Sue Crawford snorted. "It's a fat chance that Seattle won't offer you a contract. You are much too valuable for them to let you slip away to some other team."

Fredrick smiled. "If Seattle will have me I am going to stay put. I love playing for the Mariners. My demands won't be great as I feel that I am already making a very good salary."

Guy inquired, "What about the length of the contract?"

"I would be satisfied with something around four to five years. Of course I wouldn't object if they elected to tie me up for a longer period of time. I'm young and healthy and I see myself able to play until Gary reaches junior high school age or a bit longer."

"That would put you nearing the age of forty. Have you started making plans for what you are going to do when you retire? Forty is much too young to retire to the living room to watch TV all day."

Claudia burst into the exchange excitedly, "Yes, yes he has. Fredrick is taking classes at Portland State University in the off season, working on the requirements necessary to get his teaching certificate. He wants to teach math and coach baseball when he hangs up his spikes. After he gets the certificate he plans to do some substitute teaching in the off season."

Fredrick again looked into the living room and nodded. "You know, those two kids seem to have struck up quite a friendship. It is almost like they are soul mates." He winked. "You think that they might be in love?"

Claudia scolded, "Fredrick, for heaven's sake. They are only five years old. Let's give them time to grow up."

Sue grinned, offering, "I don't know if it is what you would call love or just really liking each other, but almost from birth they have been inseparable. Well, I mean since they were able to crawl. I think it is so sweet. Those two seem to really enjoy being with each other. It is almost as though they were put on this Earth to be together. I wouldn't be at all disappointed if they…….. Well, no need to get the cart before the horse. Um, we mustn't forget Lance and Greg. They are becoming best buddies as well. We are so lucky to have you as neighbors."

Guy chuckled. "Honey, you have already told them that and I totally agree, but…"

Fredrick nodded, interrupting, "I don't think that it can be over stated. Yes, we feel the same way. We are most fortunate. Good friends come along only once in a while, and I consider you folk's very good friends. I want you to know how much I appreciate the help you give Claudia while I'm away."

Claudia nodded. "Yes, I want to echo what my husband just said. I don't tell you often enough how much I appreciate all that you do for me. I feel so blessed."

Sue smiled. "That is what friends are for. I am sure you would do the same for me if the need arose."

Fredrick smiled, again looking into the living room. Finally he asked, "Have you noticed that those two seem to be exceptional in certain ways?"

Sue excitedly replied, "Yes, but tell me what you have noticed." "Well, Gary seems to be picking up all of the baseball skills without me forcing it on him. His hand eye coordination is outstanding and he is already able to make contact with the baseball when I pitch to him."

"Claudia interrupted, "And don't forget that he appears to be as smart as a whip. Um, I have also noticed that Angelina has quite a talent for drawing, and she seems to be coming right along with her ability to play the piano. Didn't she start playing when she was about three?"

Sue nodded. "That she did. I thought it might be a little young at the time, but she kept beating away at the key board, so I decided to see how she could handle piano lessons. The rest is history."

Claudia stared into space as though deep in thought. Finally she reacted to what Sue had said. "Yeah, that is truly amazing, her starting at such a young age. Um, excuse me for appearing to be distant, but I got to thinking about how they both appear to have very advanced language skills for their ages."

Sue nodded. "I'm glad to hear you say that you have noticed how bright they appear to be. I am constantly amazed at their vocabularies. Their use of words and the wide range of their vocabularies are exceptional for their ages."

Claudia added, "And they are both reading material that is at least first grade level."

Guy added, "And they are so inquisitive about everything. I swear.

Some of the questions they ask."

Fredrick chuckled. "It almost makes me feel a little backward. Some of the stuff they ask about and talk about, well, it's what I would expect us to be wondering or talking about."

Guy broke into the raving reviews, "Fredrick, don't overlook your son's speed. As a physical education teacher, I am so impressed with his quickness. I think you have a fledging athlete on your hands. You might want to watch out because I might just want to recruit him to play football."

Claudia added, "I think that you have a musician or an artist on your hands. I have heard her sing and I think that her voice is lovely, so advanced for her age."

In the living room, Angelina was extolling the virtues of being older than her friend. Smiling, she teased, "I'm older than you. What's more, I am also smarter than you are. Today, I am 22 days older than you are." She smiled, continuing, "But I won't hold that against you because you are my best friend."

Sitting around the coffee table that was in front of a leather couch located in front of a spacious fireplace, Gary blushed, "Really? Well, you're my best friend too. For a girl that can't do anything except draw pictures, play the piano and sing, you're okay. Don't you ever want to just get out and run?"

"Well, I'll have you know that what I do and enjoy is better than just playing with a silly old ball or running around like a chicken with its head cut off. Thank you for mentioning that I also sing. I didn't know that you had noticed."

Gary grinned. "Yeah, I've hear you screeching away. Ah, I think that you're just jealous because you can't catch me when you try, which isn't very often. Besides, my dad seems to be doing okay, and he just plays with a silly old ball." Suddenly all of the joy seemed to drain from Gary's face. Wrinkling up his nose to keep the tears from coming, he continued, "I just wish that he was home more. I really miss him during baseball season."

Angelina reached out and touched her friend's hand very gently. With compassion exuding from her face and in the tone of her voice, she offered, "Be thankful for today, Gary. He is here now and that is what counts." She paused and then continued, "I guess I am pretty lucky with my mom and dad both home all the time. I guess that being teachers have certain advantages."

Gary nodded. "Yeah, I think that my dad is going to teach when he is done playing baseball. At least that seems to be what I've overheard my mom and dad talking about." He paused for a moment. "So, what do you want to be when you grow up?"

Angelina smiled. "Well outside of being a painter or playing the piano or being a singer, I have decided that I would like to be married to you."

Again Gary blushed, starting to fumble with the cards that they had been playing with as his eyes darted about for some reason to escape from the discomfort that he suddenly felt. Pretending that something big was about to take place in the other room, he quickly rose and urged, "Come on, let's go into the dining room and join our parents. I think that something important is about to happen.

Angelina chuckled. "You mean like dinner?" Grinning, Angelina teased, "Am I making you nervous?"

Gary scoffed, "No! I just don't see myself getting all mushy with some girl. Besides, you don't like what I like."

Angelina frowned, offering, "I'll have you know that I'm not just a girl. I am a special girl and you are my special boyfriend. Don't you dare forget it Gary Mallon. Whether you like it or not I plan to marry you when we grow up." Storming off towards the dining room, she turned and ordered, "Come on, let's go. I want to see when we're going to eat." She hesitated for a moment watching him standing there dumbfounded. "You know? You are just a big poop. You are hopeless. I doubt that you have figured out that we love each other. In case you didn't know it that is all that matters."

Later at home, Gary snuggled up to his dad. Finally comfortable in his dad's lap he asked, "Dad, when are we going to play catch and see if I can hit a few?"

Fredrick smiled. "Well, this isn't the best weather to play baseball with the rainy season beginning, but I might be able to find a free corner at the high school where your mom teaches. They have a batting cage up there and we might be able get you in the batting cage so that you can hit a few. Even so, we can toss the ball around if you would like. Just understand that I want it to be fun without any pressure. You have a long time before you need to consider taking baseball seriously." He grinned, patting his son on the leg. "Who knows? You just might turn out to be a football player, a basketball player, or even a scientist." He paused. "Son, I would be proud of you no matter what you decide you want to be."

"Would there be anything wrong if I became a baseball player like you?"

"Gary, there's no reason for you to get in a hurry about making that decision. You'll be five in a few days and there is a lot of road to travel before you get serious about being a professional baseball player." He cleared his throat and then inquired, "So what would you like for your birthday and what do you want to do?"

Gary pondered the question for a moment and then pleaded, "Could I have a party just like Angelina had?" He paused. "I want it to be the same except I would like to go to the beach. Maybe we could invite Angelina, Lance and her mom and dad?"

"I don't see why not. You know that we'll have to see if they want to, but, yeah, that is a neat idea. Your mom loves the coast." He paused for a moment and then continued. "Maybe we can have your birthday party the day after Thanksgiving and celebrate it at the beach."

"That's okay with me. I just want to go to the beach. I think that I want pizza and berry pie instead of a cake and ice cream."

Gary's dad smiled. "Got it all figured out huh? Well, let's check with your mom and see what she thinks. If she is okay with the idea, we'll ask the Crawford's and start making plans."

The next few days passed slowly, anticipation of his fifth birthday nearly driving Gary crazy. The thought of possibly going to the beach to celebrate his birthday and having the Crawford's, especially Angelina, there to join in on the festivities was more than he could stand. Hiding his eagerness for the special day to arrive was almost impossible to pull off. On Sunday, four days before Thanksgiving, Gary's father called him into the living room. "Gary, come in here for a moment. Your mother and I have something to talk to you about."

Gary entered the living room a bit reluctantly, fearing the worst. "Ah, please don't tell me that the Crawford's don't want to go to the beach with us to celebrate my birthday."

Fredrick smiled and patted Claudia on her knee. "No, they are going to go with us, but we have to discuss how it will all unfold."

Gary frowned. "What do you mean?"

Claudia nodded her head in a positive manner, indicating that the news would be good. "Well, we have decided to have dinner with the Crawford's on Thursday, um, on Thanksgiving Day. We will celebrate your birthday and Thanksgiving at that time complete with the berry pie you like so much." She smiled. "We'll probably even have some pumpkin pie and chocolate pie as well."

"I thought you said that we were going to the beach."

His dad quickly replied, "After we have finished our Thanksgiving dinner and cleaned up the mess, we'll load ourselves into our cars and leave for Seaside. We have rented a house for Thursday evening through Sunday. We will have a small celebration of your birthday as usual on your birthday, but it we'll have the real birthday celebration at the coast. If it is okay with you, we can wait to open your presents at Seaside."

Gary pumped his fist with excitement. "Wow, you had me scared for a moment. Thank you so much. This is going to be the best birthday ever."

Thanksgiving passed uneventfully, the dinner at the Crawford's tasty as always and their company most pleasant. Soon after the dinner was done and the cleanup completed the two families loaded into their respective cars and headed for Seaside and the house that Gary's dad and mom had rented for the occasion. For the trip, Gary and Angelina were permitted to ride with Gary's dad and mom while Greg rode over with Lance and his parents. All was in order for a fantastic weekend.

In Seaside, Gary's dad pulled into the driveway of the home he had rented. To Gary's surprise and pleasure it had beach frontage and was but a short distance from the main drag of Seaside. Gary smiled. "This is so cool. Thanks mom and dad. This is going to be so much fun. Can we walk on the beach before we go to bed?"

Claudia responded to her son's query, "Of course. Within limits we can do whatever we please when we want to the next three days. Walking on the beach will be our first adventure."

The next morning Gary was up and standing at the window looking out at the ocean when he was joined by Angelina. "How did you sleep, Gary?"

"I had trouble going to sleep. The ocean is sure noisy. What about you?"

"I went right to sleep. What do you want to do today? After all, we are celebrating your birthday and you should be able to do what you want to do."

"I want to have pizza, go to the bumper cars place, and walk on the beach and…"

"Whoa. Not so fast. We have three days. We don't have to do it all in one day."

Gary frowned. "Just like a girl. I suppose you want to stay inside all day."

"No, I just think that we should take the time to enjoy what we do. You know what I hope we can do?" "No, what is that?"

"I want us to go get an ice cream cone sometime today. I like strawberry. What is your favorite?"

"I like chocolate. Um, do you want to do the bumper cars sometime today?"

Angelina smiled, offering, "Yes, I think that would be fun. I can't wait to ram my car into yours and pin your car against the wall of the bumper car track."

"Not before I do the same to you."

"We'll see. I also think that we should take a walk on the beach. What about you?"

Gary nodded. "Yeah, that would be fun. If it was warmer we could build a sand castle."

wet." water?"

"Maybe we can hunt for sea shells."

"And we can chase the water as it comes and goes without getting Angelina chuckled." Are you telling me that you're afraid of a little "No, I just think that it is fun to go out as far as you can when the ocean is going out and then race ahead of it as it starts to come in."

Angelina patted Gary on the arm. "I know something you are scared of, though."

Gary's brow furrowed as he studied Angelina carefully. "What would that be?"

"I'll bet you're afraid to let me kiss you."

"I am not. It's just that I don't want you to kiss me. Boys don't let girls kiss them."

"Why not, it won't hurt?"

"Because that is sissy stuff and I am no sissy. Kissing is icky and I don't want any part of it."

Suddenly, Angelina leaned forward and kissed Gary on the cheek. "There, take that. Now, do you feel like a sissy?"

Gary's face reddened. Stammering he replied, "No, ah no, I don't know exactly how I feel. It makes me feel uncomfortable. Just promise that you won't do it again?"

Angelina smiled. "It couldn't be that you liked it, could it?"

Suddenly she put her arms around Gary's neck and kissed him on the mouth." Slowly backing away, she smiled and asked, "What do you think about that?"

Gary immediately backed away with a look of disgust painted noticeably on his face. "Ick, that was horrible. If we're going to be friends you have to promise that you won't do that again." He paused. "Don't you dare tell anyone that you kissed me, okay?"

"I promise, um, I won't tell anyone." She paused with a smirk on her face. "Just know that I plan to kiss you again sometime."

"Not if you can't catch me."

The weekend passed. Both Gary and Angelina were in the midst of their kindergarten year. The trip to the beach had changed them forever. Without realizing it, they had become even closer than ever before. During the visit to Seaside, Gary and his dad played catch on the beach and tossed the football around with Angelina's dad. Angelina stayed indoors with her mom and Claudia while the boys frolicked on the beach. It was a great weekend. Angelina said later that she loved watching Gary play catch and run about. Gary's attitude was probably best summed up by saying, "Girls! What do they know?"

Chapter Three

Evolving

    Ah, the future and how we get there. So distant, but so near. Be careful to not get the cart before the horse, but don't wait forever to start making plans. The future will be here before you realize it. Each year of your life should be enjoyed. Twenty-one will come soon enough.

Gary and Angelina passed through the elementary grades K-5, and middle school, grades 6-8. For her age, Angelina had become a very accomplished pianist and had started to paint seriously while Gary really took to baseball. His father described his talent as unbelievable as he was able to hit any pitch thrown to him, possessed advanced defensive skills in the outfield, and had a very strong arm, a gun, that few runners dared to test.

    Most important, both Angelina and Gary excelled in the classroom and were considered by all that met and knew them to be good people.

    "Gary, come in here for a moment, will you son?" Gary's dad called to him from the living room.

    Gary was attempting to swallow the last bit of the sandwich that he had hastily prepared. With a mouth full of sandwich he inaudibly replied, "Gimme a moment, I'm just finishing my sandwich."

    Fredrick chuckled. "Don't swallow it all in one bite. I am not in a hurry."

    A moment later, Gary waltzed into the living room. "What's up?" Gary's dad sat beside his mother on the couch situated to the left of the fireplace. Fredrick looked like an athlete in a subtle sort of way even as he was on the cusp of turning forty, not displaying an ounce of extra poundage yet not displaying the bulging muscles that one expected a professional baseball player to exhibit. Gary had never attempted to describe his father before that moment, but as he approached the couch where his father sat, he noticed something more than a professional baseball player, an athlete. His father was a loving unpretentious role model that deserved and got his full attention whenever he spoke or walked into a room. He still had a full head of hair with no noticeable wrinkles. His tanned skin, a result of being exposed to the sun's constant presence, caused his blue eyes to shine like beacons. He was a handsome manly man, but always displayed a laid back demeanor that did not beg for the attention he always received. Though looking like a man's man, he had a soft and gentle side to him. He displayed that as he sat holding Claudia's hand. His presence spoke volumes.

Gary's mother did not look like a teacher, whatever that means. She was attractive, her face framed by dark brown hair. She wore little or no makeup, yet every bit of her face seemed to have had the advantage of a professional makeup artist's finishing touch. Most would have referred to her as a knockout, a foxy lady. She was the perfect complement to Gary's dad.

"There's something that your mother and I want to share with you." Gary raised his eyebrows in anticipation. "Is it anything serious?"

Fredrick smiled and winked at his wife. "No, actually I think that you will think that what I have to say is good news. We want to share it with you before I make the announcement."

"Announcement, you say. What announcement?"

Fredrick smiled. "I have decided to retire. I have reached that age, the age when I feel that it is time to consider leaving baseball to the youngsters." He again turned toward his wife and smiled. "I just got an offer from the Lake Oswego School District to start teaching math starting second semester and be the assistant baseball coach. They promised me the head baseball job next year."

Gary's jaw dropped. He was stunned. "Are you serious? The Mariners didn't decide to trade you, did they? They didn't refuse to sign you for another season did they? I know that you're 40, but you had a great year. You are a great baseball player."

Fredrick chuckled. "Thank you son, but the fact is that I am starting to feel the wear and tear on the old body. I thought it would be nice to go out on top before I was told I had to hang up the cleats. Besides, you are going on 14, an important age for a young man, and I think that it is time I become a full time father." He smiled. "Besides, I am excited about being able to be your baseball coach and be home full time." He paused. "This is our little secret. Other than your mother, your brother, to whom I will share this news with next, and the principal at Lake Oswego High School, nobody knows. The principal promised that he wouldn't make the announcement until I have told the Mariners and they announce my retirement."

"You haven't even told the Crawford's?"

"Nope, um, I will tell the Mariners tomorrow. The Mariners will probably announce it the day after, and then principal at Lake Oswego will make the announcement after the Mariners let the news out. I'll tell the Crawford's after I tell the Mariners, before the public knows. The nice thing about all of this is that the principal told me the present head baseball coach told him that he was stepping down after this year. I will not be pushing him out the door. I suppose that before the principal goes public with the news he'll sit down with the coach and let him know if he hasn't already. After all, he and I will have to work together this year. I have to, um, well it is important that the coach knows that I am going to follow his lead and not try to push my agenda forward. I want to be his assistant, his right hand man. He is still the head coach and will be for the entirety of this season." Fredrick paused. "George, I mean Mr. Johnson is a great guy and a fine coach. I really respect him. I think that we will get along just fine."

"Wow! This is really good news. It is going to be so terrific to have you home all the time, and the thought of having you for my coach is better than neat. I really like Mr. Johnson, but getting to learn form the best is so neat. I am so excited."

"Just know this, Gary. Mr. Johnson is still the head coach and what he says and wants us to do is the way it is going to be." He nodded. "Another reason that I am retiring is…" Gary's dad paused for a moment and then continued, "I have been watching you progress through the years and I want you to know that I think that you are a very good baseball player. You play the outfield as well as anyone I have seen, and have a great arm." He smiled. "Not to give you the big head, but, well, you just hit the snot out of whatever is thrown at you." Again he patted wife on the leg, and then looked directly into his son's eyes. "I don't want to put any pressure on you, but I think that you have the potential to go all the way to the top. I would like to have the opportunity to help you get there if that is what you want."

Gary nodded, an excited smile bursting across his face. "I can't think of anything that I want more. Gosh, imagine having you at home all the time and being able to learn from the best. This is the best news I have had in, well, forever."

Gary's dad cleared his throat, paused and then hesitantly continued, "I know that Guy would love to have you turn out for football, and whether you decide to or not…"

Gary interrupted, "Dad, I am not going to play football. I don't want to risk tearing up a knee or whatever when all I really want to do is play baseball."

Fredrick smiled and again patted his wife on the knee. "I doubt that your mother is disappointed to hear you say that."

Gary's mother nodded. "You've got that right." She smiled, and, as if by cue, she got up and started for the kitchen. Turning back towards them she smiled and offered, "Um, I think that the next little bit of the conversation is men's talk, so I'll leave you boys to have your private conversation."

As his mother left the room, Gary took the time to take another careful look at his mother as she left the room. She was not tall, measuring about 65 inches, was medium in stature, and a nice looking woman even for a mother. She looked like a mother, whatever than means, but not overly so. Actually she was very good looking. She most definitely did not look like an English teacher, no disrespect to the teaching profession intended. She was his mother and he loved her, but even though she would compare more than favorably with just about any other woman, she just wasn't in the same class as Angelina. Angelina's mother, also very attractive, was very similar in appearance to his mother except she was a bit taller. She also did not compare to Angelina.

His dad's sneaky athletic appearance often surprised people that didn't know that he played or had played for the Mariners. He wasn't what you would expect to see a major league baseball player look like as he was sinewy, medium height (70 inches in height) and probably weighed about 175 pounds. He didn't appear to be so, but he was fast and extremely strong,

powerful. His hair was dark brown as was his mother's, had blue eyes, and had a bronze complexion from all of the days he spent toiling in the outfield. Gary adored his father. Above all, he respected him and for all that he stood for in life. Fredrick didn't say much, but when he spoke everyone listened. Gary's mother on the other hand was a jabber Betty as was Mrs. Crawford. What a pair they were. They could have been sisters except Mrs. Crawford was a blonde. I suppose in a final appraisal of the two women, one would say that they weren't ugly children. Of their husbands, one might say that they were handsome in a subtle way. Guy was tall and noticeably muscular. He looked like a football player. Strangely he did not act like one even though his teaching assignment was physical education. Gary suspected that when he stopped playing football he left his football life in the locker room. His coaching style, as he was told, was laid back and creative. He got the most out of his players, but in a mellow respectful manner. Like his father, Guy Crawford was a good man. He and Gary's dad were married to wonderful, caring women.

Gary frowned. "Hum, what else do you want to talk about?"

Fredrick pursed his lips and stared at a fixed point on the wall. He pleaded, "Please be patient with me, son. What I have to say isn't easy, but it is important that you listen very carefully to what I have to say."

"I'm all ears."

"It's about Angelina. I've been watching you two grow up together, side by side almost from the moment you two were born. At times you have been inseparable, now more so than ever."

"That's because she's my best friend. I really like her." He smiled sheepishly. "I think that she likes me too."

Fredrick chuckled. "Don't I know, um, as it isn't obvious?" He paused to gather himself and then proceeded, "Angelina is a beautiful girl, a beautiful young woman. I know that you know that as she has all of her dimensions in the right places in perfect harmony with what any person would expect a beautiful woman to look like. I doubt that anyone in your school is even close to being in her class."

Gary nodded. "I agree. I have noticed." He grinned, "She is a looker, a real keeper."

Fredrick chuckled, nodding his head in agreement. "Angelina has become a young woman and you a young man." He paused. "The two of you are going to start having different feelings for each other. That may have already begun."

Gary nodded. "I think I see where you are going with this."

Fredrick nodded and then pleaded, "Just allow me to finish." He paused again. "It is important that you always treat her with respect and not get carried away and do something that you will regret."

Gary wrinkled up his nose and turned his head slightly the side, studying his father in an attempt to try and figure exactly what he was trying to say. "I'm not certain that I know exactly what you mean. I have always treated her with respect. I've always tried to protect her. I really like her, and I wouldn't ever do anything to hurt her."

"I know son. What I'm trying to say and doing a lousy job of it is that you see her differently now than you used to." He paused to see if what he had said registered. He shook his head in modest disgust with his inability to explain himself clearly. "Oh shit, um excuse me, um, I mean that Angelina is becoming a fully mature young woman. She is very desirable. There will be times when you are with her that you will want something more than just friendship."

Gary nodded. "Um, are you trying to say that I might want to have sex with her?"

Fredrick sighed. "Yes, that's exactly what I mean. You have already probably thought about kissing her and touching her and maybe even more."

Gary nodded. "Yes, the thought has crossed my mind, but I really like her. No, I love her. I don't want to do anything that would…." Gary paused to collect his thoughts. "The guys talk about doing it with girls all the time. You know, they talk about having sex with their girlfriends. They talk about them, the girls that they do it with as though they have no value. I don't feel that way about Angelina. To me she is special and I want to keep it that way. I would never try to do to her what the guys brag about doing to the girls that they date." He paused, clenched up his fist and then continued, "I sure as hell wouldn't talk about having sex with her even if we were. That should remain private between Angelina and me. Um, that is if we ever did have sex."

Gary's dad exhaled with relief, nodding. "That is good to hear, son. You have lots of time ahead of you to share your feelings for Angelina in a most special way. There is no hurry."

"I know. Dad, I appreciate what you have said to me. It probably hasn't been easy for you. Please trust me and know that I won't do anything bad to her. I will save all of that stuff for when the time is right. I love her dad, and I will always treat her right, with respect."

Fredrick nodded. "Are we okay?"

Gary nodded. "Always, we will always be okay. I love you dad."

"I love you too, son. Damn, this was harder than I thought it would be. I sure as hell am glad that I'm not going to try to teach health."

They both started to chuckle and then it turned into laughter. Finally, Fredrick grabbed Gary and gave him a big hug, a hug that neither seemed to have any desire to end.

Claudia entered the room with a big smile on her face. "I see that everything went okay? Come on, it's time to eat."

The next day Gary walked Angelina home after school. The silence was deafening. Finally, he took a deep breath and audibly exhaled.

Angelina looked at him curiously. "Is something wrong? You have been awfully quiet."

"Not really, but yeah in a way there is. I had a talk with my dad last night." He paused for a moment, stopped and took her hand. Facing her he said, "Can we talk?"

She nodded. "I know. If what you want to talk about is what I think it is, I believe that I went through the same thing with my mom last night."

"Really, are you serious? No, you have to be kidding."

Angelina snorted. "Yes, really, and I am deathly serious." She paused. "We had the talk."

Gary blushed. "This isn't exactly easy to talk about."

"I know, but I agree that it is time that we talk about it. So, why don't you just come out with it so we can move on?"

"Why should I begin?"

"Because you started it, Gary, and I hope you know that I love you."

Gary nodded. "I know, and I love you too. That's the problem. I'm starting to get strange feelings when we are together, when we hold hands, and when we kiss."

"Me too and that's what my mom and I talked about. She told me about the diving board."

"The diving board, what has the diving board got to do with….?"

Angelina smiled. "I thought the same thing until my mother explained it to me. After I heard what she had to say I believe it has everything to do with it."

"Would you care to explain this diving board idea to me?"

"I have every intention of doing so." Angelina paused and then began very slowly to explain, "Well, it is like this. We both are probably starting to get pressure from our friends to do it. You know, to um, to have sex. After all, most of them are doing it and they are starting to wonder why we aren't. Am I right so far?"

Gary nodded. "Yeah, there has been some talk. No, I take that back. There has been a lot of talk. To hear the guys talk, they have all done it a lot and they aren't even going steady like we are. I doubt that a day goes by without someone talking about doing with some girl. It is locker room talk. Quite frankly, it disgusts me because I think that they are making the girls they date seem cheap, like floozies."

Angelina giggled, "Are we going steady?" "Well yes, well, aren't we?"

"I sure hope so, but you haven't actually asked."

"Well, let's say that I have. No, that won't be good enough knowing you." He paused, gathered himself, and then continued, "Angelina, will you go steady with me?"

Angelina smiled. "Of course I will. I just want to know what took you so long to ask."

Gary shook his head. "Why don't you just continue? This is already getting complicated." He paused, turning a mild shade of red. "If you insist I'll tell you why I haven't asked you after you finish telling me about the diving board."

"Count on it." Angelina smiled. "Well, there is a lot of pressure being put on me to do it, and as mom explained to me, it is like being with your friends at a pool party where there is a very high diving board. All of the kids are taking turns jumping or diving off the board. They keep urging me to jump, but I really don't want to because I'm afraid." She paused. "I don't know about you, but jumping off a high diving board scares me to death. Anyway, after a while they finally talk me into doing it. So, I approach the board and start to climb up the ladder. On the way up I pause and look down upon them. They are urging me on. They even suggest that I might be chicken to do it. So, I keep climbing until I get to the top. Again I look down and they are laughing and yelling for me to jump." She paused. "You know that peer pressure is very powerful and in the final analysis we are afraid to not go along for fear of being called a chicken or a coward or even not being accepted."

Gary nodded. "I agree. Peer pressure is very powerful. We want to please our friends, but.... Anyway, I'm starting to get the picture. You don't want to jump, but they are urging you on, so you walk out to the end of the board."

"Exactly and when I look down at the water it is so far away. It looks like concrete and the thought of jumping is so scary, but they keep yelling for me to jump."

"Yeah, and then you jump."

Angelina smiled. "Yes, and then it is too late. I can't turn back."

Gary nodded. "I don't want it to be like that, Angelina. When I jump, I want it to be because I really want to jump and you want to jump with me." He paused. "Are you going to be disappointed if I tell you that even though I think that it would be great to do it with you that, um, I don't think that I am ready? I mean, I don't want to do it with you until it is right and it is exactly what we both want?"

Angelina smiled. "That is exactly how I feel. Gary, I love you. Would you please kiss me?"

Looking around, he asked, "Do you want me to kiss you here?"

"Yes, I want you to kiss me right here. By the way, why did you wait so long to ask me to go steady?"

"I wish that I knew for sure, but just know that I am so glad that you said yes. I love you."

Gary and Angelina's freshman, sophomore, and junior years passed. Angelina's report card showed nothing but A's, and Gary's average was slightly lower with but two B's on his record. Angelina was an accomplished pianist, sang in the choir, and was painting seriously. Gary had made all-league in baseball his freshman and sophomore years and all state his junior year. He was attracting a lot of attention from baseball scouts and college recruiters. Three of the colleges that were high on his list were North Carolina, Oregon State, and Stanford. Angelina had shown interest in attending the University of California at Berkley, Berklee in Boston, and Juilliard in New York to study music. Gary's interest was in law, political science, history, and government. Getting a degree was a definite goal for both of them. Professional baseball would have to wait for Gary, and a career as a pianist or a singer would have to wait for Angelina.

What couldn't wait was the inner pressure that he and Angelina felt to take their love for each other to another level. The senior season was nearing and so too was their season of love. Neither wanted their love to only last one season. Their desire was for many, many seasons. They wanted it to be a full career, a lifetime.

Chapter Four

Who Am I

Have you ever asked the questions, "Who am I? Where do I really live? Where did I come from?" The questions are valid and need to be asked, but the answers could be complex, maybe even not understood unless we are able to go beyond physical and mental barriers. The barriers, some of which have been imposed by hand me down knowledge and lore, have been imposed and enforced by the organized religions of the World of which we are a part. Perhaps those institutions can be held accountable for some of the imposed myths, ideas, or beliefs that we have a justification to question? It is important to not let the unknown be an obstruction to exploring "Who I am, where did I come from, and where do I live."

In Oregon's Willamette Valley, August is warm, sometimes even hot. Summers are delightful, but usually the term hot, ninety and above days, are not a common experience. Five to seven days in an entire summer might be described as hot to some while to others it is just the tip of the warming iceberg if you live where it is hot all summer.

An August evening has the eerie means of announcing that fall or autumn is approaching. There is a hint that the frost that will come is approaching and the beautiful orange harvest moon that emerges and hangs in the sky so near, yet so far away will soon appear.

The Wonderment of Life

The beginning of Gary and Angelina's senior year at Lake Oswego High School was just around the corner. A few days before the beginning of the school year Gary and Angelina were out for the evening walking along the Willamette River under that bright orange full moon. Resting on the horizon like a big orange basketball, it seemed to be smiling at them. It was so big and clear it seemed they could actually reach out and touch it. Gary shook his head as he walked hand in hand with his best friend.

Impatiently, in an attempt to break the silence, Angelina inquired, "What? What are you thinking about now? Why are you giving me the silent treatment?"

"Do you ever think about who you are, where you have come from, or about the meaning of all this, um what we experience but often take for granted? I am not talking about what we learned in Sunday school or what we might have read in the Bible. I'm talking about what we allow our minds to really consider, Angelina. What is the source of all of this?"

Angelina stopped and turned toward Gary, looking at him strangely. "What did you just say, you know, that bit about the source of all of this? Why did you mention The Source?"

Gary shrugged his shoulders. "I don't know. It just came out. For some reason it seemed more meaningful to say than refer, as we commonly do, to God."

Angelina nodded her head. "It is strange, very strange that you would say that because I think about The Source of all of this all the time. I think sometimes that this is just a dream. I wonder if you are really real. I wonder why I am here and why I am so lucky to be here with you. I wonder if we have met before some place that I am not even familiar with or know nothing about. Yes, I think about it all the time." She paused. "We both stopped going to church a couple of years back. Sitting in a pew every Sunday just wasn't cutting it for me. I felt that there was so much more to learn than listening to the canned sermon that the minister delivered. He actually spoke as if he knew the meaning of all of this. In actuality, I sincerely doubt if he knows any more than we do."

Gary nodded. "Yeah, I know what you mean. Will you look at that river! It is so beautiful with the light of the moon reflecting off of it. Do you know where it begins?"

"What do you mean? Where does what begin? Do you mean the river or us? You have me thinking in two dimensions now."

"The Willamette River, do you know where it begins?"

"Not exactly, but I know that it comes from somewhere east of Eugene." Angelina squeezed his hand. "I guess that begs the question of where are we from. It isn't exactly, what you see is what you get, you know. There has to be so much more."

"I know what you mean. When I look up at the sky on a clear night and see all of those bright objects, the stars in the sky, I just have to wonder if there isn't so much more." Gary paused for a moment. "You know, we are really quite insignificant."

Angela smiled. "Maybe to us we are insignificant, but maybe to the Supreme Being, The Source, or whatever we are really quite significant. Oh God, you have me doing it now. I just mentioned The Source. Why? I sure don't know." She paused. "I want you to know that to me you are very significant, very special."

Gary nodded. "I feel the same way about you. Um, let's think about where we live for a moment."

Angelina chuckled, offering, "Well for starters we both live in a house on A Street with wonderful parents that love us very much, and we both have two wonderful, but bothersome brothers that drive us nuts at times." She paused. "You know we are really quite fortunate."

Gary smiled. "Yes, we are. We've been blessed. Imagine our good fortune to live in Lake Oswego, a suburb of Portland, have the opportunity to attend a fantastic school, and as you say, live in a nice house with adoring and loving parents. We really don't want for anything." He paused. "Lake Oswego gets its name honestly because its core borders on the lake. If we go south we run into West Linn."

Angelina snorted, "Okay, bunko, let the geography lesson begin." She paused. "Yes, and to the north is Portland which is in Multnomah County which is in the State of Oregon. All that we have mentioned is on the west side of Willamette River." She paused again. "What I was leading up to is the fact that living right under our nose, so to speak, are people who are defined as homeless. They really get a bad name because they loll about on the streets, strew their trash all over the place, and some are observed to rant and rave. Many of those poor people are mentally challenged and need to be under institutional care, others are drug users or addicts, still others are military people who have come home with horrific disorders, and then there are those that due to circumstances beyond their control are cast out of their homes and forced to live on the street because of the loss of their job or a horrific raise in the cost of rent."

Gary nodded. "Yeah, and the solution to the problem is to just to move them from one place to another when someone complains." He chuckled. "Um, don't forget that Portland is on both sides of the Willamette River. The homeless people you talk about camp out on both sides of the river. Ah, sorry to interrupt. Keep going, Angelina. You are on a roll."

"Well, Oregon is one of fifty states in a country called the United States. This is a terrific state to live in if you have a job with sufficient income to pay the rent and utilities. A good job if you have one allows you to put food on the table for your family, affords you transportation to get to work and go other places for fun and recreation, and help your children get a good education to better prepare them for life. However, like the other states, there is an increasing abandonment of the mentally ill, the unemployed, and the drug users."

Gary quickly added, "Don't forget the abandoned members of the Armed Forces."

Angelina nodded, paused and chuckled with delight. "And the United States is part of North America, one of the seven continents. Um, and all of this is a part of our planet, Earth. I suspect that the problems you mention are everywhere. I would like to do something if I could, but I wouldn't know where to start."

"You already have when you said that you wished that you knew what you could do. Some Americans and peoples from other countries could care less. It is sort of the old adage, 'Out of sight, out of mind'. I suppose that if we don't see them, they don't exist."

Angelina giggled. "We forgot to say that we live in the Western Hemisphere."

Gary nodded. "Do we need to go further? I think that it all goes on and on and never ends, I mean our Universe, Galaxy or whatever."

Angelina nodded. "Do think that we go on and on?"

Gary frowned. "Well, in the church that we used to attend, they believe that we do if we're good and earn the right to go to Heaven which the minister seems to think is the termination point. Of course in that train of thought we have to wait until the end of the World and then present ourselves before God for judgement."

Angelina cocked her head as if to say, "Really?" "Do you really believe that, I mean, what about the poor souls that aren't good? What about those that have never heard of Jesus or those that believe in another God. They imply that they go to Hell. Can you really swallow that?"

"I don't know. I know that I don't believe in Hell." Gary paused. "No I don't believe in what you just said. I believe that our real existence never ends."

Angelina looked at Gary very closely for a long moment. "Do you believe in God?"

"I don't know what I would call it, but I believe in something that is so powerful, so wonderful, something that is responsible for all of this that we know and experience. I believe that it just didn't happen." He paused. "Do you think that is why we mentioned The Source?"

"I don't know, but I like the term." She paused again. "What about what the Bible says?"

"Angelina, I think that the Bible is a wonderfully simple story that helps us to begin to think about who we are, where we come from and where we are headed. Perhaps it is the Supreme Being's way of directing us along the way through input from special people. Maybe they have been sent to help us consider where we're from, how we got here, and where we should want to go. With their guidance I believe that in the final analysis it is up to us to decide the answers to those questions. After all we do have the gift of self- determination and we were given a mind and the power of reasoning." Gary paused. "Actually, I don't know what I believe. I guess I can best say that I just don't know, but I am searching and trying to figure out the mystery of life."

"Gary, could we talk about something else for a moment?"

Gary expelled a sigh of relief. "Sure, what is on your mind? I think we have exhausted that topic for now."

"I want to talk about us."

Gary nodded. "This sounds serious. Should I get ready to run for cover?"

Angelina smiled and slowly turned her head towards the Willamette River. The moon had risen in the sky, casting interesting designs on the calm waters that flowed by. In the distance the skyline of Portland was visible, the lights making the view breathtakingly beautiful. The Tilikum Bridge's was aglow with soothing bright lights. The colors of the bridge and the lights of Portland seemed to cover the entire spectrum of light. "To begin, you know that I love you, right?"

"Yes and you know that I love you?"

"I do. Um, Gary, do you remember me telling you when we were much, much younger that I was going to marry you?"

"Vaguely, yes, I recall. At the time it made me nervous. No, it made me very nervous. It almost made me want to run away."

"And now, how do you feel about the idea?"

Gary grinned. "Are you proposing to me?" Gary jabbed her in the ribs gently and began to laugh. "If you are I am going to put on my tennis shoes and start running."

Angelina's face suddenly was covered with a hurt look. "Seriously, you mean that I have invested all of this time on you to just have you pick up and run away?"

Gary stopped laughing. Suddenly his expression reflected the seriousness of her attempt to make some sense of what they were or what they might become. "No, silly, I was just kidding. Actually, I think that someday it will be a great idea."

"Good! That is how I feel. Now I want to discuss something else, something that has been weighing rather heavily on my mind for some time."

"And what might that be?"

Angelina put her hands on her hips. "Do you find me attractive? I mean, do you find me not only attractive, but sexy? Do you find me desirable? Do you ever want me?"

"Let me see. Yes, yes, yes, yes and yes of course I do. If I may be so bold, I want you to know that I think that you are the most beautiful girl that I have ever seen. Everything about you is perfect, and yes, I really want you. Did I give you the proper number of yeses?"

"I think that you added one. No, I lost count, so I will say that you gave me the right number. Um, you think that my breasts are big enough?"

Gary blushed. Stuttering, he replied, "They are perfect. What's more every time I see you in a bathing suit, well, I sort of get excited because your body is so perfect, so desirable."

"When you say that you get excited, is it like when we're making out?"

Gary blushed. "What do you mean?"

"Well, I feel your excitement pressing against me. You know, I feel your boner, your erection. My God Gary, you jab me with it when you get excited to the point where I feel almost like a matador being gored by a raging bull."

"I'm sorry. I didn't know."

"Don't be sorry. I really like it. In fact I really want to reach out and touch it, hold it in my hand."

"Wow! I think that I would really like that. I, um, really want you, but I also believe that the right thing for us to do is to wait even though I really want to touch you. What about you?"

"Would you like to touch me?"

Gary snorted. "Are you kidding? Of course, I want to touch you. I just said that I did and I really mean it. I think about it all the time." He paused and then asked hesitatingly, "Do you ever want me to touch you?"

"Yes, yes I think that would be wonderful." She paused. "Do you ever want me to touch you? Oh God, you have already said that you would."

Gary gulped. His voice shook as he replied, "To confirm what you have heard and what I have said, yes, I think that would be wonderful. I, ah…"

Before he could finish, she continued, "Gary, I trust you. I know that you would never do anything to hurt me or do anything to me that we would both come to regret."

"I agree. So, where are you going with this? Um, by the way, what caused you to bring this up?"

Angelina smiled coyly. "Well, I think that the time has come for us to start touching each other." She paused to let him have some time to digest what she had said. "I want to make you feel good. I want to hold your boner in my hand and rub it until you cum. I want you to touch my breasts and put your finger inside of me and make me cum. I love you so much. I think about doing those things with you all the time. When I am lying in bed and thinking about you and what I want you to do to me I get all wet with desire."

Gary's voice broke as he responded, "Me too. I have wanted to touch you so badly for so long." He paused. "You know that once we start, um, touching each other, well, it is going to be hard to stop."

Angelina giggled. "I know that it will be hard to stop, but I want us to touch each other." She smiled. I am sorry to inform you that it will have to wait because I am not going to do that while we are here. We have to pick a better place at some other time."

"I agree." Gary nodded as he pulled Angelina close to him. He kissed her tenderly. "I love you so much."

"Ditto, but I love you more."

"Baloney, you couldn't ever love me as much as I love you."

"Gary, could we just agree that we love each other the same and that it is so, so wonderful?"

"I'll go along with that. I don't think that we're in a contest. Neither of us has to win this debate."

Angelina and Gary's senior year began with a bang. There was the excitement of nearing the end of high school, and yet, a degree of sadness. Friday night football games, after game dances, school musical productions, special dances, and then there was also the excitement and anxiety of selecting the right college to attend. Of course not to be forgotten was and another state baseball championship to win, their third since Gary's dad had taken over the coaching duties at the beginning of Gary's sophomore year. Not to be forgotten was the anxiety of waiting to see if the right scholarship offers would be tendered.

Thinking back, Gary felt that he had been blessed. His dad had been a successful professional baseball player, and then had assumed his teaching duties second semester of his freshman year after retiring. His mom was one of the most popular teachers on staff as were Angelina's parents. Guy was an assistant football coach in addition to teaching physical education and Sue was one of the best music teacher's in the state, winning several music awards and contests with her choir. His mom's claim to fame was watching her student move on successfully to college with advanced writing skills. Greg was a sophomore and considered an up and coming football player. Lance, a bit taller, was considered an important member of the basketball team.

Gary had been approached to also play football, but, in agreement with Angelina and his dad and mom, wisdom prevailed. He put all of his energy into baseball. Why was he blessed? It all came down to knowing that no matter what his choice or Angelina's choice was or the awards tendered were, they were headed on a path supported by their parents. They felt good about where they possibly might be headed.

Angelina was beautiful. Although deeply involved in music and art, she could have easily passed for an athlete with her trim, shapely body that exposed no extra baggage. Her interest in athletics was close to zero, but she loved watching Gary play baseball and expanded her devoted attention to watching Greg play football and her brother excel on the basketball court. Her love was singing, playing the piano, and drawing. That interest had expanded to painting. She was also starting to explore, in depth, the homeless issues in the Portland area. Secretly she wanted to do something to make a difference. At that moment she just didn't know where or how to begin.

Why Gary and Angelina were close, a serious relationship item was a mystery to their friends. She was devoted to the artistic side of life having been in several school musical productions. Two of her paintings hung in the Crawford and Mallon homes. Gary was all about athletics with some occasional mention of politics. All of that aside they were not just close. They were a couple and made no secret of going steady with eyes for nobody but each other. Their love for each other was starting to strain their ability to resist moving their relationship to the next level.

Standing by Angelina's locker after school, Gary teased, "I know you're not fond of sports, but…"

Indignantly she snorted, interrupting, "Listen here Buster, I'll have you know that I have never complained about watching your brother's football games, my brother's basketball games, or your baseball games. I think that it is more accurate to say that I have no desire to participate, but for those that I love I will go to any lengths to support them." Angelina groaned. "Will it ever end?"

Gary chuckled. "When I retire it will all be over for you, and you can spend all of your time singing, playing your piano and painting."

"Does that bother you that I love to paint, sing, and play the piano?" She paused. "Um, don't forget my interest in the homeless. I don't know how, but someday I want to make a difference, to help solve the problem if I can find a solution."

"To answer your first question, No, I just don't know why you dislike sports." He paused. "As to your final comment, let me suggest that you just be the one that will come up with a solution. You have all of my support. When I retire from baseball, maybe I can enter into the political arena and help you realize your dream."

"You didn't hear me. I don't dislike sports. Actually, I quite enjoy watching other people play, especially you and our brothers. I just don't see the point in me getting out there and getting all sweaty as I run up and down the court or field or whatever. I like the peaceful solitude of the art room or the music room. Of course I love being with you." She smiled. "Thank you for understanding my desire to help the homeless and, yes, if you go into politics I will welcome your support."

Gary chuckled. "You seem to enjoy our room."

Angelina smiled. "You mean lying beside you in the back seat of your dad's car touching you and having you touch me?" She nodded as she gazed at him with a dreamy stare. "Yes, I enjoy that a lot. It's just that I want more. I want to feel you inside of me. I want to be completely connected to you. To use a sentence that I hope will become ours forever; I want you to make love to me. I want us to make love." She grinned sheepishly. "I suspect that other words might creep into the conversation when we really get into it. Just know that lately that is all I can think about when I am alone with you. Gary, you occupy my thoughts all the time."

"Are you sure that you are ready for that to happen, um, go all the way?"

"Yes, I am certain. That is exactly what I want to happen. However, I don't want to do it in a car. I want us to do in a bed. I want to get completely naked with you and feel the complete joy and wonderment that I know I will feel when we make love. By the way, I have started taking the pill."

"Wow! You are starting to cause my temperature to rise."

"Whoa boy, in case you haven't noticed, we're in the hallway of Oswego High School. I don't think that, that this is the time or place to get all excited. You know that when you get excited, well, a certain thing becomes quite evident." Angelina studied him for a moment. "Our parents won't be coming home for at least a couple of hours after the end of the school day. You told me that your parents have to go into Portland for something, my dad is doing something after school and won't be home until about 5:00-5:30, and my mom is going with your parents. We'll have either one of our houses all to ourselves. Um, we might want to use your home because I don't know what Lance is going to be doing after school. Maybe he'll be hanging out with Greg. How about it? Do you want to do it?"

"Of course I do. That is all I can think of lately as well, but are you sure that you are ready to take the next step?"

"Yes, I have never been so sure in all of my life. By the way, you didn't react when I told you, but you don't have to worry because I have been taking birth control pills. I have been on the pill for over a month now."

"Does your mom know?"

"No silly. I'm not stupid. She would have a cow if she knew." Gary nodded. "Okay then, let's go. Time is a wasting."

When Gary's parents came home the love birds were busy cleaning up the morning dishes. A distinctive aura of something special lingered in the air like the sweet aroma that the scent of lavender Febreze leaves. Gary nervously explained, "Hi mom and dad, Angelina owed me so she decided to pay up by helping me clean up the dishes."

Fredrick smiled. "That is very thoughtful of you two. It must have been quite a debt for you to help with the dishes, Angelina. By the way, how would you like to join us? We're going to join the Crawford's to go out for something to eat?"

Angelina nodded. "What about Greg and Lance, are they going too?"

Claudia chimed in, "Yes, they will be here in a few minutes." She smiled somewhat knowingly. "So, other than cleaning up the kitchen, what have you two been up to?"

Angelina blushed, shrugging her shoulders. "Not much, we just, um, we were just hanging out doing stuff."

Fredrick chuckled. "And what do you mean by doing stuff?"

Gary came to Angelina's rescue. "I don't know dad. I didn't keep a diary of what we did. We were just hanging out like always."

Fredrick nodded. "I see. Well, you both look like you were having a good time. You have probably worked up an appetite."

Gary looked at his dad and then at Angelina with a questioning stare. *"Do you suppose they know?"*

Angelina blushed. Her thoughts were much the same.

Just then, the awkwardness of the moment was dispelled with the arrival of Angelina's parents and their brothers. Saved by the bell! The looks of relief that appeared on Angelina's and Gary's face spoke volumes.

The months passed as the senior year, too short, entered the spring time of the year. Conversations about where they would attend college were almost a nightly topic. So too was the anticipation of the upcoming baseball season. Not lost in all of the activity and almost daily discussions was the elevated level of their expanded emotional involvement.

On the Saturday before the first practice of baseball season, Gary and Angelina were lying beside each other in Gary's bed. Their parents had slipped away to Sun River for the weekend to enjoy a bit of peace before the baseball season was set to begin. Greg and Lance had accompanied them, so Angelina and Gary had the houses all to themselves. Angelina and he had both received instructions to hold down the home fires. Their parents made it very clear that didn't mean tending the nighttime fire together other than what they thought would just be nothing more than two very close friends hanging out with each other.

"I was thinking Angelina, we spent last night at your place and we'll spend tonight at my place, what about Sunday?"

Angelina giggled. "Are you up to spending half of our time here and the other half at my place? We could start here and continue at my place. We'll have to be ready to greet our parents and brothers by 4:00 because that is when my parents said they would be back."

Gary nodded. "Yeah, it was nice of them to tell us that they would call when they were set to leave for home." He paused, looking into her sparkling blue eyes. "Maybe we could hang out together for about an hour after they call. I think that…"

"Good idea. Do you think that our parents know, you know, what we have been doing?"

"I don't know for sure, Angelina. My dad has that knowing smile on his face from time to time, but he has never said anything. What about you?"

"My mom gives me that knowing look from time to time as well, but my dad is clueless. I think we could be doing it right under his nose and he would be unaware."

"That's because he trusts you."

"I know. It's just that…. Um, do you think that if they knew they would be disappointed?"

Gary shrugged his shoulders. "I don't think so, but I really don't know for sure. Do you feel like we're being too sneaky?"

"Sneaky, you're damned right we're sneaky. I'm not about to let the cat out of the bag, but somehow I feel that we might be letting them down."

"What? What are you trying to say, Angelina? Are you saying that you feel we should stop doing it?"

"No, absolutely not, but don't you think that the time has come for us to decide where we are going to college and what is going to become of us after we graduate? Do we have a future or not?"

"Angelina, as you know I have offers from several place to go and play on a baseball scholarship. Right now I am leaning towards Stanford."

Angelina nodded. "Yeah, I am strongly considering the University of California at Berkley. They have a good music school and I can be close to you."

Gary studied her for a moment. "Is close all you want?"

Angelina's eyes twinkled in anticipation. "What do you mean? Where are you going with this?"

"Well, I was thinking that close wouldn't be good enough for me."

"So, what do you want?"

"I guess that this is as good a time as any to tell you that I want to marry you."

Angelina shrieked with excitement. "Oh Gary, do you mean it?" "Yes, with all of my heart. If we get married we can live together some place in between our schools. They are reasonably close geographically, probably an hour or less depending on the traffic."

"True, it's good that you mentioned the traffic. As you know we're not just talking about miles here. In California you talk about time."

Gary frowned. "So are you thinking that getting married is a bad idea?"

"Absolutely not, I think that it is a wonderful idea. We'll just have to find a way to make the necessary adjustments, particularly during baseball season."

"Where there is a will, there is a way. So, will you marry me?" "Yes, oh yes. I love you so much."

"What do you want to do about the rings?"

"Gary, I wouldn't care if we got a couple of rings at Portland's Saturday Market or out of a Cracker Jack box. We can do the diamond ring thing after we get out of college and both of us have good jobs. Right now all that counts is that we are going to get married and be together forever."

"That sounds like a plan. Maybe we should get out of bed and drive into Portland and take care of ring detail right now." He paused. "Will rings from Saturday Market really work for you?"

"Of course and what you have said is a terrific idea! I can't wait to tell my folks." She grinned. "I think that the time has come for 'show and tell'."

"Angelina, before you tell them, um, show them your ring, I need to ask your father's permission. I'm thinking that we can take care of all that when they get back from Sun River. What are your thoughts?"

"I agree. Come on, let's get moving. If we hurry we can get the rings and still get back here in time to do it again before our parents get back."

Gary chuckled. "You are too much. If I didn't know better I would think that you are trying to wear me out." He smiled. "So, I will let Stanford know that I am accepting their scholarship offer." He paused. "You know, I had all but decided after my visit to Stanford a week ago."

"Good! And I'll let Cal know. Honey, this is going to be so crazy neat. I have looked forward to this moment all of my life." She smiled. "Yes, I had all but decided on attending Cal as well when I went down there for a visit after Christmas."

"Do you suppose that maybe, just maybe that this was planned even before we were born?"

Angelina smiled. "Maybe someday we'll know for sure, right now I'm thinking that it was." She nodded. "It's almost like we will have a marriage made in Heaven as the saying goes."

At 3:30 their parents returned. Angelina's mother smiled as she walked through the door. "I told your dad that you two would be here. Gary, your parents will be right over as soon as they get their car unloaded."

"How was Sun River, Mrs. Crawford? Did you have a good time?" Angelina's dad grinned. "Yes, we had a great time. What about you? Did you get any sleep?"

Sue scolded, "Honestly, Guy, what kind of question is that? Of course they got some sleep. I swear, sometimes you can say the damn dandiest things."

There was a knock on the door, followed by a, "Hello, anybody home?" Gary's parents had arrived with their humor intact.

Gary gave them a hug and then announced, "Could we go into the living room? I have something I want to share with you."

Guy winked. "I told you so."

"Hush, Guy! Let's just wait until the cat is out of the bag before you open your mouth. This is Gary and Angelina's party so let them have center stage."

Gary shook his head. It appeared that what he had to share with the parents had already been a topic of discussion that weekend. "Well, it appears that what I have to say is not going to be a huge surprise. So, ah, Mr. Crawford I want to know if I can have your permission to marry your daughter. We have talked about this and we want to get married before we go off to college." Not waiting for a response, he pushed forward. "I promise to take care of her and love her for ever and ever."

Angelina interrupted excitedly, "Yes, and we have decided that we will attend school in California. Gary is going to accept the offer from Stanford and I am going to go to Cal." Suddenly she thrust her left hand outward. "See, all you have to do is say yes and it is official."

Guy nodded. "Nothing would make me happier. I think I speak for all of us when I say that we have suspected that this was coming for a long time and it is wonderful news. You two were right for each other right from the beginning."

Claudia, Sue, and Fredrick chimed in with their own version of "Yes".

Greg and Lance, restless throughout the drama, arose from the couch and headed for the door. Speaking almost in unison, they announced, "If it is all the same to you guys, we want to go outside. Congratulations you guys." Turning to Lance, Greg mumbled, "All of this mushy stuff is too much for me to handle."

After the boys had disappeared, Claudia began, "We know that hiding your love for each other hasn't been easy. Just know that you don't have to sneak around any longer. Angelina, both your mother and father, my husband and I agree that we have spare bedrooms that are yours to use. Yes, we have known for a long time about you two even though you have gone to great measures to keep it a secret. We would rather you express your love for each other in one of the spare bedrooms than in a car parked in some isolated place." She paused, looking around to see that what she had said was understood. "Just know that you both will sleep in your own homes. We are not upset, we're just so terribly happy that what we have prayed for is finally coming true." She paused reflectively. "I know that you two respect each other and love each other very much. We just want to make your wait for the big day a little easier."

Fredrick nodded. "That goes for me." "And me" chimed in Guy.

"And don't forget about me." Sue smiled broadly. "I am so proud. I guess we have a wedding to plan."

The Laker's baseball season, like the previous two years, went very, very well. They went into the playoffs for the state title undefeated. Gary had been named all-league and made the all-state team. His hitting and fielding made a huge impression on all the teams that he faced. Patrolling center field with sure hands and errorless judgement, it did not go unnoticed that he possessed a gun for an arm, throwing out many runners trying to stretch a hit into an extra base hit or more. His batting average was .490, hitting with power delivering the big blows that totaled 25 home runs and an additional 30 extra base hits.

On the eve of the championship game played at Volcano Stadium in Keizer, Gary's dad sat down with him to have a father to son talk. "Son, you have been everything that a father could possibly hope for and more. Happily I have also had the honor of being your coach. You have achieved in the classroom, you had a fantastic four year run in baseball, and, more importantly, you have just been a great person. I have watched you and Angelina very carefully. I am so proud of the way you have treated her. I am certain that you and she will have a very happy marriage. I am also certain that you have a terrific career in baseball ahead of you."

"Thanks dad. What you've said to me means a lot. In case you don't know it, you are my hero and I love you a lot."

"The feeling is mutual, son. You have made your mother and me so proud."

"So, what are you going to do next year? Are you going to continue to coach the baseball team and teach math?"

"No, that is what I wanted to tell you. I made a lot of money playing baseball and I was smart enough to invest wisely. Your mother and I have talked about retiring. With you and Angelina going off to college in California, the time is right for your mother and me to retire and do some traveling. Of course that will involve watching you play baseball for the Cardinals and watching Angelina's musical performances in addition to watching your brothers perform at Lake Oswego."

"Does that mean that you are going to move?"

"No, we're going to stay in Lake Oswego to watch your brother finish up. He's quite a football player, you know."

"Yeah, I know. Maybe I should tell him. It's just………"

Fredrick nodded. "I know. Little brothers get under your feet from time to time. Sadly before you know it you're both grown up and have missed out on really connecting if you aren't careful."

Gary nodded. "Yeah, Greg is quite a guy. I am going to tell him how proud I am of him."

"About your upcoming marriage and all that occurs after you are married, um, I……."

"I know what you are going to say, Dad. Having kids is going to be put off until we finish college. Angelina want to enjoy being married before we tackle having children."

"That is a wise decision, Gary. You know that you mom and I waited, and it turned out pretty damned good."

Gary smiled. "You know that you are a great coach, don't you? "Look what I had to work with. Heck a blind man could have coached our team."

"Well, that may be what you think, but the other guys and I know different. You haven't won two championships without knowing what you are doing. Today is going to be number three."

Gary's dad cleared his throat and then began, "Another thing that I wanted to talk to you about is that I may have to use you on the mound in the later innings today. All of the pitchers are worn out and I don't want to risk inuring their arms. Are you okay with that?

Gary nodded. "I will be available to do whatever you want me to do. So, what say we just go out and win? I'm starting to get antsy about playing."

Gary's dad stood up. "One more thing before we go out and win number three. You and Angelina are going to both be on scholarship, but that will not cover your apartment, so your mother and I have decided to take care of your apartment rental costs."

The crowd at Kaiser, Oregon Volcano Stadium was raucously loud and wild in a spirited way. The weather was perfect with the temperature in the low 70's. Everything seemed to go according to script as Lake Oswego jumped out to an early lead. Gary came in to relieve the starting pitcher and threw two innings of hitless baseball as the Lakers cruised to the title, winning 4-0. Gary went four for four and hit two home runs. Another chapter had come to an end with a script that could only have been written in Hollywood. The two families were very close, the future looked bright for everyone, and more importantly, Gary and Angelina were getting married. Gary often thought that perhaps Angelina had special connections as her prediction of marrying him early in their lives was soon to come true. He still wondered it something more powerful might be the actual script writer.

Chapter Five

I Do

> When a person says "I do" or "I will" they are making a promise, a pledge to do what they are saying "I do" or "I will" to do without hesitation, regret or conditions for the person they are saying "I do" or "I will" to. It is a voluntary pledge, a commitment.

Graduation from high school was special. Angelina spoke before those assembled as the Valedictorian of their class. Gary was the Salutatorian but did not speak, electing to let Angelina speak for the both of them. Her address was all about the meaning of commencement, moving on in life. She also addressed early beginnings, the importance of family and the inspiration that she had received from her teachers, parents, and friends. She talked about taking a path in life and about not fearing the many forks in the road she and her classmates might encounter. She quoted Yogi Berra's saying, "When you come to a fork in the road, take it." She added, "When you take that fork, take it with confidence and conviction and try to make the best of your choice." She added in summary, "Do not be afraid to reach out to those who are disadvantaged, and never fail to acknowledge their existence. After all they are people and all people are important and should be acknowledged and validated."

For Angelina and Gary, commencement would be the end of high school and two new beginnings. The first would be a life together as a married couple. The second would be the beginning of a new chapter in their educational lives. They were college bound and off on an entirely different journey and the many challenges they would face.

At a party held in the back yard of the Mallon's, Gary walked up to his brother. "Greg, can we talk?"

Greg nodded. "Sure, and by the way, congratulations. Wow! Only two B's your entire four years at Lake Oswego." He shook his head in awe.

"I'll be lucky if I get a total of two B's. By the way, why didn't you speak at commencement?"

"I am not much of a speechifier if that is a word. Um, besides the staff felt that Angelina could represent both of our thoughts and ideas and tell all those assembled how we felt about our years at Lake Oswego. Gary paused for emphasis of what he was about to say. "Don't sell yourself short, Greg. You are so much smarter than you think, and you are one hell of a football player. I honestly believe that you are going to play at another level when you finish high school."

"Thanks, Gary. It means a lot to hear that coming from you."

"I regret that I haven't said this before, but I want you to know that I am very proud of you. I hope that we can always be good friends in addition to being brothers. I want you to be my best man at Angelina's and my wedding. I am going to ask Lance to be one of the groomsmen." Gary smiled. "I think that you are one hell of a guy, Greg. I am so proud to be your brother."

Greg grinned. "Thank you. I feel the same way, and I accept your invitation as it's more than okay with me, um, being your best man. Does that mean that I get to speak at the reception when everyone toasts your marriage?" He chuckled. "You had better treat me right because I know and have a lot of stuff on you that I could reveal."

Gary smiled. "Yes, you get to speak as does Angelina's maid of honor. We wouldn't have it any other way." Gary smiled as he stepped forward to give his brother a big hug. "I love you Bro. You can say whatever comes to mind. I am certain it will be honest and fair."

"I love you too. Now let's stop this mushy stuff and get back to the party. This is the first time that I get to have a beer."

Gary smiled. "You mean the first time in front of mom and dad, don't you?"

Greg beckoned to Gary, indicating he wanted him to follow. "Come on, It looks like mom and dad and the Crawford's want to see us about something. Let's not keep them waiting."

As they approached, Fredrick said, "We have something that we want to talk to you about. It affects all of you. Would you like to begin, Guy?" "No, you begin and I'll finish up." He looked at his wife, Sue, and continued, "After Fredrick and I finish telling you what we have to tell you, we're going to let your mothers tell you the rest of what we want to share with you."

Fredrick began, "Well, it's like this. With you kids going to college in California, you are going to need a car for commuting back and forth between here and there and between your two schools. So, after listening to you carefully about the type of car that really turns you on, Claudia and I decided to buy you a new Honda Civic for your graduation present."

Gary cocked his head to the side, staring at his parents in disbelief for a moment. Finally, shaking his head in disbelief, he asked to confirm what he thought he had just heard, "Are you kidding me? You are giving me a new car? Oh my God. I can't believe that this is happening. This is the coolest present ever."

Guy quickly jumped into the fray announcing, "And you, beloved daughter, are also getting a new Honda Civic. It is also your graduation present."

Angelina wiped her eyes and rushed into her father's arms. "Oh Daddy, you are the best. I can't believe how kind you and mom are. I love you so much and thank you, thank you, and thank you."

Sue smiled as she accepted a warm hug from Gary and then Angelina. "You two can go with us tomorrow to pick up your new cars. We hope that other than the colors, what we have selected for you is okay."

Claudia offered with a chuckle, "Well, I suppose it is my turn." Holding out her hands to take Gary and Claudia's, she continued, "As you already know, Fredrick and I have decided to pay for the rent of your apartment wherever you end up in California whether it is in Berkley, or Palo Alto or somewhere in between. Additionally, since Fredrick and I will be doing some extensive traveling this summer we are going to let you two have the spare bedroom this summer and every summer until you graduate from college. You will have complete privacy because you'll have your own adjoining bathroom." She smiled, adding, "The bedroom even has a lock on the door in case you haven't noticed."

Sue jumped in breathlessly, "And Greg, you are going to stay with us this summer while your parents are traveling. That will give the newlyweds some badly needed privacy with the complete run of Fredrick and Claudia's house."

Claudia added, "This is our wedding present."

Sue turned to Guy and then added, "Guy and I will give you your wedding gift on your wedding day."

Fredrick smiled. "Well, I think that we should rejoin our guests for the rest of the party, don't you?"

The days passed quickly before the wedding day, June 23rd. To say the least, it was a very busy time, hectic. Gary didn't get to see much of Angelina because it seemed that she and he always had something to do to prepare for the big day. Additionally, there was the fear that seeing her might jinx their marriage.

At exactly 2:00 on the 23rd all guests and family assembled in the Crawford back yard. The decorations were fantastic. Gary's stomach was doing flip-flops and Greg was nervously attempting to keep him calm. Finally, the word came that he and his part of the wedding party had to assemble at the altar at the far end of the yard. Moments later the familiar strains of, "Here comes the bride", began.

Angelina was breathtaking. Wearing a white gown, she appeared to resemble an angel, unbelievably beautiful. Her blonde hair framed her beautiful face perfectly and the smile on her face made Gary's stomach does flip flops and his heart beat to the strains of the music. As Angelina and her father began the slow stroll down the aisle towards the altar framed with a variety of beautiful flowers, those present were overcome by Angelina's beauty, letting out a collective murmur of approval. Spellbound, Gary mumbled to himself, *"Damn, she is so beautiful. I am the luckiest man alive today, tomorrow, and forever."*

When Angelina and her father reached the altar where Gary and the rest of the wedding party stood, Guy lifted her veil gave her a kiss and then gave her hand to Gary before retreating to his seat beside his wife.

The wedding official began, "We are gathered here to witness and honor the marriage of Gary Lee Mallon and Angelina Marie Crawford.

Marriage is not an act that two people should enter into without purpose and devotion. The bride and groom have requested that they say their vows to each other, so Gary you may begin."

Gary expelled a large rush of air and then began, "Angelina I have loved you all of my life, or all of the life that I can remember. We have played together, chased each other, teased each other, been best friends, but I have always loved you even though as a young boy I pretended to be put off by all the mushy stuff, the kisses you sneakily managed to give to me. The suggestion you made, um, the promise that someday we would marry, well my darling today it comes to pass and I am absolutely thrilled. It doesn't matter that you will reach old age twenty-two days before me. You have always wanted to be first. I have been remiss in failing to say this before, but today in front of everyone, I want you to know that on this day and forever more you are the most important person in my life. When you and I have finished saying our vows, you will be number one in my life, and I promise that you will hold that honored position as long as I live and afterward. I love you now and I will love you until the twelfth of never, and that's a long, long time. I will respect you, protect you, and care for you always. You will always be my best friend and partner forever. I love you." With that said he reached for the ring that Greg held and gently placed it on her finger. "Dearest Angelina, with this ring, I thee wed."

Tears of joy appeared in Angelina's eyes as she then began her vows. "Gary, the first moment I saw you I knew that I loved you and that you would be the man I would marry. I have watched our parents and the love they show each other and know that is exactly what I want and promise to give to you. I will also love you forever, support you, and be your best friend and partner no matter what obstacles we might face. I love you." She then reached for the ring and placed it on Gary's finger. "Dearest Gary, with this ring, I thee wed."

The wedding official smiled, nodded, and said, "With the power invested in me by the State of Oregon I now pronounce you man and wife. May your marriage be blessed with happiness and joy and let it last for as long as you both shall live. Gary, you may now kiss the bride."

The rest of the day was a whirlwind of activity, a blur. It wasn't until Angelina and Gary reached their hotel room in Seaside that the activities of the day began to sink in. After carrying his new bride through the door and across the threshold of their room, he gently put her down and placed his hands on her shoulders. "Angelina, I want you to know that you have made me the happies man on Earth today. I've said it many times today, but I need to say it again. I love you with all of my heart and I can't wait for each day of our lives to begin as we move down life's path."

She smiled. "I say ditto to that. By the way, I am so grateful for the gift of our cars for graduation and the almost exclusive use of your parent's home this summer until we leave for college. You know? We are very fortunate."

"I agree, but don't forget the wonderful present your parents gave us. The honeymoon here at the beach, the trip south to find our new residence, and all of the fun we are going to have going and coming is the best. We couldn't have better parents if we had the ability to make a selection. Um, I think that it might be wise for us to head out for Berkley tomorrow morning after we get up and have breakfast so that we can find a place to live, don't you?"

Angelina smiled. "Yes my husband, I do. Now, I believe that we have some important business to attend to."

Gary nodded eagerly. *"Shit, I feel like a kid going on the roller coaster for the first time. I am so excited and so lucky. Angelina is the most beautiful woman in the World, and I love her so. Look out diving board. Here we come. I have not one reservation. I'm jumping off and looking forward to the biggest splash that we can possibly make."*

Angelina smiled knowing at him. Are you thinking what I think you are thinking, um, about the diving board? In case you don't recall, Buster, we have been there and done that. However, this will be the best of the best. This time we are doing it as man and wife. So, look out diving board, here we come." She chuckled as she took Gary's hand to lead him towards the bed, "Nobody needs to convince me to jump. I can't wait to take the leap."

Chapter Six

Beginning the Honeymoon

A commencement ceremony for high school graduation does not mark the end. Rather, it marks the beginning, a new life independent of parents and teachers. It marks the time to begin taking the next fork in the road. Life is filled with forks. One of the forks taken for Angelina and Gary was exchanging their marriage vows and beginning married life together. Challenges and minor obstacles sometimes appear and make the journey somewhat of a trial, but commitment to staying on course will make the journey worthwhile. Adding to the new adventure was getting set up with living quarters to prepare for the beginning of college life.

When they awoke the next morning, June 24th, Gary inquired as he snuggled up to his new wife, "Well, Mrs. Mallon, how does it feel to be an old married lady?"

"Old? Good Heavens, Gary, we have only been married for less than a day and you already think of me as old?"

"It was just and oft used expression. I was teasing. Have I told you that I loved you yet?"

"Honey, you told me you loved me when you woke me up to have your way with me earlier. Now it is my turn. I love you, and now I think that it is time for us to jump into the shower and get ready to head out for breakfast. Could we go to the Pig and Pancake? I absolutely love that place."

"That works for me. Um, do you want to drive down the coast or head inland and go down I-5?"

"Let's do the Coast Highway. The Oregon Coast is so beautiful and I see no reason to hurry. When we get into California I want to see the Red Wood trees and stop to see Paul Bunyan, how about you?"

Gary smiled. "Honey, that sounds terrific to me." He paused. "So, we are off for Berkley and a visit to your dean of students that wrote that she knew of the perfect place for us to live. Is it an apartment complex or a house?

You said that it is owned by one of her closest friends. Apparently he or she is saving the place just for us?"

Angelina smiled. "It is a he, and um, I think that it is an apartment. As long as it is clean I could be happy living just about anywhere with you. The nice part is that it is supposedly about the same distance from both of our campuses. I guess it is located so that it will be almost a straight shot to CAL for me and an easy drive to the Stanford campus for you in Palo Alto."

Gary nodded. "It is nice to learn that it is affordable. I don't want to put too much of a burden on my folks since they are picking up the tab for our apartment."

"Honey, it was so nice of your mom and dad to pay for our apartment. Even with their generous help, I guess you know that we have joined the ranks of poor college students."

"Yeah, we are out on our own for the first time. Kind of scary, isn't it?"

"True, but we are luckier than most. We are on scholarship and I can make extra money teaching students that want to take piano lessons. I guess that my music professor has already lined up three students for me."

"Yeah, and my coach indicated that I have a job lined up on campus. I think that we will be okay, not rich, but certainly not as poor as church mice. We might even have a little extra to do something besides sit in our apartment day after day or night after night staring at four walls and studying."

Angelina giggled. "You could always stare at me if you get bored. Um, our time together is going to be tight. With the class loads that we are going to have, our jobs, baseball practice, my performances, and travel time, we're going to have to manage our time very closely. I don't want to spend long periods of time away from you."

Gary chuckled. "You're just horny. I swear to God, every time I turn around you are suggesting that I jump your bones."

Angelina frowned, pretending to be disappointed. "Are you complaining?"

"Are you kidding? Of course not, I am very happy that you want me all the time. I can't get enough of you either. Um, you do want to wait, don't you?"

Angelina smirked. "You mean to start a family?" "Yes, how do you feel?"

Angelina looked at him with a very serious look on her face, a look of determination forming in her eyes. "I think that we should wait until we get our degrees. That is only four years away. We'll both be younger than either one of our parents were when they started a family. Besides, I would like for us to kick up our heels and have a good time before we settle down with kids. What about you, how do you feel?"

Gary nodded. "I agree completely. We've lived with the birth control pill since our senior year in high school. What is another four years? Besides, I want to enjoy you before we have to face the rigors of parenthood and the pitter patter of little feet."

Gary looked across the table and teased, "Okay, Miss Piggy, I think it is time to hit the road. I figure that we should be just inside California before I get tired of steering the car towards Berkley."

Angelina grinned, shaking her head. "Here we are only a few hours into married life and you are already complaining about my figure, Miss Piggy, indeed." She started to rise from the table, turned and leaned towards her husband. "By the way, we have an appointment in the motel this evening if my figure isn't too unattractive."

Chapter Seven

Campus Visitations

Acclimation to a new environment, a different life style, a new beginning creates anxious moments. Getting prepared to face college life, the beginning of experiencing academia outside the comfort of the home provided by your mother and father involves the challenges of finding and getting used to a new home, a different schedule, and learning what life without parental guidance is all about. Couple that with the beginning of a new marriage, the new life can be full of, and even perhaps saturated with the newness of it all.

The trip down the Oregon coast was glorious. Cast beneath a bright blue sky, the Pacific Ocean was a sight to behold as Gary and Angelina traveled south. It seemed like no time at had passed before they were weaving through the majestic Red Wood trees in Northern California. "Let's stop at the Paul Bunyan monument and get an early dinner, shall we?"

Angelina excitedly added to Gary's suggestion, "After we eat, let's find a motel and stay the night. I don't know about you, but my butt is just about paralyzed from the trip." She grinned. "Besides, I think that a little time between the sheets with you is a top priority right now."

"Just now, you mean that after the honeymoon is over, it won't be a top priority?"

"Think again, mister. I want to have my way with you as often as you are able to answer muster."

The next morning the newlyweds awoke to another beautiful day, ate breakfast and made their way towards Berkley. After a phone call to the CAL dean of students, Gary and Angelina, found and fell in love with a nice, inexpensive apartment in Oakland. Luckily for them, the manager was all too happy to allow them to have the place and not move in or pay rent until a week before they were to begin classes. All they had to do was pay first and last month's rent and agree to a three year lease.

In the office of the manager, Gary introduced himself, "Sir, my wife, Angelina, and I are here on the recommendation of the dean at CAL to see you about renting an apartment. Apparently you have been saving one for us?"

Gruffly the manager replied, "Treage, I am known around here as Treage. If we're going to get along you'll have to drop the Sir nonsense and just call me Treage." He looked over his prospective new tenants very carefully. "Yes, on the recommendation of Sally, um, the dean, I reserved it for you. Looks like you are just the tenants that I have been looking for." He nodded. "So, you two are going to be going to school in the Bay Area. Which one of you is going to CAL?"

Angelina stepped forward. "That would be me, Treage."

"Good girl. I see that you are smarter than the average bear, no pun intended." He paused, directing his attention toward Gary. "So, you are going to be playing baseball for Stanford. I'm not too fond of the Cardinals, but if one of my tenants is going to be playing for them I guess I'll have to… By the way, CAL doesn't have much coming back this year, so I expect to see you shine when you play the Golden Bears."

Treage, as he liked to be called was a burly man possessing a gruff, outward aloof manner. As they prepared to sign the lease papers, Treage explained, "Baseball players usually only stay for three years before they turn pro if they think or have been told that they have what it takes to make in the majors. I hear that you have what it takes, Gary. So, the three year lease is for your protection. If something happens that you don't go out at the end of three years, I will give you and Angelina a first option to rent the place for an additional year."

Gary smiled, looking at Angelina. She nodded, their thoughts about the manager apparently reaching the same conclusion. Treage was an old softy. Obviously his bark was more severe than his bite. This was going to be a good relationship. Treage, as he preferred to be called was going to be like their away from home father.

After the lease papers had been signed, Treage extended his hand to Gary, inquiring, "So how long is your stay going to be?"

Gary smiled. "Angelina and I are on our honeymoon. We were married two days ago." Gary paused. "Um, as soon as we visit our respective campuses we will head north and see some sights before returning home to Lake Oswego."

Angelina excitedly added, "Yes, we hope that by visiting our respective campuses, we can get our classes squared away for fall term." She smiled. "Of course the trip north is not going to be set on a specific course, if you know what I mean." She paused. "I think that we will begin the campus visitations tomorrow morning."

Treage nodded. "Well, congratulations. Why don't you plan on staying in your apartment tonight and tomorrow evening before you head back? I can round up some linens and some toiletries for you so that you can make the bed and be able to shower and whatnot. You can consider that my wedding gift to you."

Angelina rushed forward thrusting her arms about his neck and kissing him on the cheek. "You are truly a sweet man. Thank you so much."

Gary chuckled. "Well, I guess we accept. Thank you so much."

Four problems solved. First, the extended lease agreement gave them a comfortable place to live during school for a very good price. Second, they had the comfort of knowing that they didn't have to go apartment hunting every year. Third, they weren't even obligated to pay for their apartment in Oakland while they were back in Lake Oswego for the summer. Finally, when they went home for the summer, Gary's parents had promised them the use of their home, free of rent and having the peace of mind knowing that they could move into their apartment in Oakland at their leisure and be ready to face classes at the beginning of fall term completely settled into their new life.

The anticipation of what their college campuses would be like at the beginning of the school year was already starting to cause their excitement barometers to rise. Gary and Angelina could hardly contain themselves as they scoured each other's campus the next day and met their respective academic advisors to get their class schedules all set up for their first day of classes.

First up the next morning after a restful night in their new apartment was a visit to the CAL campus. Angelina and Gary left their car parked near the coliseum where CAL played their home football games.

While Angelina went off to meet with her academic advisors, Gary wandered about the campus and paid a visit to the infamous Henry's, a place identified as the place to go in Berkley before and after a CAL game. Later, when he and Angelina met up, he told her how impressed he was with the Berkley environment. "Your campus has a definite Roman appeal, especially the coliseum where the Golden Bears play their home football games. You also have to love Henry's. What a cool hangout. I can't wait to see the Stanford – CAL game this year and test out the environment of Henry's on game day. I hear that the CAL pep band marches in at the end of a game and plays their fight song for the patrons."

"Wow! How neat is that?" Angelina excitedly continued, reporting, "I got all of the classes I wanted. I will be taking 17 hours with a very nice schedule. I should be able to be home by 5:00 every evening unless I am involved with a musical production. That should give us plenty of time together until the start of the regular baseball season, you know, when you start playing games."

"When is your earliest class?"

Angelina frowned. "I have an eight o'clock class every day." She sighed, "At least I will be done early so that I can do the music lessons and still get home at a respectable hour. Now it's time to head for Palo Alto and see what your schedule is going to be like."

He smiled. "I'm a step ahead of you. I called my coach while you were getting your schedule sorted out and already know what my schedule is going to look like. All we have to do is visit the Stanford campus, check in with my coach and academic advisor. I am set to go."

"Well, how cool it that! So, what's your schedule like, smarty?"

Gary grinned. "I will be done by noon as my last class, history, begins at 11:00. I am also taking a four hour math class, English, a science class, and a political science class. All of my classes are on Monday, Wednesday, and Friday except I do have to take the math class on Thursday. That will be the day that I put in the most of my time for my job on campus. Damn, things are working out really well. Now, tell me what courses you are taking."

"Well, I got all of the classes I wanted. I am taking history, English, math, Science, music history, piano, and voice. All my classes end at 2:00. If I counted correctly you are taking 16 hours?"

"Yes, I think that is plenty considering that baseball is going to occupy so much of my time."

Angelina nodded. "That is smart." She grinned devilishly, "It appears that we will have most of our evenings together." She paused and smiled at him. "So, you like my campus?"

"I love it. I really like the fact the campus appears to be so closely connected to Berkley. You can finish a class and hit the coffee shops or a pub without having to walk hardly any distance at all. What about parking? It looks like it could be a nightmare."

"They have student parking. I got a sticker for my car, so all is good."

Later, after taking care of business at the Stanford campus, Angelina grabbed Gary's hand as they strode towards their car. "Um, by the way, I like your campus as well." She winked. "You know, I think that we made the right choices. Being a Cardinal and a Golden Bear is going to be exciting. I promise not to give you a bad time when our schools meet in an athletic contest. Tell me your thoughts about what you have experienced."

"Honey, it was crazy. Thank God for my academic advisor who figuratively took me by the hand and ushered me through the registration process. I'm thinking that being on scholarship has certain advantages." He paused. "You know, I got to thinking about what it is going to be like when the bulk of the students report to register for classes. I can't wait to just sit back most of the day watching the craziness unfold as the kids scurry about trying to get registered. I'll bet the environment will be electric. I think I am going to love going to Stanford, and I also think that you are going to love your experience at CAL."

"I experienced pretty much the same things that you did. You know, the campus and downtown Berkley pretty much intersect or appear to just blend together as you said. I met a couple of nice gals that I went to coffee with and just observed all of the hustle and bustle going on in Berkley. Just think of it. All of the excitement and school hasn't even started. College life is certainly different than high school. Like you, I am going to enjoy this college life. I am very excited, but not nearly as excited as going home to you every day. I love you so much." She paused. "By the way, you say that Henry's is a cool hangout? You aren't of age. How does that work?"

"I just had a burger and sipped on a coke. I hear that Henry's is pretty much open to all ages prior to the game for food and non-adult beverages for those of us who aren't twenty-one." He frowned. "Too bad we won't be of age when CAL plays Stanford in football this year. I guess we'll have to wait until our senior years before we get to enjoy the complete ambiance of Henry's on game day." He grinned. "That is unless we sneak in to watch the CAL band march in a play the CAL fight song."

Angelina nodded. "That sounds good. Maybe you will want to take me to a CAL game sometime?"

"You have a date. I will for sure when Cal plays Stanford this year." He paused. "Are you thinking of joining a sorority?"

"I got a packet of info. Looks like rush will begin on the Wednesday before the first day of classes. I think I am going to pass. What about you, are you interested in joining a fraternity?"

"Well, my coach advised me against joining fraternity as it will just add to the time that I would be away from you. I am also going to pass."

"Good! I am certain that we can have a campus connection without joining a Greek organization."

"Angelina, I have been thinking about what our apartment manager said when we signed the lease. This year I am going to accumulate 48 hours and you are going to end up with 51 if we don't change our schedule. Since we're taking the basic required courses, I don't see why we would, do you?"

"No, but what is your point?"

Gary smiled and suggested, "Please take out a pen or pencil and some paper and write down what I am saying."

"Okay Einstein, fire away, I am ready."

"Honey, suppose I decide to go out in three years. To graduate I would need 132 hours more with two years to do it in. That means that if I took 66 hours a year, I could get my degree in two more years and go pro at the end of my junior year." He winked. "We could start a family a year sooner."

"Honey, that means you would have to take 22 hours per term. Are you sure you want to tackle that?"

"Angelina, we could always do a summer school session. If I took 12 hours one summer I would only have 120 hours left or 60 hours per year. That is 20 hours per term. If we did two summer sessions, taking 12 hours, I would only have 108 hours remaining or 54 hours per year. That would be 18 hours a term. That is manageable."

"Wow! That is still a load. Are you sure that you want to tackle that? I'm as anxious to start a family as you are, but…. Let me see, I would need how many more to graduate at the end of my junior year?"

"It is enough to know that you would have fewer hours per term than I would. So, what do you think?"

Angelina nodded with a look of reluctance etched on her face. "Gary, I think that we need to face this year first and then decide what direction we want to go or can go. You know that all work and no play, makes for a very dull boy."

"I hear you and I totally agree. There is no sense in getting the cart before the horse." He grinned. "By the way, all work and no play can also make for a dull girl."

After their brief but productive introduction to their universities and another night in their apartment, they headed their car north and home the next day. After spending the night in Shasta City, the newlyweds arose, ate a hearty breakfast and again set their course for home. Nearing Ashland, Gary inquired, "What are your thoughts about turning east when we reach Medford?"

Angelina looked at him strangely before inquiring, "What do you have on your mind my husband?"

"I have always wanted to see Crater Lake. To my knowledge you have not seen that beautiful place either."

"That would be correct, but I have always wanted to go there. It is strange that we have lived in Oregon all of our lives and yet we have never been to Crater Lake."

Gary smiled. "Like so many other Oregonians, yeah, here is what used to be one of the Seven Wonders of the World and we have never been there."

"I have seen pictures of it. It is really weird, an island located right in the middle of the lake. What's the island called?"

"Wizard Island, yeah and the lake is so very, very deep. Did you know that years and years ago Mt. Mazama blew its top and formed the lake? It is a national park, you know." Gary smiled. "I've been doing my research. I figured that we will only get one honeymoon, so we might as well make it a good one with many memories to have of this wonderful occasion."

"I am all for it. Where would we stay?"

"I'll try to get us a room at the lodge. The lodge is on the edge or the rim of the lake. Heck, we might even go exploring and take a boat ride if you want."

"Whatever you want, I want. Thanks for making the suggestion. I was not really excited about ending our honeymoon quite so soon." Angelina paused, cocked her head as though suddenly having a new thought. "I think that going to Crater Lake is a terrific idea, but what are your thoughts about going home through Central Oregon and paying a visit to Bend and perhaps Sisters?"

Gary nodded. "'That would be more than agreeable with me. After all we still have the rest of June, all of July, and a large portion of August to enjoy in Lake Oswego before the rigor of college life smacks us in the face." He paused. "Yes, I don't know what your people at CAL told you, but the folks at Stanford suggested that I, um, we report to school the last week of August to get the jobs squared away, buy books, and generally get acclimated to the college life."

Angelina purred, "The rest of the summer is going to be fun and filled with new adventures and adjustments to married life that we can thankfully experience before classes began. I am looking forward to going home, but another day or more is just what the doctor ordered."

Gary nodded. "Well then, we have a plan. Next stop is Crater Lake." "Good idea. If you don't mind I think I am going to lay back, close my eyes and take a little nap. Wake me when we are a few miles from Crater Lake, will you? I don't want to miss the sights as we get close to Crater Lake."

"You've got it. Enjoy your nap." As he drove onward his mind started to wander, considering the future that lay in front of them. *"Classes will begin the second Monday in September, proceeded by rush and orientation. With the extra week we are going to capture by reporting the last week in August,* we'll have ample opportunities to visit each other's campus and indulge in some very personal interaction. College life promises to be good. We'll be able to call home and share with our parents what we're experiencing and catch up on our brother's experience as juniors at Lake Oswego High School."

Gary shook his head. He could almost hear it now. *When I call, dad will proudly report that Greg is the starting fullback. He'll extol about Greg's accomplishments and the accomplishments of the Laker team. Angelina's ear will be pressed to the phone next to his and will wait anxiously to hear a report about her brother Lance. If the report isn't filed quickly enough, she'll inquire about how Lance is doing and how everything is at home."*

Gary smiled as this thoughts continued, *"Dad will give a report about how well Lance is doing in school and how supportive Lance is of Greg's accomplishments. He'll probably mention when basketball season is set to begin and how Greg and Lance's roles will be reversed. After we've exchanged some other news with my mom, I'll hang up. Now it will be time for Angelina to call her parents. The conversation will be just about a repeat of we've heard from my parents."*

Gary chuckled quietly to himself. *"When all the reports have been filed, I'll probably turn to Angelina and mention that it is good to know that all is well at home. Then I will give Angelina a hug and tell each her that I love each her. Angelina will nod her head and then say something like, yeah, it sounds like everyone is very happy. I sure am happy that they are coming down for Thanksgiving. I will really be missing them by that time."*

Angelina chuckled. "You must be having a lot of thoughts running through your head. I have been trying to concentrate on taking a nap, but every so often you break into my concentration with some chuckle, grunt, or brief comment. Just so you know I miss our family too. It also goes without saying that I love you very much as well."

The summer months passed quickly. Taking up residence in the Mallon home was easy on the pocket book and gave them the opportunity to maintain close family ties. Many might feel that living with parents as a married couple would be stressful and awkward, but it actually turned out to be quite pleasant as Gary's family spent a considerable amount of time traveling. Greg's summer was filled with football camps and hanging out with Lance. All in all it was almost like having the Mallon home all to themselves with little or no interference from Gary's family. Angelina spent some time exploring the homeless issues as her interest had not waned. As she set about visiting the encampments of the homeless and talking with the different shelters she was starting to formulate a plan for solving the homeless issue.

At last the summer break came to an end. The sendoff to college was a tearful affair. Gary and Angelina had to swear on their first and second born that they would maintain frequent contact and find a way to return home for a visit when the opportunity presented itself.

Prior to launching their trip south in their cars, Angelina suggested that they stop again at the motel in Shasta City that they had stayed in during their return home after visiting their respective campuses. As they started to get into their cars, Angelina offered, "I'll give you a call when we are close to Shasta City so that we can navigate to that motel we liked so much. What do you think? The accommodations are inexpensive and quite nice. It is also close to really nice restaurant. You did like it, didn't you?"

Gary smiled. "Yes, I liked it a lot, and it sounds like a plan. You know that you can call me prior to that if you get bored and want to talk, right?"

"Count on it. Well, let's hit the road. We have a few miles to cover."

Chapter Eight

Classes Begin

When university classes begin, the orientation pleasures turn to work. Attending classes, listening to lectures, doing assignments, writing papers, and preparing for and taking tests brings forth the pressure. The pressure to excel at Stanford and CAL is enormous. Add to that a job and practices for music or an athletic endeavor and you have what is called a full load.

Monday, the first day of classes, finally rolled around. The craziness of orientation and rush had at last spent its considerable energy and the two campuses were back to normal. The weather was warm, the sky, cloudless, and the soon to be experienced atmosphere would be more somber. The pursuit of the degree and expanded knowledge was ready to burst out of the starter's gate.

Gary lay in quiet repose, allowing his mind to wander while waiting for the alarm to go off. Set for a 5:00 revelry, he suddenly felt the wonderful warm presence of a familiar body enveloping him. Angelia purred, "Are you awake?"

"Yes, I have just been lying here planning out my day." He turned toward her and kissed her tenderly on the lips. "Good morning. I love you."

"And I love you." Momentarily he felt the presence of her hand slowly find its way inside his shorts. Innocently she teased, "I didn't want him to get lonely. Want to mess around before we have to get up, shower, eat, and get ready to hit the road for school?"

"You read my thoughts." Slowly he began to massage her breasts as she continued to stroke his expanding offering.

Shortly after he had begun to pleasure her, she started to breathe in short gasps, pleading, "You make me feel so good. I never seem to tire of the pleasure you give to me." She gasped. "When you touch my breasts it sends an electric pulse throughout my body. It begins in my vagina and travels up my body until it reaches my chest cavity. Whether you know it or not, you can make me cum by just playing with my boobs." She momentarily pushed away from him and inquired, "Do you suppose we'll ever get tired of this?"

"Not if I have anything to say about it."

Moments later, after resuming their engagement with foreplay, Angelina moaned with pleasure and excitement. She gasped, "I want you. Oh God, I want you. I want to feel you inside me. Oh Gary, I want to feel you inside me."

No further encouragement was needed. Moments later the orchestrated music made by the couple's movement against the resistance of the bed and moans of pleasure filled the room. Angelina moaned, "Oh God, don't stop. Don't stop! I love what you do to me and how wonderful you make me feel."

Responding almost simultaneously, his body stiffened as she thrust her hips upward to completely contain him. Stalled to savor the moment, they both began to shudder with complete satisfaction, Angelina moaning and whimpering with joyful satisfaction with the completion of their perfectly coordinated performance.

Suddenly the room became a tomb of nearly complete silence. Only the faint sounds of two spent warriors trying to catch their breath while awaiting the beating of their hearts to return to normal could be heard. Moments later, Gary grinned as he rose up on his elbows and looked into his beautiful wife's eyes. "It is always so good with you. You spoil me. Promise you will never turn me away?"

She purred, "I promise." Suddenly, her mood changed. Pretending to be hurt, she whined, 'Oh, have there been others?"

Indignantly he responded, "No, you know better than that. You have always been the only one. I haven't even considered…"

She giggled. "I know, and ditto to your nice complement. If you play your cards just right you might convince me to offer you a return engagement tonight."

"Twice in one day? What do you think I am an athlete?"

"Honey, it isn't a record. We've done it much more often before. With school and work and what not, I'm afraid that, except for the weekends, we'll have to be happy with twice a day or maybe only once."

He nodded. "Yeah, you are probably right. Do you want to hit the shower?"

"If you'll shower with me, I will go willingly. I want you to wash my back."

He grinned. "Is that all you want?"

Pretending to be irritated, she stomped into the entry of the bathroom, stopped and turned toward him. "Well, what are you waiting for, an engraved invitation?"

At 7:00 they were off for their respective campuses. Higher education and the quest for a degree had begun. On their respective campuses it was like a well-orchestrated play. They popped into a classroom, took a seat, frantically took notes while trying to consume all that their professors offered, popped out, ran to the next class, popped in, and so forth and so on. At the end of their academic day, they were spent, exhausted. After the frenzied activity of attending classes had ended, Angelina gave three piano students their first lesson of the year while Gary puttered about the athletic department doing odd jobs. Fall practice was not set to begin for another week.

That evening, during dinner, they began to discuss their day. So, Gary, tell me about your classes, you job, and how the meeting went with your coach."

I really like my history class and political science class. I will manage to get along in science, and, well, math is math. What can I say? It isn't my favorite subject even though dad is a math teacher. Oh, I forgot English. That is going to be a neat class. My professor emphasizes writing and you know how I love to write."

She nodded. "Hum, sounds terrific. What about the job?"

"I just worked in the athletic office doing odd job. I won't be starting fall practice until next week. I learned today that on Saturdays when we have a home game I will be busy doing something to be decided later. Um, what I do or will be assigned to do will always take place at the stadium where they hold the games. Would you like to get in a few more hours? I told them that I was married and that you might want to work if there is anything for you to do." He grinned devilishly. "I told them you were going to CAL and that they might want to keep an eye on you as you might be working undercover. You know, like a spy."

"Absolutely, I would love to do that. I sure as hell don't want to sit here in this apartment all alone." She chuckled. "Funny you should mention me working undercover. Maybe I could pick up a little extra cash if I told the CAL athletic department what I was doing. I suppose you are right. That would make me a spy."

"Some spy you would make. What you know about football I could put in a thimble and there would still be room for what you know about basketball. Besides, I doubt they have any worries. I doubt that either one of us will be doing anything more involved than taking tickets, ushering or whatever."

Angelina pretended to ignore his comment about her knowledge of football and basketball inquiring, "So, what about the meeting with your coach, um, how did it go? Do you like him?"

"We'll begin drills next Monday after my teammates' classes and my classes are done. I think that we'll begin after we get some lunch. The practice will last until about 3:00 or 3:30." He paused. "You know the coach is a big burly guy with a gravelly voice. He looks more like what you would expect a football coach to look like than a baseball coach. In some ways he reminds me of Treage." He shook his head. "His looks belie who I think he really is, however. I really like him."

"How so, what do you think he is really like?"

"Under his the rough, gruff exterior he tries to present, I think that he is very gentle. He is more like a pussy cat, but I'm sure that when it is necessary he can roar like a lion. He really seems to care about all of us as people, not just baseball players."

Angelina chuckled. "Yes, he does sound like Treage." She paused. "So, you'll be able to be home somewhere around 4:30, um, 5:00 at the latest?"

"Yeah, I can even start dinner if I beat you home. Maybe we should plan a week's menu so that we know what to prepare no matter whom gets here first."

Angelina nodded, "Good idea, but don't you think that we should build in one day for us to go out for dinner? It could be our date night."

"That's a great idea. So, tell me about your classes and your piano students."

"I love my classes, especial theory of music, and my piano and voice classes. I begin my day at 8:00 and my last class ends at 3:00. My music professor scheduled the piano lessons for Tuesday and Thursday. I did, however, meet my students and learn a little about their skill levels today. They seem to be neat kids, so eager to learn. Sounds like both of us will have a light Tuesday and Thursday schedule." She smiled. "Isn't college fun?"

"Yes, so far it is. I am so glad that you are happy with your classes. I think that this is going to be a great year. Please know that whenever you have a musical performance I will move mountains to be there for you."

She smiled coyly. "And pray tell why would you do that? Don't tell me that you have decided to go into the Earth moving business."

"Because I love you and because you always support my activities. It is the least I can do. Just know that it is not an obligation. I will do it because I want to."

Fall term sped by like an SST, passing quickly as Gary quickly got into the groove with the baseball team, impressing the coach with his hitting ability and his rifle like arm. His classes also were going very well and the few Saturdays that he and Angelina had to work during home football games were fun and added to their resources so that they could do something besides go to class, study, and work at their extra jobs. Angelina had never been happier, bubbling over every time she spoke of her classes and music lessons.

Gary and Angelina wanted to fly home for Thanksgiving and Christmas, but had to stay in Oakland for Christmas because of baseball practice. The plans quickly were revised with their families coming south for Christmas. To ease the burden on their parents and to accommodate Lance's basketball practice regime, they decided to fly home for Thanksgiving. Thoughts of a home cooked meal made the wait excruciating. They were homesick. They were also tired of their cooking.

Their parent's decision to come to them for Christmas would allow for an almost complete Mallon and Crawford Christmas holiday. Lance's basketball schedule posed a bit of a problem, but a neighbor had offered to let him stay with them as Lance had a couple of games over Christmas break. They agreed that they could have two Christmas celebrations to accommodate Lance, one before they left to join Gary and Angelina in Oakland and the other in the Bay City. Thanksgiving posed no problems for anyone as all of the Mallon's and Crawford's would gather in Lake Oswego. Gary was excited to learn that he and Angelina might be able to see Greg play in the playoffs for the state championship if Lake Oswego advanced that far.

Life was good. Angelina and Gary had started looking into attending summer school, reasoning that if they did they could graduate in three years instead of four by cutting back on the number of hours they would have to take during the regular school year. It appeared that attending two sessions of summer school was under serious consideration.

Angelina had met a CAL coed that was married and had a child. The lure of motherhood was starting to make a huge impact on her. Many of their conversations started to center on what being a mother and father would be like. Gary, although willing to please, was less excited about starting a family. Conversations with some of his teammates who had taken on the responsibility convinced him that waiting was not a bad idea. He felt the increased need to experience and enjoy being a student, enjoying his teammates, and enjoying life with Angelina as a couple without the burden of a little one. That seemed to make more sense to him than rushing into fatherhood. His defense of the idea was not lost on Angelina. She enjoyed the freedom they enjoyed. She also did not object to delaying the entry into parenthood.

During one of their discussions, Angelina reasoned, "As much as I want to have children with you and enjoy the rush of motherhood, I also know that what we are sharing now can never be replaced, at least not until the children leave the nest. I want us to welcome our children with eagerness and a feeling that we are completely ready for the responsibility of being a mother and father."

Gary's nod of approval sealed the deal. Additionally the appeal of attending summer school and loading up on extra hours to graduate early was starting to lose more and more of its luster.

Chapter Nine

Stand in There and Take Your Cuts

College baseball is very similar to the experience that a baseball player might encounter in the minor leagues although some might argue that the competition is not as severe or as demanding. The leap from high school ball to college ball is huge. Even more severe is the jump to the professional level. Some toil in the minors with nary a whiff of the big time, the majors. Even though college baseball players are on scholarship and expected to produce, the biggest difference, that which really sets the levels apart, is the sudden realization that a player is no longer the king pin when he enters the professional world. In high school a player probably had little or no completion for his positon. In college, there is possibly a person in the depth chart waiting to take your position. In pro ball a player had better not blink or else he will ride the pines and probably be traded or dismissed from the organization that drafted him. The guys that Gary met at Stanford were good.

Gary burst into their apartment on a sunny Thursday afternoon, excitement on his face and his voice ringing with enthusiasm. "I won the center field job. Can you believe that I beat out last year's starter, an all-league performer?"

Angelina whooped in joy. "Way to go slugger." She paused, cocking her head. "So what is what's his name going to be doing?"

"He is going to be our designated hitter. Brett, um Brett Pine is a great guy. With him in the lineup as the DH we will have a potent offense."

"Is there a reason that they don't just move Brett to one of the other outfield positions and let someone else be the DH?"

Gary frowned. "Hmm, you always ask the most difficult, thoughtful questions." He shrugged. "I don't have an answer. Maybe the coach thought that was best for the team. At any rate, Brett is handling the change quite well."

"Well, again, congratulations, slugger, I knew you could do it. What was the determining factor, your glove in the outfield or your hitting ability?"

"Coach said I had the stronger arm. In all other respects, we were pretty equal. Besides, with me playing center field and him being the designated hitter we have the luxury of having two center fielders or two designated hitters. Damn, I am so excited."

Angelina frowned. "Hmm, you are sure that Brett was okay with the news?"

Gary smiled. "He was okay with it. He has turned out to be my biggest supporter. Of course I am now his biggest supporter as well. After all, as the coach told us, we are teammates and part of the bigger picture. We are Cardinals." He paused for a moment. "Um, I have some other good news. I got you a season pass so that you can see all of my home games if you want."

Angelina nodded with a big smile on her face. "Well, I suppose that is the least I can do since you have been at every one of my concerts. By the way, have I told you how wonderful your support makes me feel?"

Gary nodded. "Yes, several times. Have I told you that I love you today?"

She smiled as she walked slowly towards him, putting her arms around his neck and looking into his eyes. Yes, my love, you have, and I want you to know that I love you too."

"Let's go out to celebrate, shall we?"

"Not before I share my good news with you."

Gary's face immediately assumed a hint of guilt, disappointment in his self-centered display of excitement. "Damn, I was so excited about my accomplishment I forgot all about your day. I am so sorry."

Angelina smiled at him. "Apology accepted. Besides, how were you to know? It even caught me by surprise."

Gary looked at her with a quizzical look on his face. His brows furrowed and he turned to the side. "So, tell me. The suspense is killing me."

She grinned with that look that indicated that something special was about to be revealed. The Chasseur smile that spread across her face was very revealing.

"You didn't."

She lowered her head, started pumping her fists as she kept rhythm with her feet, and excitedly announced, "Yes, yes, I did! I was selected for the lead in the spring musical."

"Oh, my God, how good is that? Oh honey, congratulations. That is the best news of the day. Now we really have something to celebrate. Damn I love you. So, that means you are going to play the part of Maria in the 'Sound of Music'?"

"That is about it. The gal that I was up against and I were equal in acting ability, but the head of the production, Mr. Riche, felt that my voice was stronger. She is good, but her voice is a bit weak. She doesn't sing with ease. It comes off as being forced."

"Well, again congratulations, and again, I love you."

Pre-season games and the daily rehearsals dug a deep trench into their schedules. It was not rare for Gary to be away on a road trip for a weekend or longer, and it was a common occurrence for Angelina to have night rehearsals. Creativity soon became their password for salvaging time, meaningful time together.

The PAC-12 was purported to have the strongest conference in the nation that year according to preseason polls. Three of the twelve teams were ranked in the top ten. All but two of the remaining eleven participating schools were in the top twenty-five. From top to bottom, there wasn't room for error. All the teams would have been vying for a championship in another conference, so each game of each series promised to be a battle, no series captured easily. When the time came for the NCAA selection committee to select the regional participants, several PAC-12 schools figured to be in the mix.

During pre-season Gary did his best to suppress his excitement about the Stanford baseball team and his accomplishments, only casually mentioning the results of an away game and not dwelling on the home games when they concluded. He felt that Angelina needed to have as much support for her upcoming performance as possible, constantly pumping her for the latest as her performance neared and how the musical was coming together. In casual terms, she dismissed the anxiousness she felt, constantly checking to see how her husband felt about his performance as the seasons moved along towards league play. Their conversations had somehow become emotionless, resorting to small talk, the weather often mentioned or short, terse responses such as "fine", "nothing new to report", or "you know, same o same, same o".

Gary was troubled. He started feeling like he and Angelina were just communicating on the surface, going through the motions of being married. Even their sessions in the bedroom had lost some of the luster they had enjoyed previously. On the trip home after an away game in Hawaii, Gary opened up to Brett Pine. "Brett, I am trying so hard to support Angelina's upcoming performance, and I sense that she is trying so hard to support me." He paused, lowering his head. "The bottom line is that we have started to become distant. I don't know what to do. Do you have any advice to offer to a troubled teammate? After all, you are an old married man compared to me. The last thing that I want is for my marriage to end up on the rocks."

Brett grinned. "You know partner, I could give you my opinion, but when I faced the same thing that you're facing right now I went to the coach and had a heart to heart chat with him. He really helped me. Take my advice and go see him. It is no accident that he has been happily married for thirty- five years and counting."

"Thanks Brett. I think your advice is sound. Think that he is in the mood for that conversation now? I am desperate. I want to go home with a plan so that I can turn this issue around."

Brett nodded. "I will go get him for you. All he's doing right now is catching some shuteye."

Moments later the coach approached Gary and took a seat on the plane beside him. "So, you wish to talk about some issues in your marriage? Brett filled me in."

"Yeah, I need some advice as to how I can support Angelina without our conversations always turning into small talk or just resorting to flippant responses. I think that she's facing the same issues, but I want to set things right when I get home. I need a plan."

The coach nodded. "Well, when you go home tonight do you intend to share with your wife the details of our series with Hawaii?"

Gary shrugged. "I know she will ask. Um, I'll probably just say something like it went okay."

"Come on, Gary. You know that it was better than that. Our team swept the Rainbows and in the three game series you went nine for thirteen with three home runs. It is admirable to be modest, but..." The coach shook his head. "Honesty never hurts my man. It isn't wrong to talk about your successes and your failures with your wife." Coach Ralston continued, "If two people love each other they share the good and the bad. Just because you go home excited about your performance or are down in the dumps when things didn't go well, it shouldn't be taken as being self-centered and not caring about your wife. By the same token, it isn't wrong for her to share her ups and downs with you as well. Just know this. If you share and then show an interest in what she did then you will be engaged in honest communication." He paused. "Do you know what I think your problem is?"

Gary shook his head. "Coach, I am asking you for some advice because I don't have a clue."

Coach Ralston smiled. "Son, you are too damned modest. Even around your teammates, you don't open up and share. Share all of your thoughts and then ask her to share. Let her know that what she has to say is the most important message that you will hear today." Coach paused. "One more thing, Gary, you have to learn to play for the love of the game like your dad did. He was a great player and he always played for the love of the game. Loosen up and let it out. I will love it, your teammates will love it, and you will come to love it.

Gary looked at the burly man, a person that was so warm and genuine. His gruff outer demeanor somehow just didn't fit the man that sat next to him on the plane. Nodding, Gary replied, "Thanks coach. What you have to say makes a lot of sense. Maybe because this is the first real rough spot we have experienced, I just forgot how to communicate, really communicate with my wife. Thank you so much."

The rest of the plane flight was very relaxed and enjoyable as Gary began to think about how he would talk to Angelina and what he would say so that he could get his marriage back on track. When the plane was in its final approach to the San Francisco Airport the butterflies started misbehaving in Gary's stomach. He knew what he wanted to say, but he was not confident in his ability to pull it off. *"Come on Gary, the coach was right.*

Honesty is the best policy. Just level with Angelina and tell her how much she means to you and how badly you want your wife back, the wife that you have known all these years. If you can hit a baseball you should be able to open up and let her know how you really feel."

Gary hit the door of their apartment in Oakland at 9:00, greeted by Angelina who kissed him passionately on the lips. "Gary, I have something that I have to say, something that has been bothering me for all too long now. I have to tell you something while I still have the courage to say what I have to say."

Gary's heart sank. *"Shit, am I too late. Damn, I didn't even get to tell her what I wanted to say."* Um, what do you want to talk about? I have something that I want to talk to you about as well, but you can go first if you like."

"You do, you have something you want to talk to me about?"

"Yes, I have been thinking about it all the way home from Hawaii. Um, you can go first if you want."

"Honey, if you have been thinking about what you want to say all the way from Hawaii, I think that the least I can do is let you go first. So, let me hear what you want to say, and just know that it had better be good because what I have to say is really good."

"Hum, well here goes. I, um, I've been thinking that lately our conversations have been filled with small talk and flippant responses. Even our love making has suffered with a lack of emotional involvement. I feel that we are just going through the motions. I think that you are trying too hard to down play how great the musical is going and spending too much time trying to make me feel good." Gary cleared his throat and continued, "Angelina, you should know that in the series against Hawaii I went nine for thirteen with three home runs. I didn't make any errors and I nailed a runner at home that decided to test my arm." He curled up his lip displaying confidence and self- assurance. "We swept the series. The team was great and Brett had one hell of a series, but it didn't mean a damned thing because up until now I have been afraid to share because I don't want you to think that baseball is the center of my universe. I want you to know how important your success in the upcoming musical is to me. I have been dishonest with you and me. Of course I want you to be successful, I want you to be successful to the max because I love you so much and I am so afraid of losing you. I never want to put me before you. I guess you could say that being a professional baseball player, being a success at Stanford means nothing if I can't share it with you and have you in my life. I want you to share all of your successes with me as well."

Tears were running down Angelina's face as she fell into his arms. "Damned you, I was going to tell you that I was going to give up the lead in the musical if we could just get back to where we were. I don't like the way things have been lately. Things have been going so well with the musical, better than anyone could expect, but none of it means a thing if I can't have my best friend and the love of my life back. I love you so much."

"Well, do you think that we can just start sharing openly and honestly so that we can both celebrate each other's successes?"

"You have a deal. Um, I think that we have an appointment in the bedroom. I want you to see what I am like when I put everything I have to give into making love with you."

Stanford was perfect going into their first league series against Oregon State with their record standing at 15-0. Gary was hitting .420 and had powered ten homers over the distant fences. Brett, hitting in the cleanup spot in the batting order was leading the team in RBI's and also hitting above the .400 mark. In the field Gary was flawless, his arm considered lethal to any base runner brave enough to dare try to take an extra base. The Beavers were tough, touting a near perfect record with only two losses. It was going to be a tough series and Gary felt mixed emotions playing against his home state rival. The bright side of the conflict was that the three game series was to be held in Corvallis. Angelina was making the trip north and both her family and his family would be in attendance. Thanks to the generosity of Gary's dad, Angelina's airfare had been taken care of thus assuring a Mallon and Crawford reunion. Angelina had touched base with all of her professors and the spring musical director and had given his blessings for missing her Friday classes. It would be a jam packed weekend, but by taking along some of her books to study when she could grab a few minutes would ensure that everything would be in order when she returned. Gary suggested that she grab a little library time in the Oregon State library on Friday and Saturday.

The first game of the series, a Friday night affair was a typical spring day in Corvallis as the sky was cloudy with dark menacing clouds seemingly always present. Periodically the clouds, apparently tired of holding all of their moisture, unloaded. In addition to the intermittent rain and a howling wind, the temperature hovered near 40 degrees. It was miserable.

Oregon State had been held in check for eight innings as had Stanford. With the score tied at 0-0, the Cardinals came to bat in the top of the ninth. The lead-off hitter fooled everyone in the park by laying down a perfect drag bunt, beating the throw to first base by half a stride. The second hitter laid down a perfect bunt to sacrifice the runner at first to second. On deck, Gary knew what he had to do. Perfect at bat thus far, he needed to get a hit so as to drive in a run, a run that would allow Stanford to take the lead and perhaps grab the win.

Coach Ralston called time and approached Gary. In his usual deep gravelly voice, he implored, "All we need is a hit. Their pitcher is going to give you a fast ball high and outside. If you go with the pitch you should be able to slap the ball into left field. They have the shift on so you should be able to easily find a hole."

Gary nodded. "No time to go for the fences now. The ball isn't carrying with the wind blowing in, and it's so damned cold I don't think the ball would carry if I hit it on the nose and it was wind assisted."

Coach smiled, nodding his head in agreement. "I think they will pitch to you because there is no advantage in giving you a walk and having to face Brett, our clean-up hitter. Just know that the pitcher isn't going to give you anything good to hit." He patted Gary on the back and growled, "Now go up there and deliver."

Gary pawed at the dirt trying to get a comfortable stance. As he prepared to take his position in the batter's box, he noted that the relief pitcher was a southpaw and was known to throw bullets. He also had a wicked slider. *"Hmm, coach thinks that he'll throw me a fast ball up and away. If he gets ahead I'll face nothing but sliders. No matter, I just have to go with the first pitch and put the bat on the ball."*

Finally ready, he assumed his stance waggling his bat to release some tension. The pitcher came to the set position and checked the runner at second. Finally, he came to the plate with his offering.

The resounding sound that a metal bat makes with a baseball is unmistakable. A person without sight would know that the contact was solid. Sadly, a blind man would not know the direction the ball was headed. The crowd did, rising to their feet and letting out a resounding roar as the ball exploded off his bat headed down the left field line towards the corner. By the time the left fielder had corralled the ball, the runner on second base had crossed the plate and Gary was standing on second base. Stanford would go into the bottom of the ninth with a 2-0 lead thanks to Brett coming through with another timely hit.

In the bottom half of the ninth, OSU led off with a walk. The next batter also walked. Gary, starting to feel a sickness welling up in his stomach, stood helpless in the outfield trying to focus on what he was supposed to do. *"If the guy hits a fly ball to me I've got to make my throw to third to hold the runner on second. If he gets a hit I have to go home with the throw to keep the runner on second from scoring. If he hits one into the gap I've got to go to second so that I can keep the hitter from advancing past second or perhaps have a chance to catch him trying to take an extra base. Worst case scenario is that we will be tied with a runner on second."*

The count reached 3-2 and the mostly OSU crowd was in frenzy. The deciding pitch was low, but the batter, fooled by the nasty slider, swung awkwardly at it with nothing but air making contact with his bat. Strike three! Gary stood there in shock as he saw the catcher whip a throw to first, attempting to catch the runner who had strayed too far from the bag. The umpire spread his hands and waved them above the ground to indicate that the runner was safe. Now it was one down and the situation was better, but still dangerous with runners still on first and second. A hit by the OSU hitter would surely cut the Stanford lead to a single run with runners on first and second or first and third. Depending on the quality of the hit, the game could be tied with a runner on first or second. *"Focus*

Gary, it's time to focus! Just consider the situation. If the ball is hit on a line in my direction I have to try to hold the advancing runner at third, or go home. If it is hit in the gap I have to hold the advancing runner that's on first at second by throwing to third, possibly catching him if he tries to take an extra base. Hopefully the worst case scenario is that we will still be up 2-1 or tied with one out with a runner on second."

The Cardinal Pitcher quickly got ahead in the count 0-2, a pitcher's count. The third pitch, a waste pitch, was too good and the hitter hit it solidly into the outfield to Gary's right. Racing as hard as he could to his right, he reached out and snagged the ball on one hop. Wheeling nearly 270 degrees as he exchanged the ball from his glove to his left hand, he planted his right foot in perfect position to rifle the ball towards home plate. The runner on second had taken off with the crack of the bat and was rounding third when Gary launched his throw.

The crowd hushed as the perfectly thrown ball arrived on one hop at home plate. The catcher did not have to move his glove, as straddling the plate and braced for the impending impact, he merely held out his glove awaiting the runner to slide into it and hear the beautiful sound of the umpire announcing, "You're out!"

The catcher alertly did not wait for the expected announcement, whipping the ball to third to catch the runner who had foolishly attempted to advance. The umpire raised his right arm to gesture that the final out of the game had been recorded. Game over and the Cardinals were still undefeated.

Stanford won again on Saturday and Sunday. At the airport he bade Angelina goodbye as she prepared to leave the waiting area to board her plane. "Please wait for our plane to arrive at the airport. We should arrive just a bit after you do. I just want to know that you landed safely. I love you."

"I love you too. By the way, you had a great series. You don't know how proud your father is of you." She smiled. "I am very proud of you too."

Gary smiled. "Yeah, I do." Nodding his head, he continued, "Dad is a man of few words, but he lets you know what's on in mind with his eyes." He grabbed Angelina and kissed her. "Thanks for saying what you did. I am so proud to be your husband. Be safe. I can't wait until we get home."

Chapter Ten

The Sound of Music

A partnership formed by marriage should not be just about one of the partners. Each deserves their time in the sun, a time in the spotlight. A sport almost universally generates great fan support and revenue. A simple college musical performance may not have the luster or generate the interest as that of the seventh game of a World Series, but to the participants and to those who support the arts it is significant and worthy of support. It goes without saying that the support of a loved one is appreciated when given willingly.

The spring musical, "The Sound of Music" was a resounding success. Each of the three night performances were sold out. Angelina's performance as Maria was marvelous. Gary attended each performance and nobody in the audience could have been prouder. Her acting was superb, but it was her voice that stole the show. She was a bonfire star.

After the final night's performance, a cast party was held in the home of the director of the musical. All of the cast and their significant others were present. As Gary circulated about the gathering, allowing Angelina to receive the plaudits she so richly deserved, his pride was pinned to each lapel of his suit and painted in broad letters on his forehead. The director approached him, interrupting the proud trance he had fallen into. "Excuse me, Mr. Mallon. My name is Larry Reich, the director of the musical. I just wanted you to know what a talented wife you have. As you probably realize, she carried the musical with her acting ability and her voice. Oh, that voice. Her voice reminds me of another voice that I've had the pleasure of hearing."

Gary nodded. "Gary, um, my name is Gary. Yes, I am very proud of her. If I didn't know better I would swear that I was listening to Julie Andrews when Angelina sang those numbers in the musical."

"My thoughts exactly, yes, I think that we totally agree on that topic. Um, I understand that you are a baseball player." He smiled. "You are all that Angelina can talk about."

Gary's face reddened. "She gets a little carried away sometimes. I, um, I am giving it my best shot."

"Too bad you don't play for CAL. I understand that you are having a terrific season."

Gary grinned. "You wouldn't know that because of a little bragging by my wife, would you?"

Larry nodded. "It isn't wrong for a husband or a wife to brag about their significant other once in a while. Well, I must move on. You know, people to see and hands to shake. Good luck with the rest of your baseball season. Oh, and thank you for sharing your wife. She is terrific. We all love her."

At home Gary again told Angelina how proud he was of her. "I think that you have a career waiting for you. With your talent you can't miss."

Angelina frowned. "Listen mister, I love to act, sing, play the piano, and love my art, but my complete devotion is to you and being your wife. In time that will all have to be shared with our children. One career person in the family will be plenty for this lady thank you very much."

"Well, just know that I will support whatever you aspire to do, but I do like the goal you have set. I just hope that I able to help you achieve that goal."

"Don't you worry you'll be a part of achieving that goal every step of the way." She paused. "After we graduate and you start playing with one of the teams in the majors I just might do a little performing in one of the local productions. Just know that it won't interfere or disrupt our family. Our children when they arrive deserve to have one if not two parents at home with them all the time."

Gary nodded. "I agree, but I just want you to know that I don't ever want you to think that I am placing my career ahead of yours."

Angelina smiled. "I know that and I love you so much for that."

Chapter Eleven

An Omaha Landing

Setting a goal and making a well-developed plan to achieve that goal is what can lead to success or at least give the person or persons setting the goal a fighting chance to achieve what they are striving for. In WWII, the United States had a strategy, a well-developed plan to achieve a goal, landing successfully on Omaha Beach and then marching into the heart of Germany to defeat the Nazi Government. That achieved goal, success, was instrumental in winning the war in Europe and defeating Nazi Germany. Stanford had a goal for their baseball season. The goal of the team was to go to Omaha, not a beach landing to achieve victory in war, but a landing in Omaha, Nebraska to win the national title in college baseball.

The season passed. Stanford won the PAC-12 title finishing with a 29-4 record, earning top seed in the western regionals and selected to host the regionals at their ball park, the Sunken Diamond.

Sweeping through the regionals they then hosted the super regionals. Another sweep of the assembled teams earned the Cardinals the right to go to Omaha, Nebraska for the College World Series. Five goals achieved, having a winning record at the end of the regular season, winning the PAC-12 championship, earning a trip to the regionals, earning a trip to the super regionals, and finally earning a trip to the College World Series. Now they had only one goal left, winning the national championship.

Angelina met Gary outside the dressing room after the final game of the super regionals, her excitement impossible to contain. "Oh Gary, I am so proud of you and your team. Just imagine. You are going to the College World Series."

Gary took her in his arms and kissed her tenderly. "Do you think that you can find a way to go to Omaha?"

She giggled. "Try to stop, me mister. Of course I am going. I talked with my professors and they are going to let me take finals when we return from Omaha. What about your finals?"

"The professors are letting all of the guys on the team to do the same. By the way, have you heard from you parents or mine about their plans for getting to Omaha?"

Angelina frowned. "I am so sorry. In all of my excitement I forgot to tell you. Yes, they called me during the game and said that they were going to get plane tickets for our brothers and me in addition to them. It appears that they will be taking different flights to Omaha, but they will all get there by the time the first game is played. I guess I am staying in the motel with them. They got three rooms, one for me and my parents, one for your parents, and one for Greg and Lance."

Gary smiled. "That is great news. There is nothing I would like more than to have the family in the stands watching us play. How do they have the rooms set up?" Gary chuckled. "Oops, you have already covered that item. I guess I am a bit excited as well."

Angelina grinned. "Well, in case you forgot the details, I am staying in one room with my parents, your parents will have their own room, and they are letting your brother and my brother stay in the other room."

Gary nodded. "Sounds like a plan." He paused for a moment. "Did you tell them that you and I are seriously thinking about going to summer school?"

Angelina nodded. "Yes, and they weren't exactly pleased, but after I told them why, they seemed to understand. I told them that we would be able to get home to Lake Oswego at the end of summer session and spend some quality time with them before we have to begin fall term."

"Thanks for doing that, Angelina. I think that it would have been really tough for me to tell them. I know that mom and dad are really looking forward to spending a lot of time this summer with us. I doubt your parents were overly excited either."

"You can say that again." She paused. "Come on sport, let's get home. I think that we have some catching up to do before you have to leave for Omaha."

"Yeah, I won't be seeing much of you after we leave for Omaha except for brief moments after we play our games." "When do you leave?"

Gary smiled. "Good news, we get to have the next couple of days together before I fly out with the team."

Angelina smiled, a devilish facial expression conveying a most exciting plan. "Well then, let's get a move on. I think that I can keep you busy for the next couple of days."

The team left for Omaha two days later, Angelina the day after. She was scheduled to arrive the same day as her parents with Gary's brother and her brother on the same flight with her parents. Gary's parents were scheduled to leave the day after, set to arrive just in time to see Stanford's opening game in the series. An invitation by the Seattle Mariners for Gary's dad to be honored with his number being retired caused their delay. Gary elected to not try to figure out how all of the travel and room accommodations had come as it appeared to be similar to trying to figure out a complex puzzle or solving a complicated mathematical equation. He elected to simply go with the flow, allowing the events and plans to unfold. It was all out of his hands.

On the morning of the opening game of the series, a 3:00 game against the number two team in the nation, North Carolina, Gary awoke with a start. He was soaked in sweat as he frantically tried to recall the dream he had just experienced. All he could recall about the dream was an explosion and then a huge ball of fire followed by an inflamed image of a tote board focusing on Southwest Airlines. Suddenly a most surreal event started to unfold. His life was flashing in front of him as clearly as though he were sitting in a movie theater watching a movie.

He smiled as he saw Angelina and him playing together as little kids and seeing their parents in the background with loving smiles on their faces. The replay seemed to flash forward to when he and Angelina were in junior high school. She was such a pest, always trying to kiss him. He pretended to resist because that was what boys were supposed to do. The replay quickly moved on to Angelina's and his graduation. My heavens she was beautiful as she stood before the audience and delivered her valedictorian speech. Then there was a family meeting on the day of their graduation and a huge surprise.

Their parents had bought Angelina and Gary VW Jetta's for a graduation present and had informed them that they would have a room at the Mallon house during the summer after they returned from their honeymoon. His dad explained, "We figured that you were going to need two cars to transport yourselves back and forth to your respective campuses. We opted for new because we don't want you to have issues with a balky car."

Mr. Crawford then intoned, "And Angelina's mother, um, we decided to chip in and pick up the cost of your honeymoon. Your scholarships don't cover all of your living costs, so we decided to make this, well I guess it is just a gift that we want to give to you for being such wonderful kids."

The replay moved forward with brief glimpses of their wedding and their freshman year to a phone conversation he had had with his dad prior to leaving for Omaha. His dad advised, "Your opening game against North Carolina will put you up against the best pitcher in college baseball. His ERA is .087 and he has a blazing fastball with a nasty slider. If he gets ahead of you in the count, all you will see is that slider. If it were me, I would sit on the first pitch that will probably be his fastball. He will try to pitch you high and outside so that he can take away your power. You will have to be content to just go with the pitch and try your best to get on base. In this old game we have to sometimes give ourselves up for the betterment of the team." His dad had paused and then continued, "I love you son. You have made your mother and me very proud. We are not only proud of your accomplishments in baseball, but we are just a proud of your other accomplishments. You are a fine human being."

Tears welled up in Gary's eyes as he lay in bed. *"Hmm, that was so strange, weird. I wonder what that dream was all about?"*

The rest of the morning Gary was in a zone. For some reason he couldn't seem to focus on the game ahead. It was weird because he never before had experienced problems getting ready mentally for a game. At a team lunch prior to the game, he just sat in the restaurant toying with his food.

In the motel where Angelina and her parents were staying, Mrs. Crawford urged, "Come on you guys. Let's get a move on. We have to be at the ball park in less than an hour."

Suddenly there was a knock at their motel room door. Angelina walked over to the door and opened it. Greg stood before her, tears streaming down his cheeks. "Turn on your TV. Oh my God, they're gone. Mom and dad are gone."

Angelina's heart sank as she raced to turn on the TV set. Everyone huddled about the set to see a broadcast reporting the disaster that had happened. The plane Gary's parents were on exploded while taxing to where they were to take off. The reporter covering the story was talking about a governmental concern that it was a terrorist sponsored attack. First reports indicated that there were no survivors.

Angelina sank to her knees and buried her head in her hands. "Oh my God, dear God, what am I going to say to Gary?"

Angelina's parents rushed to where Greg stood and embraced him. Mrs. Crawford, choking back tears murmured, "Oh Greg, we're so sorry. We loved your parents so much."

Greg sobbed, "What am I going to do. I don't have a mom and dad anymore."

Mr. Crawford put his arms around Greg and whispered, "You have us, son. We'll take care of you. We love you like you were our own son."

Angelina, tears streaming down her cheeks, asked, "What are we supposed to do? Do we tell Gary now or wait until after the game?"

Mr. Crawford replied, "Honest to God, I don't know. I am so shocked I can't even think."

Mrs. Crawford, displaying unusual calm said, "We will wait until after the game. I am almost certain that there won't be a report of this reaching the team until after the game has been played. We have to be strong for Gary now and go on no matter how badly we feel. There will be time for tears and grieving after the game."

Greg displaying unusual maturity nodded his head. "You're right. We are all hurting right now and Gary will be devastated when he hears the news, but telling him can wait until after the game. If we see him we have to be strong and not let on that anything has happened." As he finished his lower lip started to quiver and then he broke down and again began to cry. Lance put his arm around his best friend and just held him as tightly as he could.

The North Carolina pitcher was everything as advertised. Going into the ninth inning he had completely handcuffed the Stanford hitters except for two scratch singles. Gary had made contact, but had lined out every time he had faced the hard throwing southpaw.

Coach looked at his players and calmly explained the situation they were in. "Well men, we are down to our last three outs. With them leading 3- 0, we have to go out there like there is no tomorrow and figure out a way to scratch out some hits, get on base. He has been living with that fast ball on the first pitch all day. I think it would be wise to go up to the plate and expect to see it. If he gets ahead of you all you are going to see is that nasty slider."

Seemingly all of the starch had gone out of the Stanford hitters as the North Carolina pitcher retired the side on twelve pitches. Game over! The Cardinals were one game from being eliminated from the series.

Outside the dressing room of the Cardinal team, a saddened party of greeters awaited Gary's emergence. The first person to come out the door was Coach Ralston. Mr. Crawford stepped forward. "Coach, my name is Guy Crawford, good friends of Gary Mallon. I am afraid that I have some very tragic news." He paused to collect himself. "The plane carrying Gary's parents was blown up today before it left Portland. Terrorist activity was suspected. All passengers perished in the explosion."

"Oh my God, I am so sorry." Hanging his head, Coach Ralston mumbled, "What lousy news. Who in the hell would do a thing like that?" He paused. "Um, wait here. I'll go get Gary."

A moment later, Gary emerged from the dressing room with Coach Ralston and Brett Pine. Following closely behind was the rest of the Stanford team. Gary looked around, a quizzical look on his face. "Where are my folks?"

Angelina stepped forward, burying her face in his chest. "Oh Gary, I have bad news." She started to cry, looking up into his eyes. "Their plane was blown up by terrorists earlier today. All……."

Gary dropped to his knees and began to cry. "Oh no, oh no, it can't be true. Tell me it isn't true. Please Angelina tell me it isn't true."

As Gary continue to cry and plead for the news he had received to not be true, Angelina knelt beside him, holding him in her arms as his teammates gathered around to give their support. "Is it really true, Angelina?"

Angelina nodded her head, tears streaming down her face. "Yes honey, I am so sorry. I loved your parents so much."

Coach Ralston's voice wavered as he suggested, "Fellas, you go back into the dressing room. I'll join you in a moment." He turned toward Gary and dropped to his knees. "Gary, you go with the Crawford's and your wife to their hotel. I'll come see you as soon as I get your teammates settled into our quarters. Son, I am so sorry. At a time like this, um, words escape me. Just know that we all love you and……."

Gary nodded his head. Looking up at coach with tears running down his cheeks, he replied, "Thanks coach. I, I appreciate it."

The Crawford motel room was very somber. Only an occasional sound of someone crying could be heard. Finally, Angelina broke the silence. "Gary and I are going to go to the motel room that his parents reserved. Greg, you are welcome to join us. You can come too, Lance. Before you come, if you decide to, please give us an hour or so to be alone. You don't mind, do you mom and dad, um, Greg and Lance?"

Mrs. Crawford nodded her head. "Yes, you need to be alone. Give us a call if you need anything. Gary, I am so sorry."

In the motel room, Gary sat on one of the beds and stared into space. Finally he shook his head as if to confirm something. "I had a dream last night. I saw the explosion and the Southwest Airlines tote board." He lowered his head, continuing to mumble, "All morning I have experienced the weirdest feelings. It has been like I was in a movie. My entire life was displayed on the screen." He reached up to wipe away a tear. "Angelina, I'm not going to summer school. I want to go home. We have a lot of things to take care of, and I guess I am the head of the house now. You don't mind, do you?"

Angelina nodded her head. "No, of course I don't mind. We belong at home with family. Your brother will need us. Just know that I am your wife and I will stand by you no matter what comes up. We will work together to take care of whatever has to be done."

Gary looked at her with a look of appreciation and deeply felt love. "I love you so much." He paused for a moment. "Angelina, I know this may sound crazy, but all of my life I have felt that I was on a predetermined path. Somehow I feel that we met a long, long time ago in heaven or wherever. It is no surprise that we are married. I have loved you since the first moment I can recall playing with you in our parent's homes. You are the love of my life. Even as bad as I feel right now about losing my parents, I feel that there is a reason, a reason for us to go on and accomplish what we were sent here to accomplish."

Angelina nodded, a smile spreading across her face. "I'm glad that you finally realized that we were meant to be together. If you recall, I told you a long time ago that I was going to marry you."

There was a knock on the door. Greg and Lance entered. "I hope we are not intruding. There is something that I want to say to you."

Gary looked towards his brother. "Before you begin, um, let me tell you something that is very important." Gary paused. "Greg, um, we have to go back to Oakland to get some things straightened away, take our finals, and then we'll drive home. We are not going to summer school. We want to be at home with you. Will you be okay?"

Greg nodded. "Yeah, the Crawford's said that I could stay with them."

"Just know, little brother, when Angelina and I get home, you can stay with us in Mom and Dad's house. We're family and we have to stick together."

There was a knock on the door. Greg went to the door and opened it. Coach Ralston stood outside with Brett Pine, Gary's best friend on the Cardinal team. "Is it okay if we come in?"

Gary nodded, "Certainly, come on in, coach." He smiled. "You too, Brett, I suppose there is room in here for two more. I guess we have a few things to talk about, huh?"

Brett walked across the room towards the bed that Gary had occupied and that Angelina still occupied, joining his friend and putting his arm around him. "I love you man. I am so sorry."

"Thanks Brett, I'm sorry too. Other than my wife, I lost my best friends today." As the tears again started to well up in his eyes, he continued, "I am going to miss them so much. Um, I guess I have to, to, um, Coach, what am I supposed to do?"

Coach Ralston paused, lowered his head and starred at the floor briefly before replying, "Your only job is to heal. What you have ahead of you is much more important than any baseball game. The guys on the team love you and want you to know that…"

Gary shook his head defiantly. "No, my dad would want me to play. If you want me in the lineup, I want to play. Um, maybe you should move Bret to center field and put me in the lineup as the DH."

Brett took his arm from around his teammate and gave him a mild but defiant shove. "Listen here. If you are hell bent on playing then you are going to play center field. Listen you knot head. You beat me out and won the job to play centerfield, delegating me to the designated hitter role. You've earned the right to play there if you want. It's all up to you and coach."

Coach Ralston smiled. "I agree with Brett. If you want to play, you will play. The decision is yours to make. There is no pressure. Like I said, what's best for you is more important than a silly baseball game."

Stanford, the number one team in the nation going into the College World Series, was eliminated in the next game 4-3. In the dressing room after the game, Coach Ralston began, "Fellas, you don't know how proud I am of you. Together we accomplished so much. More important than any single game whether it was a win or a loss have been your personal growth and the growth of our team. In life, that is what matters most. To me it is more important than hitting .300, hitting home runs, or striking batters out. Winning isn't everything. Everyone loses in life just as everyone wins. The important thing is how you take your successes and your failures and how you play the game. There will be a tomorrow, and a next season." He paused. "Gentlemen, we're going to go back to the motel and gather up our stuff and get the hell out of this place. I don't know about you, but I want to go home." He paused as a soft gentle smile slowly spread across his face. "When we get back on campus and after you have finished your finals I want to talk to each of you individually. My talk with you can wait until we get back on campus and you have finished taking your finals." He grinned sheepishly. "Hmm, I guess I already covered that. Well anyway, after my talk with each of you, I am going to say, 'Have a nice summer, be well, and stay safe. I'll look forward to seeing you when school takes up again in the fall.'"

When Gary's finals were over, he walked over to the athletic office and knocked on Coach Ralston's door. "Hi coach. Well, I'm done with my finals. I am going back to my apartment in Oakland and pack up and head for home. Angelina and I have decided not to go to summer school. We have a lot of things to clean up at home. I suppose that I am the head of the family now."

Coach nodded. "You are coming back next year, aren't you?"

"Yes. I really felt good about this year and appreciate all that you have done for me. I guess that since I'm not going to summer school you can count on me for the next three years if you want me."

"You know very well that I do. So, you decided not to turn pro after your junior year?"

"Yeah, I've got time. I want to get a degree. One thing that I know for sure is that they can't take away the degree if my body breaks down and I can't play or if I'm not good enough to play in the majors."

Coach Ralston smiled, nodding his head. "Smart decision, but don't even consider the fact that you aren't good enough to make it to the majors. If I were to bet on anyone making it, it would be you." He got up from his chair and extended his hand. "Have a good summer and just know that coaching you this year has been a real pleasure. With you and Bret in the lineup again, we could be tough next year."

Gary nodded. "Thanks coach. It has been great having you as my coach. You have a nice summer as well."

As Gary walked out of the athletic complex a smile spread across his face as he considered his feelings about coach Ralston. *"Coach is a gruff old warrior, but inside he is soft as butter that has been sitting out for a spell in a warm room. To look at that old bear you wouldn't think that he could exude the caring feelings that he does. I think that he honestly loves every one of us. Like a father, he makes us toe the line and do all the right things, but he also allows us to be individuals, to find the proper way to do the right thing. What a neat guy. Damn, in his heyday I'll bet he was one hell of a football player in addition to excelling in baseball."*

Chapter Twelve

Moving On

Overcoming grief caused by the loss of someone of indescribable value, great importance in your life is a process. Much like overcoming an illness, it takes time to recover. The loss and its impact will in time be overcome because life is for the living. Coming to realize that instead of personal contact memories will have to take their place. Reflection will help as will staying active, but being around loved ones is the salve that makes the recovery take place more quickly and completely. Coming to grips with realizing that the loss of a loved one takes time, time to realize that although the departed person will not return, memories of them can be locked in the vault of your memory forever. When the time is right, the vault can be opened and the memories recalled and enjoyed.

Lying in bed the night prior to leaving for Lake Oswego and summer vacation with his family thoughts circulated in Gary's head making the arrival of sleep impossible. The thoughts also robbed him of his normal enthusiasm to make love to his beautiful and most desirable wife. Bombarded with her unusual silence he somehow sensed that she was also deep in thought. "Honey, if it is all the same to you I'd like to just close my eyes and do a little thinking. My mind is like a beehive with all of the thoughts I am having circulating about in my head."

"Good idea, I was thinking the same thing. Um, just know that you have the night off, but I'll get even with you in the morning. I plan to have my way with you mister."

Gary nodded, emitting a half-hearted acknowledgement as his mind began to spin, thoughts fluttering about like the assemblage of bees returning to their hives. *"I know that Angelina really wants to have a child, actually two. One each as she puts it, but when I look around at the people we know that have children and what they go through, I start thinking that it isn't a real good idea right now. Thank goodness she agrees and feels that we should wait until we get our degrees. With both of us going to school and the activities that we're involved in I just don't see how we could manage it and still enjoy our lives. My teammate and buddy John Bledsole has two kids with one on the way. That poor bastard always looks like he is running on fumes. I honestly don't know how he does it. He sure as hell plays a great first base, but he is struggling in the classroom. No wonder, when he goes home he never gets a chance to crack a book until the kids are in bed. He told me once that he loves his kids to death, but he sure wishes from time to time that he and his wife Betty had waited. He really envies the life that Angelina and I have. We are as free as a bird and I love every minute of it. But, I suppose that if Angelina wanted….."*

He mumbled inaudibly, "Yeah, if you want, yeah, if that's what you want. I wish I knew what you want for sure. I'd do anything to please you. Damn, I hate the thought of the drive to… I wonder what you really want."

Angelina giggled. "Honey, are you having a dream?" You are talking about some woman and what she wants. Do you care to share? Is there somebody that I don't know about?"

Somewhat more coherently, Gary replied, "I just want to please you and only you. If you want to start a…."

"Gary wake up, we need to get this settled once and for all. I told you that I want to wait to have children. Every time I look at the people we know that have kids I get a little envious until I discover what they are going through. No, no, and no again. I do not want to start a family until we are just a tad bit away from getting our degrees or have our diplomas in hand."

Gary sighed deeply, a sigh of relief. Clearing his throat, he offered, "I just wanted to make sure." He paused. Turning towards her, he confessed,

"You know, I get the weirdest feelings from time to time that mom and dad are right here. I know that isn't true, but I sense their presence. I feel my dad's guiding hand from time to time. I feel that they are on another journey, but I still can't help but feel that they are close at hand." He nodded. "You know that he was my hero don't you?"

"I do, and for what it's worth you couldn't have had a finer role model. I know that he and your mom never said so, but they really wanted to be grandparents. I wish…"

"I know. You know, somehow I feel that they have met the kids we are going to have. They didn't get a chance to know them down here, but somehow I believe that wherever they are…, well, somehow I feel that they have met them already. It's sort of like it was with us. Do you ever get the feeling that we met before we were….?"

Angelina nodded. "Yes, and I know exactly what you mean. I've always felt that we met before we met down here if you know what I mean." Angelina giggled. "Why do we always say, down here?"

Gary chuckled. "I don't know. I suppose that we have been taught about heaven and assume that it is up there. Actually, I believe that heaven or whatever is all around us." He paused. "About meeting before, I know exactly what you mean. You know, I think that we're all a part of some master plan. We're kind of like puppets on stage doing our thing." He took a deep breath. "Honey, it's time to close our eyes. We have a long trip ahead of us tomorrow. I love you my adorable wife."

"I love you too, my handsome husband."

Gary did as he suggested to Angelina, but in his sleep his thoughts began to take a journey. *"Dad, you have told me that you think that I have what it takes to go to and play on the grand stage, the major leagues. Please tell me again what you see that I am not so certain that I feel about myself."*

Gary's dad smiled. "Son, I could name a bunch of qualities that you have that it takes to go all the way to one of the big clubs. To start with, you have unbelievable hitting ability, terrific speed, outstanding fielding ability with the instincts and ability to cover a lot of ground in the field, and your arm is outstanding. Nobody dares to challenge your arm unless they are just plain stupid or have a desire to kill a rally. All of that is important, but you have something else that you either have or you don't. You have heart and a belief in yourself. You know that when you go to the plate you are going to get a hit.

You know that when a fly ball is hit in your direction you are going to catch it and make a play. You can't teach attitude or confidence. You either have it or you don't. Son, you have it."

Tears rolled down his cheeks as Gary lay motionless beside his beautiful wife. *"Just know that I love you, dad. You have always been my biggest supporter and it has really meant a lot to me. I sure hope that you know how I feel."*

Sleep, welcome sleep had enveloped Gary, but that didn't stop the dream, a conversation with his father. There was no fitful tossing and turning.

He felt completely at peace. He slept like he was in a coma.

The next morning as Angelina and Gary finished putting the last items in their cars, Gary nodded to his wife and suggested, "We need to go see the manager and let him know that we're leaving before we hit the road for home. I think that Treage still thinks that we're going to stay here for summer school."

Angelina nodded. "Good idea. Um, where do you want to stop tonight?"

Gary grinned. "How about Shasta City, would that work for you?"

Angelina shrieked, "Are you kidding? That is my favorite. That would be more than okay." She smiled. "Do you know why Shasta City is my favorite place to stop?"

"I could speculate, but no, why don't you enlighten me."

Angelina smiled. "Because Shasta City is just before or after we pass by that beautiful Mountain. It's too bad that Shasta isn't always completely visible."

Gary nodded. "I agree, but don't forget Lake Shasta. It is also quite a site." He paused. "Come on honey, we have to pay the manager a visit and time is a wasting."

Moments later they were in the manager's office. "Mr. Treage, we're going home to Portland for the summer. I know we told you that we were going to summer school, but with the...." Gary ducked his head, staring at the floor as he continued, "We cleaned out all of our stuff and wanted to drop the key by for you."

The manager quickly corrected Gary, "Gary, Gary, Gary, can you tell me how many times I have told you that I answer best to Treage."

He paused briefly looking at Gary and then at Angelina. "Please, I am Treage. Um, I don't want the key. I rented the apartment to you with the understanding that it was yours for the time you two were here to go to college. When will you be returning?"

Angelina replied, "We should pull in about the middle of August. We want to shake out all of the kinks to get ready for our sophomore year." She paused. "By the way, we're going to do the four year plan. So, if we can have the place…"

"It's yours. You kids have been great renters. I would be out of my mind to not let you have the place for another year. By the way, I'm so sorry to hear about your parents, Gary." Treage suddenly disposed of his gruff, unapproachable demeanor. "I know what it is like to lose a parent, um, parents. My loss occurred later in life, but any loss….." Treage dropped his head. When he again looked up there were tears in his eyes. "I still miss them. Thank God I have great memories to refer to from time to time. Hang onto yours. They will console you when times get tough or during lonely hours in some distant place."

Gary nodded, choking back tears. "Thanks, I appreciate….." He paused. "Treage, you are a special man. Other than my dad, Angelina's dad, and my coach at Stanford, well, you are special."

Treage, as he liked to be called, nodded and then replied, "Thank you. That means a lot to me. Um, as I just said, you two have been great renters. I wish that I could get more like you. Um, I've been thinking. Going to college these days isn't cheap. I think that I'll pass on charging you rent for July and August. You have already paid me for the month of June."

Gary looked at the burly man whose heart was certainly made of gold. His demeanor was so different than his caring ways. After a pause, Gary replied shaking his head, "That is awfully nice of you, but Angelina's parents already paid the rent ahead."

"Yep, and I have already sent them a refund check. Like I say, having you here is more important than the rent check that I collect. If you don't mind me saying so, I think of you as I would if you were my children." Again tears appeared in his eyes. "I never had the joy of having kids, but…"

Gary gratefully shook his hand and stepped back to allow Angelina step forward to give him a hug and kiss him on the cheek. She whispered, "See you in August. Have a good summer you sweet man. We love you."

The Wonderment of Life

As they started to get into their cars, Gary hollered at Angelina, "When we get on the road, give me a call on your Bluetooth. We can alleviate some of the boredom by talking while we're traveling to Shasta City. If you need to make a pit stop or take a break, we can discuss where to stop."

"Sounds good to me, I don't like driving on the freeways in California. Having company will be nice."

A few minutes later, headed for the I-5 freeway north, Gary's phone rang. "Hello?"

"You asked me to call. So, what do you want to talk about?"

"This may sound corny, Angelica, but have you ever wondered why we are here?"

"All the time, and I think that I have an answer."

"What would that be? Um, you're not going to lay some heavy spiritual stuff on me are you?"

"Do you want me to tell you my thoughts or not? After all, sweet cheeks, you started it all last night."

"Okay, my love, have it your way. Let me hear your theory."

"Well, Gary, I think that we are here for a reason. I feel even stronger that you and I were meant to be together."

After a brief pause, Gary responded, "I'm sorry about giving you a bad time about the heavy spiritual stuff. I want you to know that I feel the same way. Um, this is a bit tough for me to say right now, but I think that my parents didn't just die by accident. There was a reason."

Angela inquired, "What do you feel the reason was, pray tell?"

"Well, I think that I have a job to do that goes well beyond just playing professional baseball. Don't get me wrong, I'm going to play, but there is something far more important that I have to do. All baseball is going to do for me is open some doors."

"What has their deaths have to do with the job you feel you have to do and what do you think that you have to do anyway?"

Gary paused for a moment. "Are you still there?"

"Yes, Angelina, I am still here. I was just gathering my thoughts." He paused momentarily and then began, "Well, here goes. My parent's deaths sort of made me focus on things that may be more important than playing baseball. I think that you will agree that the government is pretty messed up right now in our country. We pass laws only to see people willfully disobey them. People have difficulty telling the truth, or they make excuses for the things that they do wrong. The United States has an image of being a bully, a nation that wants everything their way and are willing to do whatever it takes to get their way. We are becoming a nation that is not governed for the people and by the people. Sadly it is now run or strongly influenced by a few huge corporations that only care about acquiring power and the bottom line which is directly related to acquiring wealth. Right now we might be the most hated people in the World except for the terrorists that kill for no apparent reason other than to just show the people of the World that they can. We have lost that image of being the nation that leads the people of the World by doing the right thing. I don't think that we are a beacon for the peoples of the World to follow any longer. I want to help change that if I can. I want to work towards finding a way that we can achieve harmony, love, and peace in this World of discord. I don't want our nation to be accepted because we jam it down people's throats. I think that it is time that someone goes to Washington to represent the people instead of the money people that get him or her elected. I think that there are some good people with admirable intentions prior to going to Washington. Once they get there they get swallowed up by the party they belong to and are forced to go along with the party's agenda so that they can get reelected. Maybe a person needs to back there not owing anybody for getting there. I think that if that I was true to myself by setting a positive example, the representatives sent to Washington might just join me and start a movement that changes the culture in Washington. Maybe that movement would help make things work again in Washington and work for the people they are elected to represent." Gary paused. "There are a couple of things that could get this change rolling. I think that insuring that more than two parties can have the same opportunity to be a viable force in our government would be one step. The other would be to cast out the Electoral College system, replacing it with the popular vote. Why should a plurality of one vote in a state guarantee that the winner takes all of the Electoral College votes for that state?"

"Wow! It sounds like you want to go into politics. Do you know that I love you? What you just said makes me love you even more. I just hope that you will let me help you achieve your goal because that is a terrific goal and I am completely on board." Angelina paused. "Do you know what my passion in life is?"

Gary quickly responded, "I know about your desire to act and sing on stage." He paused. "I think that......"

Angelina interrupted him with excitement in her voice gushing forth. "Excuse me for interrupting, but you must know that what you just mentioned is only part of it Gary. I want to help find a way to solve the homeless issue. They are the forgotten people many of which served in the military and returned home so messed up that living on the street is all they aspire to do. Many others are mentally ill and have been booted from institutions that can help them. I want to help find a solution."

"Well my darling, I will do whatever it takes to help you achieve the goals of your passion. By the way, I love you too. No, I love you more than I love life itself. Um, I am going to tweak my major a bit. I am going for a straight degree in history with a minor in political science and constitutional law. I think that it is important to start preparing for my second career. I mean my third career."

There was a moment of silence at the other end of the phone. Finally, Angelina inquired, "Tell me about your first career. I think I have it figured correctly when I say that you are going to have a career in baseball and then go into politics, but what's the third endeavor that you plan to pursue?"

"Look silly, I am married to you. As such I have a career of being your husband. That is the most important career that I can have and I will do everything to always make our marriage a top priority, the highest priority." He paused. "I suppose that I should have said four careers because when we have children I will also have a very important career as a father. I want to be the best father that I can, always trying to be better. I hope that I can be as good a father as my dad was."

"Honey, you are so sweet. You really know how to charm me. Let's hurry down the road so that we can make some whoopee. I am getting horny."

"Do you want to sign off for a while? I have some thinking to do about some things that need to be done when we get home."

"Sure, I'll hang up for now. We don't have too much further to go, do we?"

"Sorry to give you the bad news, but we won't be at Shasta City before dark. I won't be away long. I'll get back to you in an hour, okay? I love you."

"Roger that, and I love you too."

An hour later as promised, Gary pushed the call button on the steering wheel. A voice replied, "Main menu."

Gary replied, "Call Angelina cell."

The voice replied, "Call Angelina Cell, calling Angelina Cell." A couple of rings later, a familiar voice replied, "Hello?"

"Hi good looking, how are you doing?"

"Outside of missing you, I am doing great. My butt is getting a bit tired though."

stretch?""Want to stop for a burger or a break to get out of the car and Angelina answered emphatically, "Yes, yes, yes, I want to stop." After the brief stop, they continued on, arriving at Shasta City at 8:00. After securing a room for the night they took the motel clerk's advice and headed for a favorite restaurant. A dash through the menu with but two selections each, salad and an order of fish and chips, and they were off for their room and the comfort of a nice hot shower and then a long awaited visit to the bed.

Angelina opted to begin the night without any clothing which Gary found much to his liking. After some much needed exercise between the sheets, Gary and Angelina took a break to replenish their energy. "Gary, do you enjoy doing it as much as I do?"

"Are you kidding? Of course I do. You don't know how much you turn me on."

"What do you think about while we are doing it?"

Gary smiled. "Funny you should ask. I think about how beautiful you are, how much I love you, and how wonderful it feels. I also revel in listening to your funny noises while we do it. What about you?"

Angelina smiled. "Well, it is almost like a multi-tiered wave of thoughts that rush through my head. First of all there is the excitement I feel when we kiss, when you massage my breasts, and when you run you finger in and out of my vagina and across my clitoris. All of that is just so damned good because you take the time to make me feel so good." She paused with a twinkle in her eye. "Then there is the anticipation of when you are poised above me and you slowly slide your body between my legs and I take you in my hand and guide you inside me." She smiled. "My God that is so good, but what follows is what blows my mind. When you start moving inside of me I feel like I am riding a rocket headed towards the moon." She paused. "What do I think about? Actually, I think my mind goes blank with only the thoughts of how good it feels and how much I love you."

Gary chuckled. "I know one thing for sure. You really like doing it, don't you?"

She nodded. "There is nothing better. Sometimes I just want to scream at the top of my lungs, 'I love you, I love you. Oh God, I love you.'" She paused for a moment. "So, when you said that you needed an hour to ponder what to do when we got home, what were your thoughts?"

"Well, I was just trying to put things we have to do in some sort of logical order. If you agree, I think that we want to put mom and dad's car in Greg's name. Next, I think that we have to put Greg, you and me on the title to the house."

Angelina nodded. "I agree. I think that is what your mom and dad would have wanted. So, is there anything else?"

"Yeah, there is the matter of my mom and dad's investments. My dad made a lot of money playing baseball and he was smart enough to invest wisely. We need to talk to the man that manages his investments and get all of the investments in our name." He paused. "Um, Greg needs to have his name on the investment accounts as well. This is where your parents come in. While we are away at college, I hope that we can get them to watch over my brother and treat the money coming to him as an allowance and a savings account. He is entitled to receive the same amount as we do, but he is too young to get it all in a lump sum each month."

Angelina nodded. "I am certain that my parents will be happy to take care of that." She frowned. "What do you plan to do with the house?"

"This is another place where your parents can help. I think that if they are willing, we need to have a family meeting and figure it out. I have some ideas, but I want to hear what they have to say along with what my brother thinks." He paused. "I didn't mean to leave you out. What you think is important to me because we are partners and a very good team." He paused. "Right now I am leaning towards keeping the house. What do you think?"

"You have come up with some great ideas, a good plan. I can't think of a thing that I would suggest that we do differently." She smiled. "You seem to have accomplished a lot in that hour."

Gary smiled as he playfully started to rub her breasts. "Are you up for another go round?"

"Always, I could make love with you all day and all night."

The next morning they got up at the respectable hour of nine o'clock, showered, dressed, and checked out of their motel. After breakfast they once again headed north.

A short while out of Shasta City, Angelina dialed his number.

"Hello?"

"Are you seeing what I'm seeing?" "You mean Mt. Shasta?"

"Yes, isn't it beautiful? It is completely unshrouded by clouds. It is so majestic."

"Makes you wonder, doesn't it?"

"Yes, God or whatever you want to call him, her, or it, well, it worked and still works wondrous magic."

Gary nodded, and then responded, "The greatest accomplishment of The Source was the creation of man. Damn, there I go again mentioning The Source."

Angelina chuckled. "I think that is so much better than referring to the creator as God. I like referring to it as The Source."

Gary replied, "Me too, yeah, I like referring to the Supreme Being as The Source."

Chapter Thirteen

A Summer Place

There is nothing like going home. When you have been away there is nothing like the feeling that going home brings to you. It is comforting to be reunited with friends and familiar sites. Going to visit where you used to live brings back many memories. Even going home when the loved ones that you used to visit aren't there is special as it brings back warm memories.

Just outside of Salem, Gary called Angelina. After she had answered, he offered, "I have an idea."

Angelina giggled and then in a teasing manner, replied, "That's refreshing. I was wondering when you were going to come up with an idea. You aren't exactly known as an idea man."

"Funny, you are really a riot. Where did you get your humor? Is it canned or is it original?"

"I get it from listening to you. So, what's your idea?"

"What would you say about you and me going on a cruise to Hawaii or some like place after we get all of the details taken care of at home?"

"Are you serious?" She shrieked, "I would love it. My God, it will be our second honeymoon." Angelina paused. "When you say, "Or a like place" are you implying that visiting the islands where it is warm and offers the opportunity to swim in the ocean and…?"

"I think that I should have just said that I wanted to visit the Hawaiian Islands. We couldn't do all of them, but maybe Oahu and the big island would be good. So, what do you say?"

"I am still on board with the idea."

"Good, we can start making plans after we wade through the stuff we have to take care of at home. By the way, are you sure that your parents will be okay with sitting down and having a family POW WOW?"

"I'm positive. In case you haven't realized it, you are family. My parents love you as though you were one of their own. In many ways they consider you a son. They will be so flattered."

"Well, the feeling is mutual. Your mom and dad have always been like a second mom and dad to me. I love them a lot."

"Honey, I suggest that when we are close to home we give mom and dad a head's up. They know we will be there sometime early in the afternoon, but wouldn't it be nice to have them greet us?"

"You mean that you want the greeting party to be waiting for us in the driveway?"

"Exactly, there is nothing like a greeting party for a home coming." "I agree. It will be so good to see them and our brothers."

An hour later, they drove into a familiar driveway. Standing there to greet them was the family, Guy, Sue, Greg, and Lance. It was so good to be home. Their presence in the driveway made the homecoming extra special. All that was missing was the band. Gary grinned, offering, "If we had given them a little more warning they would probably have had a band there to greet us."

Angelina chuckled. "I think that you are right. Look at their faces.

They are as excited to see us as we are them."

As they opened the doors to their car, everyone was there to give hugs and help unload the car. Carrying in the last of what had found its way into their cars in Oakland, Gary turned to Guy and asked, "Guy, would it be okay with you and Sue if we sat down to have a family talk? I need some help to wade through some of the stuff that needs to be attended to, um in particular how Angelina and I are going to deal with the house. I trust that you know a hell of a lot more than I do about some of these things. I would really appreciate it if, um, that is if you would feel comfortable with the idea."

Guy grinned, his beaming smile stretching from ear to ear. "It would be our pleasure. We have some things that we want to discuss with you as well." He paused for a moment. "Why don't you and Angelina take some time to get used to being home? If you like you can plan on having dinner at our place. We can have our family talk after that."

"That sounds good to me. Thanks Guy for all that you and Sue have done."

After dinner the family gathered in the living room of the Crawford home. Guy began, "Before you begin with what you want to discuss, Sue and I want you to know that we have asked Greg to stay with us. With you and Angelina away at college for most of the year, it just seems natural for Greg to stay here with us. It will also give you two some privacy when you come home for a visit. While you are away at college we will check in on your house from time to time to ensure that all is okay."

Gary nodded. "We discussed this a bit after we were eliminated from the College World Series. Angelina and I appreciate your offer, and we accept. Um, I see that Greg has already cleaned out his room."

Angelina chuckled. "That is called being prepared, Gary. I also think that it is a good idea. It will take a lot of pressure off of us." She turned to Gary and suggested, "Honey, why don't you share with mom and dad what we talked about?"

Gary nodded. "Good idea." He cleared this throat. "Well, to begin, I think that we should go to DMV and change the registration of mom and dad's car and put it in Greg's name. I'll talk about the insurance later. It is my understanding that all we have to do is supply them with the death certificate."

Guy nodded. "That is my understanding as well. If I am wrong we can always jump through the hoops to make it happen."

Greg pumped his fist in excitement as he looked approvingly at Gary. "Thanks, Bro. I promise not to go crazy now that I have a car to drive."

"Well, just know that if you do go crazy your insurance will go through the roof and you will be completely responsible for the increase."

Greg, still pumping his fist, replied, "That is more than fair. I promise to be a responsible driver."

Gary grinned. "Since you are staying with Guy and Sue, I expect you to listen to what they say. You might think of them as your mom and dad from now on if that is okay with them."

Sue grinned and quickly responded, "That is perfect. We gain a son for the daughter you took away from us."

Angelina shook her head. "Mom, you know better. You and dad willingly gave me away to the man I love."

Gary cleared his throat. "Um, I think that is enough talk about territory and who belongs to whom. The next thing I would like to talk about is the money that comes out of mom and dad's investment account each month. Right now, it is automatically deposited in their checking account which I will transfer to Angelina's and my account. Mom and dad had my name on their account." He paused to insure that everyone was on board with the idea. "I think that it is only fair that the money be divided evenly between Greg, Angelina and me." Turning to Angelina, he smiled. "You know that what's mine is yours."

She nodded approvingly, chuckling. "And just don't you forget it, mister."

"Greg, I think that it makes sense for Guy and Sue to manage your share, putting you on an allowance with the rest going into your savings account. Your allowance should include enough money to pay for your car insurance, gas for the car, and a reasonable amount of spending money."

Guy and Sue nodded their heads. Guy offered, "It sounds to me like you have thought this out, and I want you to know that I think that your ideas make a lot of sense."

Greg nodded his head. "Yeah, that sounds more than fair to me."

Gary began again. "This next piece is something that Angelina and I hope you will help us decide what is best to do. It all has to do with the house. It appears to me that since the house is paid for, the only major expenses would be insurance, taxes, utilities and a modest amount of upkeep. That means that we could get rid of the burden of selling the house. If we do that, Angelina and I would have our own place to come back to when we come home for breaks at college and for summer vacation. What would you recommend?"

Guy looked at Sue for confirmation as he began, "I think that you and Angelina should keep the house. I believe that is what your mother and father would have wanted. There is more than enough monthly disposable cash coming from their investments to easily pay for the expenses incurred by keeping the house.

Gary nodded. "Yeah, that and much more, dad invested wisely." After a pause, he continued, "My problem is how to transfer the account to Angelina's and my account."

Guy nodded. "I am sure that the investment representative can help you with that and make the transition very smooth and easy."

Sue nodded her approval.

Guy continued, "Let us think of the money that comes out of your parent's investment account in this way. After the house expenses are paid, you could then divide the rest between you and Greg. Greg will live on an allowance with the rest of his share going into his bank account. You and Angelina would do the same with your share." He paused. "Sue and I will be happy to watch the house carefully in terms of keeping the yard up, and keeping the temperature in the house at fifty degrees during the colder months. Of course we'll make sure that all of the necessary cleaning and upkeep of the house is covered."

Gary shook his head adding, "Damn, I forgot to add that the newspaper, TV, and internet can be put on hold when we are not at home."

Guy nodded. "All of the utilities will continue whether you are at home or not. Why don't you set up your checking account with all house expenses taken out automatically? During this summer we can watch the expenses and get a fairly good idea of what to expect. Of course we can keep you informed so that you can move money back and forth in your checking and savings accounts by using your computer on line. Sue and I will help you set all of that up." Guy paused for a moment. "Um, it would be good for us to set up a checking and savings account for Greg at the bank where you have your account so that you can move his share into his account each month."

Angelina smiled. "Thank you. You don't know what a relief it is to know that basically we won't have anything to worry about while we are away at college." She smiled. "I guess you might say that it will be like being at the coast watching the tide come in and go out."

Gary nodded. "I agree, but I have one more thing that I think fair to mention. Guy, you and Sue are taking on a lot of responsibility. You are watching our house, taking care of Greg, and helping us with the budget. I think that you should receive something for your efforts."

Guy shook his head. "No, Sue and I won't hear of it. We are doing this because we love you and Angelina. For the longest time we have thought of you as a second son. Now we can expand that to think of having three sons and a daughter."

Sue nodded. "I will second that. Now, I think that it is time to put this topic to rest for a while. We can start doing the necessary things tomorrow or the next day. Heavens, by the time June has passed you and Angelina will be completely organized with nothing to worry about."

Angelina looked at Gary and inquired, "Are you going to tell them or am I?"

Gary frowned appearing to be confused. Suddenly as though a light was turned on he nodded his head. "Oh yeah, um, I think that you should tell them."

Angelina smiled. "Just like a man to defer to a woman for the important stuff." Chuckling she continued. "I'm just kidding. Um, well, Gary and I are thinking of taking a cruise to Hawaii to visit Oahu and the big island. Would you like to go? Of course Greg and Lance are invited as well."

Guy smiled. "Sue and I were talking about doing something like that just a day or so ago. I think that it is a great idea. As soon as we get all of your things in order, we can arrange for the airline tickets." He paused. "Are you certain that you want to go to Hawaii? You haven't thought of going to Mexico?" He paused, shaking his head. "You did say a cruise, didn't you? Well, if that is what you want we can get the tickets for a cruise."

Gary smiled. "Yes, we did mention a cruise and no, we sort of have our hearts set on going to Hawaii. We are thinking of it as a second honeymoon or at least an extension of our first one."

Sue smiled. "Gary and Guy, it appears that you need a woman to organize you. I think that we should arrange the trip by getting the tickets and then do all of the necessary things to clear up your obligations. If this is going to be a second honeymoon, I like your idea of going on a cruise. Spaces on cruises fill up quickly, um, that is if you are certain that you want to go on a cruise. Maybe that is what we should decide first. Do we want to go on a cruise or fly and then take a land cruise?"

Guy frowned shaking his head. "Just like a woman. Honey, I think that Gary and Angelina should decide. I could care less whether we do a cruise or fly over to the islands. After they tell us what they want we can make arrangements."

Angelina interrupted the discussion offering, "I vote for taking a two week cruise to Hawaii. We can check out the arrangements for visiting both Oahu and the big island."

Gary nodded his head. "I agree. Are you and Sue okay with the idea."

Guy and Sue nodded their heads. Sue smiled, "I guess that I got a bit pushy and should have not started to make plans for you Gary and Angelina. I apologize."

Gary shook his head. "No apology is necessary. I think that we are all excited about the trip. Now all we have to do is make the arrangements."

Greg and Lance smiled with Greg offering, "I am sure glad that you adults have finally come to a decision. I thought that we might be here all night deciding."

Lance chuckled. "I will second that."

In the middle of July the newly formed family departed on a two week cruise to Hawaii. Of course all of the changes in title to the house and car, arrangements for the payments to be automatically withdrawn, the conversation with the investment counselor, and the budgets for Gary and Angelina and Greg had been put in order. With minor monthly adjustments in the payment amounts for different obligations, all was set. The islands beckoned. Aloha.

Chapter Fourteen

Aloha

The Pineapple State offers plentiful exposure to the sun, wonderful tasty fruit (pineapple a favorite of the touring family), hula girls, Luaus, and the opportunity to meet some of the friendliest people on the planet. Put on that lei, don't forget your swim suit, and enjoy the relaxed environment. Oh, I almost forgot. Snorkeling to see the beautiful variety of fish is almost a must experience.

The monument to the Arizona is historically significant and brings back painful memories to those who were old enough to experience the attack on Pearl Harbor. The war is over. Time has passed and we have entered into a positive relationship with the Japanese, so leave your grudges behind. Countries that were once enemies can learn to love and respect each other. Forgiveness is important, putting a conflict in perspective as it is the governments that wage war using innocent citizens to do the dirty work.

As the merged family soon discovered, a cruise puts a lot of pressure on your midsection. Perhaps it the pressure on your will to resist that is put to the test as the delicious and wide range of food offerings is served nonstop. Resisting playing "follow the leader", fellow cruisers who parade through the serving area and adhering to the three meals a day regimen is difficult.

Never the less unless you wish to go on a yearlong diet after the visit to the islands via a cruise, it is a necessity to impose self-restraint. With exception of Greg and Lance, still growing boys, the family was content to adhere to the "three meals a day" regimen. Even following that plan, they felt it necessary to make sure their plates were not filled. Moderation was the word of the day for the entire cruise as well as making sure that exercise was on their schedule.

Other than eating at every opportunity, Greg and Lance were perfectly content to commit to the varied deck activities offered such as volleyball, swimming, shuffleboard and even a moderation of girl watching. Guy, Sue, Angelina, and Gary focused on enjoying the swimming pool after partaking in a tasty brunch, walking the perimeter of the ship, enjoying some of the offerings such as instructions on how to play bridge, socializing with the patrons in their age group, and the evening entertainment which included dancing and listening to exceptional performances by a couple of fine singers and a wonderful band.

One afternoon on the deck beside the pool, Angelina looked at her husband as he lay soaking up the rays of sun. "So when we dock in Oahu, what is on your bucket list to visit?"

Gary squinted as he turned towards her. "I would like to go see the Arizona memorial, see the hula girls, and attend a luau. What about you, what do you want to do?"

"I like your choices, but I would like to hit the beach sometime and take in the public bus tour of Oahu. From what I have heard it is a real bargain. You get to see pretty much the same thing as the more expensive private tours at a fraction of the cost." She paused to reflect further. "Um, I can't wait to visit the big island. A visit to the volcano, snorkeling, and another luau would be at the top of my bucket list. What are your thoughts?"

"As usual, I love your ideas. I am glad that we decided to focus on visiting Oahu and the big island. Too many islands in one visit would be stressful, um, vacation overload. We'll be plenty full of the islands after spending a week at Oahu and a week on the big island." He paused as he took a moment to look at his wife carefully. His thoughts about the upcoming year and the quest to return to Omaha would have to wait to develop fuller as his focus had taken an abrupt detour. Nodding his head to confirm his thoughts, he just knew that there was much more to Angelina than her outward appearance. "Um, I think that renting a car and driving to the volcano would be fun." Gary groaned as he turned over onto his back. "I have just about had enough sun. How would you like to go back to our room?"

Angelina smiled wickedly. "And just what do you have on your mind, mister?"

Gary smiled. "I think that you know, and I am surprised that you haven't already made the suggestion. Usually it is you that brings up the subject."

"You seemed so peaceful lying there. I didn't have the heart to disturb you."

Gary chuckled. "That would be a first. Actually, I think that you are the one that began this conversation."

Indignant, Angelina protested, "I did not. You are the one that suggested that we go to our room."

"True, but you were the one that asked about my bucket list." He smiled slyly. "Did you know that you interrupted some interesting thoughts I was having about you?"

"No, I didn't. So what were your thoughts all about?"

"I really didn't have time to formulate any concrete thoughts before you interrupted and broke my concentration."

"What's a girl supposed to do when she has had more than enough sun? Besides, I wanted to spend some private time with the man of her dreams."

Gary grinned. "Come on. There is no point in trying to discover which came first, the chicken or the egg. Let's go to our room."

Later as they lay beside each other in their room after enjoying a joyful romp between the sheets, Angelina murmured, "This is just like a honeymoon."

Gary nodded. "Yes it is. You know, I think that we should plan on going somewhere special at least once a year. I think that having a honeymoon every year would be so cool."

Angelina nodded. "You know I was looking forward to becoming a mommy in a couple of years. It looks like we have added another year to that date. Don't get me wrong. I think that we have made the right decision. Having you all to myself for another year and a bit more will be wonderful."

Gary pulled her close and whispered in her ear, "I don't disagree. We are in a position to start a family whenever we want. Waiting so that we can get the most out of college life and having the opportunity to enjoy each other without the patter of little feet until we get our degrees will be ideal. I have noted that the people that we know who started a family just after they got married seem to feel that they have missed out on so much."

"I totally agree with what you are saying. I just want you to know that I want to have children with you, and an occasional discussion about starting a family won't hurt. I want everyone including our children to know that starting a family was a planned event and that our children were really, really wanted as opposed to being a mistake because we couldn't manage our sexual attraction to each other."

"Yeah, I second that in spades. Besides, I think that by now everyone knows that we both plan to stay in school for four years. There is no reason to rush it. Maybe by staying I'll be a more valuable pick in the draft."

"Don't forget that by staying the full four years will put far less pressure on us to take huge numbers of credit hours to graduate early. Personally I like the idea of having fun and enjoying college life. I don't want the experience to be like having a job." Angelina smiled and then kissed him. "That means that we can start the process of having a baby during our senior year. Um, what month would you like to have the baby born?"

"What do you think about November? Both of us were born then." "I like it." She furrowed her brows and pursed her lips as she pondered what she was about to say. "If we have a baby in November, I believe that we have to get pregnant in February?"

"That is what I figure." He paused. "That means baseball season will be over when the baby is born."

Angelina smiled. "Okay, we have a plan, but I want you to make me a promise."

"What is that?"

"Starting February first of our senior year we have to do it every day, every night, and maybe more."

Gary chuckled. "Am I going to be able to attend baseball practice and go with the team on away games?" He jabbed her gently in the ribs. "You know, you are something else again. I want you to know that I love you, correct?"

"Yes, I know, and you know that I love you, right?"

"Yes, I do. Angelina, I will love you for a long, long time, until the Twelfth of Never." He paused, a smile forming on his face. Finally he added, "And that is a long, long time."

"Oh my, aren't you the poetic one?"

"No, I am just quoting a line from a Johnny Mathis song. The big difference in listening to the song and listening to me is that I am saying it directly to you. Just don't ask me to sing it."

Angelina chuckled. "Not to worry and thank God that you chose not to sing."

Gary looked at her for the longest time, considering what to say next. Before he could open his mouth, Angelina frowned and asked, "What? What are you thinking about?"

He began slowly and thoughtfully, "Actually, I have two things to say. "

"Well, I am waiting. Should I be concerned?"

"Heavens no, I'm just trying to confirm something." He paused again. "Angelina, do you really love me or is all that we are experiencing just an extension of our beginning? I don't think that we really began our existence here on Earth. I think that it all began before we arrived, before we were born."

Angelina nodded in a most reflexive manner. "Just know that I am certain beyond a doubt that my love for you is real. It might have begun before we arrived, but just know that I have loved you since the first moment that I saw you." She smiled. "You know, you were really kind of pathetic. All you wanted to do was buzz around like an agitated bug. You were crawling here, there and everywhere." She shook her head. "To top it all off, you were running to and fro like a crazed pup chasing its tail. I was so intrigued, always wondering if I would ever get you slowed down so that I could catch you and put my claim on you. I have always loved you so much." She paused. "Enough of that subject. I'm not going to ask you when you fell in love with me because you were so busy running here and there you probably didn't have the time to figure it out. I had to do it for you."

Gary shook his head. "Little did you know? I was just playing hard to get."

Angelina shrugged her shoulders in resignation. "No matter, so what was the second thing that you wanted to tell me?"

"I was just thinking about how selfish I have been and when you brought up the "not singing to me" bit. It reminded me that I didn't pay enough attention or give you the compliments you deserved for your outstanding performance as the lead in your school's production of "The Sound of Music." I was so caught up in my world of baseball and then with the death of my parents… I just want you to know that you were fantastic! I mean it, I was so proud of you. You were terrific. You were the true personification of Maria."

Angelina smiled. "Well, thank you kind sir. I knew all along how you felt, but it is so nice to hear the words. I love you so much."

"I love you also, my wife."

Angelina cleared her throat as if to announce that something profound was about to be said. "Gary, I have made a decision that I haven't shared with you until just now. Um, I have been asked to be in two major musicals this coming year. One is in the fall and the other is in the spring." She paused. "Of course I would have to go through the formality of trying out for the parts, but…."

"Wow! That is terrific. After your performance in "The sound of Music" I can see why you are in demand."

"Well, it is nice to be wanted, but I have other plans. I have decided that I will only do one of the musicals, the one in the fall. I want to devote all of the spring to watching you play baseball and root for a Cardinal return to Omaha. You and your teammates have some unfinished business to attend to and I want to be your most vocal cheerleader."

"Are you sure that is what you really want to do? I would not be the least bit disappointed if you did both, um both musicals and also served my most ardent cheerleader."

"No, I have made up my mind and that is final. So, let's enjoy the rest of the cruise and have some fun back home before we have to go back to school. Actually, I should not have implied that we have to go back to school. I am really looking forward to it. We have made some fantastic friends, live in a great place, are getting a terrific education, and, well, life is good, so very, very good."

Gary smiled. "Ditto to that, life is good and I can't imagine that it won't get better."

Chapter Fifteen

Back to School

Summer break is a time to relax and recharge the batteries. It is also a time to reconnect with family and friends. The time away from the world of academia is refreshing and thought provoking. Not unlike birth, the entry into the world of academia is a shock. The infant is bombarded by sights, sounds, and feelings never felt before in the comfort of the womb, or at least that exposure is not apparent. To the freshman, the first year is also a shock. All of a sudden the newbie is exposed without prodding to the rigor of going to class, taking notes, studying, passing tests, and writing that first dreaded college paper. Many infants learn to walk and begin organized toilet training during the first year. So too does the student rookie gradually acclimate to the world of academia.

The break between the first year and the beginning of the second is short for the toddler as the organized quest for knowledge begins or has already begun. So too is the summer break for the first year college student, but returning to school is another step towards becoming an educated man or woman and finding the career path that will allow for the contributions that one must make in following their path in life.

The cruise ended and preparations were made for Greg and Lance's senior year. Greg was going to be the returning starting half back on the Laker's team, and Lance was going to be the starting power forward on the basketball team. Both expected to have good years chasing state championships. Guy and Sue were preparing for another school year, and Gary and Angelina were busy packing for the trip south to their Oakland apartment. The departure date was only a couple of days away and the activity around the two houses was hectic. A send-off barbeque was scheduled for the next day, so that heightened the frenzied activity even more.

After the barbeque Gary sat down with his brother, Greg, for a heart to heart discussion. "Greg, your senior year is going to be special. You are going to have a fantastic football season. Please remember that you also have to tend to business and also have a great year in the classroom. Getting good grades will give you choices and expand your opportunities to select the college that you want to attend. Just remember that the college you want to attend will offer you a football scholarship if your grades are good. Otherwise, you might have to settle for a second choice. It is entirely up to you."

Greg nodded. "I pretty much know where I want to go. I want to go to OSU and become a Beaver."

Gary smiled. "That is a good choice. Do you know what you want to pursue as a field of study?"

Greg nodded. "I am interested in sport's medicine. It is going to require a master's degree and I know that OSU may not be the best choice for that pursuit, but there a lot of courses that I can take that will pave the way. I am also interested in sports medicine so that I can become an athletic trainer."

"It is good that you have set a course and have goals. Work hard and you will achieve those goals." Gary paused. "Please do me and the Crawford's a favor."

"I know. You want me to act as though they were my parents."

Gary nodded. "They are doing you and me a huge favor by offering to be your adoptive parents. They are offering to serve in that capacity because they know what a fine person you are and because they loved mom and dad." He smiled. "You would also be doing Angelina a big favor."

Greg nodded. "You really love her, don't you?"

"Yes, I love her more than words can describe. She is my best friend and I just hope that someday you will find someone as special for you as she is for me."

The next morning Gary and Angelina said their goodbye's to the Crawford's. There were probably enough tears shed to water a good sized plant together with enough hugs and kisses and handshakes to last until Thanksgiving. That still didn't stop Gary and Angelina from going back for more and leaving with great hesitancy.

On the road, Gary's phone rang. "Hi, what's up?"

"I want to know where you think we should make our first pit stop."

"Hum, what do you think about Ashland?"

"That is okay with me if we can spend the night again in Shasta City."

Gary chuckled. "You really like that place, don't you?"

"Yes, it is really a cool place to land. I like the motel we stayed in, the restaurant we ate at, and quite frankly I would like to stop before we get so tired that neither one of us has an interest in making love. I am already missing you."

"Well, I miss you too. Just drive safe. I can't bear the thought of losing you."

"I promise, but the same goes for you. We don't have to be in a hurry."

Chapter Sixteen

Treage and the Sophmore Year

The return to some place previously visited is not filled with the same anxious excitement as the first visit. However, it is good to return to a familiar place, perhaps a second home. It is also nice when visiting or returning to that familiar place to see a familiar face.

The journey down I-5 was a mixture of the boredom caused by driving on a long, straight freeway broken only on occasion by a gentle curve or two. The tedium of the dry brown terrain that embraced the passage from Cottage Grove to Roseburg and beyond was thankfully broken by the awe inspiring beauty and majesty of Mt. Shasta unshrouded by clouds. By then, thankfully the discomfort inflicted on their derrieres resulting from being behind the wheel too long was soon to be relieved by a stop at Shasta City. It was there that the excitement of two loving bodies entangled in intimacy within the comfort of their motel in Shasta City was at last realized.

Another day on the road was at last over when they pulled into their parking space at their apartment in Oakland. The fatigue of the long trip was greeted with relief and the excitement of facing another school year. Of course that excitement was heightened by a visit to their apartment manager.

"Hi Mr. Treage, we're back."

Treage frowned. "Treage, the name is Treage or have you already forgotten?" His grin hid an attempt to gruffly add, "I hate formalities as you might have gathered." He paused to carefully inspect the duo that stood in front of him. "It is so nice to see you. I've missed correcting you with the name." He smiled. "I haven't changed. I'm still the same old Treage. Did you have a nice summer?" Extending his hand to meet Gary's out stretched hand and then giving Angelina a hug, he offered, "Again I say, it is so good to see you. You look rested and ready for another go at academia, sports fame, and stage recognition."

Angelina nodded. "We had a wonderful summer. We were able to go to Hawaii with our, I mean with my parents." She hesitated and then continued, "After we took care of getting our family business straightened out with, you know, Gary's"

Treage nodded. "Yes, I'll bet it was tough, but just think it's all behind you. Now you can concentrate on being students and all of the other stuff you do. I hope you will take my advice and enjoy the journey that you are on. These years can't be duplicated. Before you know it you will be entering the world of work, accepting the responsibility of raising a family, and all of the stuff that follows your college years. Enjoy it as it only happens once in your lifetime."

Treage paused looking lovingly first at Gary and then at Angelina. "You know, at one time I had it all going for me. I went to CAL on a football scholarship as a linebacker. I was all state in high school and showed the promise of really being something in college. The first week of practice I blew out my knee. I was devastated. I was so afraid that my football career was over."

Gary nodded. "That must have really been tough."

"It was, but by the time I had undergone the surgery and suffered through rehabilitation on my knee I had lost all interest in school." He dropped his head and pounded his hand on a nearby desk. Looking up with glistening eyes, he continued, "So, um…, I quit." His eyes filled with tears as he continued, "There isn't a day that goes by that I don't regret my decision. So, don't you two quit! You continue and get those degrees. It is worth it and something that nobody can take away from you."

Gary smiled. "Thanks for the advice. What you said sounds like something that my parents would have mentioned to us." He paused. "By the way, you guys don't need to tip toe about when you refer to my parents and be so sensitive. My parents are dead. I am okay to talk about it. They lived a great life and loved my brother, Angelina, her family, and me unconditionally. Um, about the rent, do you want it up front like the last time or…?"

Treage smiled. "Let me see, you paid first and last when you moved in last year, and I let you have the place without rent for the summer, so that means you are already a month ahead. Let's say that the rent is due the first of September."

Gary shook his head. "You are too kind, Treage, but I'm not going to complain. We appreciate everything you have done for us." He paused. "By the way, thanks for reimbursing Angelina's parents for the summer rent. Somehow I feel like we are taking advantage of you."

Treage smiled. "It has been my pleasure. You two are the nicest tenets I have had in a long, long time. So, unless I see you out and about, I'll see you the first of September. Oh, by the way, let me get the receipts for the electric bill. I paid it for you. You can just add it on to the September rent." He paused and turned slightly away. "I always support the CAL programs, but with you playing for Stanford Gary, I think that I'll just become a Cardinal fan for a while."

Gary grinned. "Well, it looks like I have another ticket to wrestle up for our home games. It will be great having you in the stands Treage."

Angelina stepped forward and gave him a hug. "Thanks Treage. You are a sweet man. It's too bad there aren't more people like you."

After unloading their cars and putting everything away, Angelina suggested, "I think that we should go to the store and stock up on groceries. I don't know about you, but I think that I would like to wait until tomorrow before we go to our campuses to get set up for our fall classes, etc."

Gary nodded. "Yeah, I'm bushed. I think that after we get the groceries and put them away, I'd just like to just veg out and…."

Angelina smiled. "I like your inclusion of 'and'…. You read my mind." She paused and then with furrowed brow inquired, "I have never asked before, but politically what party do you support? You are so tight lipped when it comes to politics and religion that I just thought it would be nice to know. I also don't mind discussing the issues with you because I know that you won't try to convert me to your way of thinking." She grinned. "It would be a fat chance that you would be able to convert me even if you wanted to."

Gary nodded with a serious look of reflection etched on his face.

"My parents were registered Democrats but always voted for the person they felt was the best candidate. I suppose I would call myself an independent. Guess I will have to select a party when it election time rolls around. I just hate the fact that in Oregon you have to be a member of one party or another to vote in the primaries." He paused. "As for religion, well, let's say that I believe that religion was created by man. I choose to say that I am spiritual with self-formulated beliefs that we have talked about from time to time. What about you? You haven't exactly been talkative about religion and politics either."

"My parents were and are Democrats. I suppose that because of the mess the Republicans have stirred up in Washington I will be a Democrat, at least for now. Like you I know that I will always vote for the person that I feel is the best candidate."

Gary smiled. "It sounds like we are on the same page. Electing a person to an office is too important to just vote the party line."

Angelina nodded. "As for religion, well, I am pretty sure that I feel the same way you do. I just know that we were put here for a purpose and I, we are doing our best to figure it all out. I suppose that is what we could call the mystery of life."

The next morning Angelina headed for the CAL campus and Gary took off for the Stanford campus. Luckily for them the heads of their departments were prepared to sit down with them and plan out their year and register them so that they didn't have to go through the hectic registration process that most of the other students had to face. Angelina had to make contact with her piano teacher to set up a schedule with her students, and Gary had to check in with the athletic department to set up his work hours, hoping that the same offer would be extended to Angelina for the home football games. Even with the newly found income from his parent's estate, working part time was a way to have some extra money without dipping to severely into the estate money except in the case of an emergency.

That evening, after returning from their respective campuses, Gary and Angelina began to report about their day's adventure. "So my dear wife, how did it go? Did you get your schedule all figured out? Um, before you begin I want to confess something to you."

"Hmm, sounds serious."

Gary smiled. "No, quite to the contrary, it isn't serious at all. Um, I just wanted to tell you that last year was a real wakeup call for me. The staff at Lake Oswego High School did a terrific job of preparing me for college, but college was still such an eye opening experience. I feel blessed that I had the good fortune to have a lot of support and help from the Stanford coaching staff, the counselors and my professors. Without it I would have surely dug myself into a huge hole."

"Don't feel like the Lone Ranger. All of those A's I got at Lake Oswego came so easily for me, it was like, well, like I had to start all over again and learn how to study. I never mentioned it, but there were times last year that I was nearly in panic mode, especially when I was rehearsing for the spring musical. Honestly, I don't know how you did it. Your season was so long."

Well, the good news is that we made it and we are better prepared this year. So, tell me about your day on campus."

Angelina smiled. "Well my dear husband, I was able to set up my schedule. It looks like I will be taking the same number of hours this year as last with about the same time schedule. What about you?"

"Yep, my schedule isn't much different than last year, just different courses."

Angelina smiled. "My classes begin at 8:00 each day. On Monday, Tuesday, Wednesday, and Friday I am done at 1:00. On Tuesday I am done at 12:00." She paused. I got all of the classes I wanted with plenty of library time so that I don't have to spend so much time studying in the evenings. How about you, did you get what you wanted?"

Gary nodded. "Looks like our schedules are pretty much the same except I don't get that library time after we begin baseball practice. I will be getting home by 5:00 though."

"Gary, I'll bet your coach is excited about you staying the full four years."

"Yes, he was elated. He told me that there is no way that I won't get drafted high enough to go out early, but that by waiting I could enhance my position." He smiled. "It's funny, but he told me the same thing that Treage mentioned. He said that doing the full four years in college was a good idea." Gary paused. "He did add, however, that he would be keeping tabs on my draft possibilities so that if I changed my mind about staying the full four years that…" He paused. "You know? Coach Ralston comes across and looks like an angry grizzly bear, but down deep he is a real softy. That gravelly voice suits him to a tee and helps him come across as a stern task master. When the chips are down, though, he is always there for us and our biggest supporter." Tears welled up in his eyes. "Yeah, he was really there for me when my folks were killed."

"My, his status has improved. The last time you thought he was a pussy cat." She paused and then continued, "Seriously, you aren't still thinking of going out early, are you? Good God, Gary, if you did go out early you would go out without a degree. I don't like the sound of that."

"No, I'm not even going to go there. I will be here for the full four years. Coach just told me that he wants me to realize my dream and he will do everything in his power to ensure that I reach my goal with the best possible options. There is no way that my options can be any better than staying the full four years unless I were to get injured my senior year. There is no way to plan to avoid that, so I will be staying the full four years."

"What about your extra job in the athletic office?"

"No change, it will be the same as last year. Looks like you and I will have the opportunity to be doing some Saturday Cardinal football games again. Is that okay?"

"Absolutely, that is perfectly okay with me." She smiled. "I kind of like being a mole. Um, are you going to be able to get tickets for Treage?"

"Yep, it is all covered."

Angelina smiled. "Did I tell you that I love you today yet?"

Gary nodded. "Only about three or four times, you were really wound up in bed this morning."

Angelina smiled. "That's because you do wonderful things to me. I didn't notice you shying away from telling me that you loved me either, sport."

The months slipped by. Thanksgiving came and went with Gary and Angelina again playing host to the family. Christmas was spent in Lake Oswego, a welcome break and an opportunity to make sure that all was okay with Greg, the house, and of course, Angelina's parents. Greg had made the all-state team and had the scholarship offer he wanted from OSU. Lance was heavy into basketball and the offers were coming in for him as well. He was also leaning towards OSU as well. As Lance put it,

"There is no way that I plan to break up the brotherhood by going to some school that Greg isn't attending."

After returning to Oakland after Christmas, the baseball season began with Stanford again destroying the competition. Going into the regionals, again hosted at the Sunken Diamond, Stanford had posted a record with only four blemishes on it. They were prohibitive favorites to go to and win the College World Series.

Stanford roared through the regionals displaying the power and pitching that had earned them the number one ranking in the nation. That was followed by resoundingly smashing all opposition in the Super Regionals hosted at the Sunken Diamond.

After the game Coach Ralston addressed his team, "Well guys, here we are again. We're going back to Omaha. I remind you that we are again going back as the number one team in the nation with a huge bull's eye painted on our backs. This time we are going to win it all." He turned towards Gary and dropped his head. "I'm sorry. That comment was completely uncalled for, I'm so sorry."

Gary rose, looked at his coach and then faced his teammates. "Guys, last year I lost my mom and dad. I didn't perform in the game against North Carolina like I should have, but I promise you that this year it will be different. We are going to kick butt. Coach, we're going to win this one for you. If you don't mind, I am also dedicating my efforts to my folks. Um, I think that I can speak for the rest of the guys in saying that we might have lost last year, but all it did was make us all the hungrier. Coach, this one's for you, and my parents."

All the members of the Cardinal team rose to their feel, raised their right arms in the air with clenched fists and shouted, "Team!" Stanford was Omaha bound and on a mission.

It is only fair to say that Angelina performed admirably in the fall Musical, "Singing in the Rain." She didn't have to play the lead role as a rising male actor took over the headlines. However, it was noted by many in attendance that her supporting role or lead female role at times stole the show. Her voice as usual was magnificent.

Chapter Seventeen

How Do You Stop A Runaway Train?

How do you stop a runaway train? You don't. It comes to a halt when it runs out of fuel, crashes into an unmovable barrier, when some predetermined destination has been reached, or when someone trying to enact a scene from the Old West manages to pull back on the reins of the train as if to say, "Whoa."

Eight deserving teams, double elimination, and the goal of a national championship paraded out onto the lush Omaha baseball field in front of a packed stadium. Overhead, the sky was blue and completely cloudless. In the ninety degree temperature the breeze that blew in from the outfield was a welcome treat to all except those who hoped to launch the long ball.

Somehow Gary felt a twinge of nostalgia invade his body as his thoughts raced backwards in time to a similar scene a year ago when the Cardinals were eliminated in the second round of the double elimination tournament. This year there was no nightmare prior to the game. This year there wasn't the thrill of being able to perform in front of his parents. This year, somehow, everything was different. This year he was focused and totally ready to perform.

Gary and Brett had experienced terrific years, becoming the most fearsome hitting duo in all of college baseball. Brett, hitting cleanup as the DH, had managed to accumulate a .401 batting average with 35 home runs and 70 RBI's. Hitting in the batting order in front of him, Gary had amassed a batting average of .408 with 30 home runs. He had driven in

60 runs, played flawlessly in the field and had thrown out ten runners attempting to take an additional base. A third and welcome addition to the power structure of the batting order was John Bledsole. Hitting in the fifth spot in the batting order he had managed to clean up any and all runners left stranded after Gary and Brett had finished their work.

Somehow all that the trio had accomplished during the regular season, the regionals and the super regionals meant nothing at that moment. All that mattered was what would happen in the next few days. None of the other seven teams cared about the Cardinal record as all that mattered was what any of the teams was able to do in the World Series. During the pre-game ceremonies, Gary had butterflies bouncing around in his stomach like frogs doing some ritualistic dance. He turned to his friend, Brett Pine and inquired nervously, "Are you feeling what I'm feeling?"

Brett posed an awesome figure, a stocky, muscular specimen that broadcast power. Additionally his demeanor exuded confidence almost to the point of being cocky. He mumbled, "You mean butterflies the size of a horse trying buck off its rider?"

Gary grinned. "Something like that, um, did your lady manage to come for the series?"

Brett smiled. "Partner, you must be nervous. My lady is sitting with your wife, her parents, and your brothers in the stands alongside the first base line. Damn, I hope you get it together before we take on Mississippi State. Those bastards have one fine team and I hear that their pitcher is lights out."

"I'm okay." Gary paused and then poked his friend in the arm. "I'll get on base if you'll drive me in."

"Are you kidding? The number of times that you've allowed me to do that this year I think I can count on one hand. You should be hitting clean up." He paused and then slapped his friend on the back. "Gary, if you get on and haven't cleaned the sacks, I will deliver just to show you that I can."

"Come on, Brett. If I wasn't on base it didn't seem to matter. You either started another rally or were so pissed that you knocked the cover off the ball anyway." He grinned. "As I recall, you led us in home runs and RBI's. You are a hell of a player, my friend. If you don't go high in the draft this year I'll eat my hat."

"I hope you're right. So, is it true that you're thinking of doing the entire four year gig?" Brett grinned. "When I found out that you were thinking staying around for the entire four years, I started thinking about maybe staying on another year myself. Wouldn't it be cool to win back to back championships?" He nodded his head as he pawed at the well-manicured dirt in the infield. "Enough talk, rookie, let's take care of business and get this thing done. We need to show our teammates how it all works."

Gary smiled. "Lead by example, huh?" He frowned. "By the way smarty, I'm not a rookie. I think that if you recall I am a sophomore. I think that I more than paid my dues last year."

"That you did partner. So what are we waiting for? Let's get going. I think that we have an appointment at the awards ceremony." He smiled. "I'm talking about the trophy for winning the championship."

The game wasn't close. The Cardinal hitters opting to not challenge the incoming breeze by playing small ball bunching hits together to score one or more runs in each inning. The Cardinal Pitcher did his part by holding the Bulldogs to a mere run produced by a walk, a sacrifice, a stolen base and a sacrifice fly to the outfield.

After the jitters of the first game had been settled with the blowout victory over Mississippi State, Stanford raced through their bracket and was set to face their old nemesis, North Carolina in the elimination game. North Carolina had to defeat Stanford or they were done and the Cardinals would be the national champions.

Before the game coach Ralston had taken Gary aside. "Gary, it is my understanding that you did some pitching in high school."

Gary nodded. "Yeah, I pitched a few innings when we were shorthanded with worn out arms on our pitching staff."

Coach Ralston nodded. "So I've heard. I want you to know that today we are shorthanded. I can't in good conscience ask any of my starting pitchers to throw today. Do you suppose that you could throw a few innings so that I can then bring on the bull pen to finish up? We have a cushion in that we don't have to win this game. If I throw my starters, even by committee, I run the risk of not having anything left for tomorrow if we lose today."

Gary looked at his coach, squinting up his eyes and pursing his lips in deep concentration. Coach, I'll give you all that I've got, but you have to let Brett take my place in center field."

Ralston nodded. "You give me five good innings and I think that the bull pen can do the rest. As for Brett, you read my thoughts."

Gary nodded. "Coach, just so you know, you won't need the bull pen. I will go out there and finish the job. North Carolina is toast. I have a score to settle with them."

North Carolina was good. Not only were they good, but were on a mission to prove that last year's championship was no fluke. Stanford responded by answering everything that North Carolina offered as a challenge. They were very aware that the Tar Heel pitcher had allowed but two scratch hits while walking both Gary and Brett every time they made a plate appearance. Gary was just a bit better as nobody on the North Carolina team able to reach base in any manner. In the top of the ninth inning, Stanford's leadoff hitter the eighth man in the batting grounded out to the shortstop to open the inning. The number nine man in the order flied out deep to the right fielder. With two outs recorded, Stanford was set to send the top of their order to the plate.

The leadoff hitter managed to draw a walk as did the number two hitter in the batting order. Now there were two outs and runners on first and second with Gary coming to the plate. You could sense the tension and pressure, stifling as the coach for North Carolina opted to come to the mound. After a brief conference, he returned to the dugout to watch his pitcher intentionally walk Gary setting up a force out at each base.

The Tar Heel coach called time and strolled to the plate rubbing his left arm to signal that he wanted the best relief pitcher in college baseball to enter the game in relief with the bases loaded, two outs and Brett due to bat next. Things were looking up for the Cardinals. There was no way that the Tar Heel pitcher could walk Brett and force in a run. He faced with the task of pitching to the best RBI man in the nation.

Brett had a look of determination on his face that was an unmistakable sign that he was more than ready to meet the challenge. Just as Brett was about to step into the batter's box, Coach Ralston called time and motioned for Brett to come to him for a conference. In the conference, Coach Ralston nodded his head and patted Brett on the back, relating to him a suggestion, "Brett, he has a wicked slider, a knee buckling curve ball and a great changeup. He is a terrific three pitch hurler and he spots the ball where he wants to. My scouting report indicates that he will come at you with two straight sliders followed by a curve ball down and away. He'll hope that you chase that pitch. If it isn't exactly where you want it lay off it. You will then be expecting to see the slider, but he will give you his changeup. Sit on the changeup Brett. That is your pitch."

Brett stepped into the batter's box and took a couple of practice swings before settling into his batting stance awaiting the delivery by the pitcher. "Strike one" the umpire bellowed. Brett stepped out of the batter's box, adjusted his hitting gloves and stepped in to face the pitcher again. In quick succession the umpire rang up another strike and a ball, the curve ball a tantalizingly good waste pitch. The count was one and two as Brett prepared for the pitcher's next delivery. In his mind Brett recalled what coach had told him to anticipate. The noise was deafening. Standing at first base Gary looked around the infield at his teammates who occupied second and third base. He shook his head as thoughts of the situation swirled about in his head like an eddy in a river, *"Crap, this noise would awaken the dead. Now is the time for Brett to produce. Everyone is counting on him. I just have to remember that there are two outs. I have to be off for second if Brett makes contact. Thank God Brett is at bat. If anyone can deliver it is Brett."*

The pitcher wound and came to the plate. The noise just a split second prior to the pitcher's delivery had hushed so that the fans close to home plate could almost hear Brett grunt as he swung the bat. Crack! That beautiful resounding sound, so sweet and so indicative of what was about to happen broke the eerie silence. Suddenly, for just a moment, except for the wondrous sound of Brett's bat meeting the ball, and atmosphere had been created that was like all life on Earth had ceased to exist. It was like being in the silent void of space. Only the sweetness of the Omaha air at that moment made drawing a breath as enjoyable as smelling the aroma of a magnificent rose. The silence was instantaneously replaced with the gasp of the thousands of fans as the runners took off as if on a mission. Their quest was to reach the next base, more if ball had found a hole. No fool hardy risk was needed as one run was all that was needed. Gary too was off like a flash. Nearing second, he got the signal from the third base coach to go for third. Rounding second, he felt like he had wings. Responding to the signal from the coach at third, he hit the dirt to beat the throw from the outfield with ease. The stadium had erupted into an avalanche of delirious noise. Two runs had crossed the plate and Stanford was leading 2-0 with Gary standing on third and the hero of the moment, Brett standing safely on second. Gary nodded to his teammate. Brett had come thorough just as he knew he would.

The next batter, John Bledsole, flied out to center field to end the top half of the inning. Three more batters and the Cardinals would be national champions. As he walked to the mound, there was no awareness on Gary's part of the perfect game he was pitching. All he could focus on was that there were three more outs to record.

Gary struck out the first and second batters he faced in the bottom of the ninth. The ninth batter in the Tar Heel order worked Gary for a walk. The first man to reach base had ruined his perfect game, an accomplishment that, at that moment, Gary was totally unaware of because of his total concentration on the next task at hand.

The next Tar Heel hitter was their most productive hitter. He not only got on base, but he produced with a modicum of power. This was going to be a huge challenge as the wind had changed directions, blowing out towards center field.

Coach Ralston called time and strode to the mound. "Gary, don't get cute with this guy. Do not give him anything good to hit. It won't be a sin if you walk him, just don't give him anything good to hit."

Gary nodded. "Do you want me to give him an intentional walk?" "No, I don't want the winning run coming to the plate. Just pitch to him carefully. He is eager to get a hit or give one a ride, so just don't put one down the pike. Make him work for it.' Coach Ralston smiled as he patted Gary on the back. "Oh hell, why not just strike him out and end this thing?"

Gary sized up the hitter as thoughts raced through his mind. *'I have retired him three times before. Each time I got him with my fastball on the outside of the plate. Hmm, let's see if I can't help him put a nail in North Carolina's coffin."*

On Gary's first pitch, the North Carolina leadoff hitter made contact, a sickening sound that caused Gary to want to retch. Turning towards the outfield he saw Brett race back towards the fence. At the last moment he leaped and somehow managed to snare the ball in the webbing of his glove. Out number three had been recorded. Stanford had climbed the mountain. They were the new national champions.

How joyous it was to see his teammate's race towards him, to feel their bodies make contact with his, to be smothered at the bottom of the huge celebration pile, and to look up and see Brett's joyous smile. Brett chided, "You son of a gun, oh, you son of a gun. Do you realize what you just did?"

Gary replied, his brow furrowed as he tried to move under the pile, "What, what did I do? You are the one that got the winning hit and you were the one that saved the game with that magnificent catch. You are the son of a gun, oh you marvelous son of a gun."

"You don't know?" Brett shook his head. "No matter that you just pitched a no hitter. No, no matter because we won and that is all that counts. You are my hero Mallon." He paused. "You settled the issue for me. I'm coming back for another year. I'm hungry. I want to be a part of two national championship teams."

Gary nodded. The weight of his teammates was too stifling for him to give a verbal response. Just then coach shouted above the joyous celebration. Let's allow the guys on the bottom of the pile to get up. He continued, "Okay guys, this is what we've been playing for all year. It doesn't get any better than this. I am so proud of you that I could cry."

Brett shouted back, "Coach, please don't do that. You'll ruin the image you have established. All the guys will think you are an old softy."

Outside the dressing room, Gary and Brett greeted their special ladies and the rest of Gary's family. Somewhat subdued Gary inquired, "Well, what do you think?"

Mr. Crawford nodded his head. "Well, it was more than what I expected or hoped for or thought I would see. Don't get me wrong. I didn't doubt that you would win, but to march through the tournament without a loss? It was one hell of an accomplishment." He paused. "You really put the icing on the cake with that gem you threw today. Can you believe a no hitter in the championship game? I am so proud of you."

Angelina frowned trying to hide her excitement. "Yeah, I doubt that the Carolina bunch felt it would turn out that way either." Finally unable to restrain herself, she thrust her arms around Gary's neck and whispered, "I am so proud of you. You pitched one hell of a game. You were perfect."

Gary chucked. "Almost, they did get a walk off me."

Brett laughed. "Hey, what are we complaining about, we won. In my opinion it was like the most beautiful thing that has ever happened to me."

Gary slapped his friend on the back. "You did a hell of a job out there today. Not only did you do your job at the plate, but you were a great leader in the dugout. You played a hell of a game in centerfield today my friend. You saved my bacon on that last play. What a catch you made." He paused. "The guys really look up to you for leadership and you always produce. You said I was your hero. Think again. You are my hero."

Angelina nodded. "I think that I have to amend your statement Gary. You are both my hero."

Gary smiled, putting his arm around his friend and his wife. "I would like to correct that statement. I think that Brett is the man of the year. What a season you had, partner. I am so proud to be your teammate."

Brett frowned. "Are you kidding me? You hit for a higher average, were perfect in the field, and won the last game of the season with a no hitter. I honestly believe that you were probably the most feared hitter in the league. That doesn't even take into account how many runs you saved with the phenomenal job you did in the outfield. Nobody unless they were stupid dared try for an extra base with that arm of yours. Sure you don't want to try pitching full time next year?"

Mrs. Crawford shook her head. "It doesn't matter who was better at whatever. The point is that you played as a team and every person contributed. You wouldn't be champions if everyone hadn't stepped up to the plate." She paused. "Let's get out of here. I'm so hungry that I could eat a horse. I think that coach will let you guys escape to go out for a bite, don't you?"

After garnering the national championship, the Cardinal baseball team returned to a welcome usually reserved for a major league baseball team after winning the World Series or some other professional teams accomplishing a like feat. Sitting on the stage erected in the middle of the football field, Gary turned to Brett and mumbled, "Can you believe this? I'd guess that there are almost as many people here as there are for a football game."

The Wonderment of Life

Brett smiled, "How does it feel to be a celebrity?"

Gary shook his head, muttering, "Yeah, sure. What are you doing for the summer?"

"I'm going home for a bit and then I think I'll play a little ball on the east coast. I want to impress the scouts so that I can go high in the draft next year. I think I could be chasing a big contract." He paused. "I don't know if you heard me in the pile at the end of the championship game, but I have decided to come back next year. I want to help you, coach, and the rest of the guys win back to back championships."

"I heard you, but I have been waiting for you to make it official." Gary paused. "Are you completely serious? You won't even change your mind if the right team drafts you and the money is right?"

"I have made up my mind. It will be nice to get a degree. One never knows just how long a person can milk a baseball career. The one thing they can't take away from you is that sheepskin."

Gary nodded his head in agreement. "Those are my thoughts." He paused and looked reflectively at his friend. "You know, when I face the draft in a couple of years I'd be really disappointed if I weren't drafted by the Mariners or Giants. I would prefer the Mariners, and right now I'm hoping that Seattle is interested, but I wouldn't be at all disappointed to play in Frisco. How about you, do you have a preference?"

"I suppose that I'll just be happy to go to the team that drafts me." He paused. "It would be nice to go to the Giants or the Mariners, but quite honestly, I would like to play for the team that you are on."

A week later, finals concluded, a goodbye said to Treage and with the last goodbye said to Brett and his wife, Angelina and Gary climbed into their cars and headed for home. A half hour into the trip the phone rang. "I know you want to stop in Shasta City for the night, right?"

"That is true, but I want to stop before that for a pit stop, okay?"

"Fine with me, um, have you been thinking about where we might go this summer?"

"Funny you should ask. I would like to take a road trip and visit the east coast."

Gary chuckled. "There's a lot of road between where we live and the east coast. Any places in particular you want to see?"

"I want to see Boston, New York, and Washington D.C. and any place that seems interesting in between."

"Angelina, how long do you think that this road trip should take?"

"I think that we could do it in a little less than a month. Can we afford it?"

"Well, let's sit down and do a little research when we get home and see. We do have to spend some time with your folks, our brothers, and friends."

"What would you say about having them all join us, um, I mean all of our family?"

Gary paused. "Hum, are they talking about making a trip?"

"Yes, but they want to do it by train. They want to pick some stops along the way, stop, explore, and then move on."

"Wow! That sounds like fun. Somehow I just can't see doing all of that by car. Um, what about our brothers, I don't think that it would be good to leave them behind?"

"We wouldn't do that, silly. I'm sure they will want to go."

"Well, let's talk to your folks and see what plan we can decide to do. By the way, I'm all for a family trip. I love your folks, and I love hanging out with our brothers."

Angelina chuckled. "I echo your feelings. By the way, we only have two more years before we get to start a family."

"Correction, my dear wife, since you have suggested that we start working on it in February of our senior year, I think a more accurate statement would be that we can start a family in nineteen months."

Angelina chuckled again. "That means twenty-eight months before I get to be a mommy and you a daddy. I like the sound of that. Damn, I love you so much."

"And you my wife, the woman that I love without condition and hope to help me keep the fire burning for fifty or more years, I say I am signing off until we reach our pit stop."

Chapter Eighteen

Another Summer Vacation

> Everyone needs to recharge their batteries from time to time. College students use summer vacation as a time to accomplish that feat. For those of you that finished or attended college, weren't they the best years of your life? During those enlightening years didn't you look for special things to do to recharge your batteries?

A wonderful summer at home after leaving their respective campuses awaited Gary and Angelina. It appeared that the agenda that awaited their arrival in Lake Oswego was to focus on or at least explore the possibility of going on a cross country train journey to see some of the geographical sights that Angelina had her heart set on seeing. Gary was on board with her visitation interests, but realized that her parents and the brothers might have other ideas or interests. The amount of time away on the cross country trip and the cost of such an adventure were issues that the family had to discuss and face.

The welcome mat was out when they drove into the driveway of their home in Lake Oswego. Of course the Crawford's and Greg were out front awaiting their arrival. A phone call just south of Lake Oswego guaranteed the ceremony in the driveway would occur. Shortly after their cars were unpacked and all of their belongings had been put away they gathered at the Crawford home to catch up.

Mr. Crawford took a deep breath before beginning. "I don't know about you, but I am very happy that the unloading of your cars is over. It seems that you brought more stuff home with you this year than last." He paused. "Would you like to discuss possible plans for a trip this summer?" He paused. "Maybe you would rather take a deep breath and do it later?"

Angelina smiled. "Dad, you read our minds. Gary and I are ready to see what you have in mind and share our ideas. So, since you brought up the subject, why don't you begin?"

Mr. Crawford nodded. "Um, what do you think about doing a barbeque and having an adult beverage or two as we talk about our summer plans? It appears that from now until the first part of August, we're open to kick up our heels and play. Do you have ideas other than what you have briefly told us about Angelina?"

"Dad, we don't have anything planned as of yet. We have some ideas, but we want to hear your ideas." She paused. "Please realize Greg and Lance that we want to hear from you as well. Maybe your summer basketball and football camps will have some bearing on our plans.

Mr. Crawford nodded and then began, "The last time we talked you did mention a road trip. Um, I would like to throw out an idea about taking a train trip. It could be a lot of fun and probably far less exhausting."

Gary grinned. "That sounds good to me. I mean both the barbeque and your idea about the train trip. What about you Angelina?"

Angelina nodded. "I could go for a train trip. Um, we have some wine and beer in fridge from the last time we came home. Can we bring that over for the barbeque?" Again she paused. "We would also like to hear your ideas Greg and Lance."

Sue Crawford shook her head somewhat emphatically. "That won't be necessary. This is our treat, our welcome home to you. It is so good to have you home. We have missed you so much."

Guy chimed in, "Yes and congratulations again for you and Cardinal team winning the National Championship. It was quite a feat. We are so proud of you. That game you pitched was special. It will be a memory that you can put in your scrapbook to share with your kids when they arrive."

Greg nodded with a sly smile etched on his face. "It has already been stated, but just let me say that it is so good to see you."

The Wonderment of Life

Gary paused and winked. "Yeah, I've missed you guys a little bit." Chuckling he added, "Bro, you did very well, um, terrific this year in football. I followed all of your games that I could. And Lance, you had a great basketball season."

Lance nodded. "Let's stop with all of the back patting stuff and get going with the barbeque. I am starved. I also am curious as to what you all have up your sleeves as it relates to a summer trip. I am going to have a basketball camp or two to attend this summer. I think that they are planned for June, so I am hopeful that we can work around that."

Angelina shook her head, a sly grin enveloping her expression. "Just like a man. All you can think of is sports. Don't worry that little head of your little brother, we won't plan anything that will get in the way of your precious basketball camps."

Sue jumped in, serving as the referee before the sibling battle got out of hand. "Enough already, it is time to eat. Let's save the tennis match for later."

After dinner, Sue opened the conversation, "So, tell us about school, what you did, and what is ahead."

Gary looked at Angelina. "Do you want to begin?"

Angelina nodded. "Well both Gary and I are on track to graduate in two years with no difficulty at all. I'm still giving piano lessons, singing in the choir, and have had some involvement in the CAL musical productions. Gary had a great year and it appears that he'll go high in the draft in two years, barring an injury. Um, I guess that about covers it." She turned to Gary and asked, "Do you have anything to add, sweetie?"

"Angelina is being too modest. She was the star of the fall production and that is not an overstatement." He paused for a moment, blushing as he began, "Well, we want to start a family." Looking at Angelina for confirmation, he continued, "I think that we're going to start trying after the first of the year during our senior year. We think that it would be nice if the baby could be born in November. I'll be home with baseball season over and........."

Mrs. Crawford smiled. "That is wonderful news. Just imagine. I'm going to be a grandmother."

Gary dropped his head momentarily. When he looked up his eyes were filled with tears. "Yeah, I just wish….."

Angelina reached over and squeezed is hand. "Honey, they will know and they will also be so very, very proud."

Mr. Crawford nodded his head. "Well, I think it is time to start talking about that cross country train journey we have been talking about." He glanced at Gary, and then continued, "You and Angelina have discussed the trip, um, about all of us going as a family, haven't you?"

"Yes. I think that it is a terrific idea." Turning towards Greg and Lance, he inquired, "Are you two wanting to join us for a trip?"

Greg excitedly replied, "I am totally okay with the idea. Like Lance, my football camp is scheduled for June."

Lance nodded. "Yeah, I have always wanted to see the east coast. I'm in. Um, don't worry big sister, I won't bring up basketball camps again. I just hope that we…"

Angelina smiled. "Not to worry Lance. We will work our trip around both of your camps. We want to go as a family and that means that we want you to be with us."

Gary inquired, "You wouldn't happen to have a map of the United States, would you, Guy?"

Guy nodded. "I have one and I also have contacted the train people. We have come up with a possible route we could take. Along the way we can stop, visit sites we want to see, and then get back on a train and proceed towards our other destinations." He paused. "Why don't we go into the living room so that I can show you what I have come up with so far? It will be more comfortable in there. Um, of course we want your approval because we want everyone to be happy with the final plan." He looked at Greg and Lance. "You two have a say in this as well, so don't swallow your tongues. If you don't voice your desires, you'll have nothing to complain about if we don't go where you want to go."

In the living room, they all knelt around the coffee table looking at the map of the United States that had a sizeable red travel route marked on the map. Angelina offered, "It looks like the plan might be to go from Portland east and north to Eastern Washington, across northern Idaho into Montana, across to North Dakota and then through Minnesota, Wisconsin, Illinois, Ohio, New York, and then into Boston before we head south to Washington D.C." That's basically a northern journey through our country."

Mr. Crawford nodded. "Honey, realize that Portland and New York are basically on the same Latitude. Also note the line in green. It shows that we basically retrace the route we took to Boston once we have left D.C. and travel a bit north to Chicago." He paused. "There will be some transfers involved. It isn't going to be a straight line journey."

Gary nodded. "It looks good. Do you have any idea what the policy is concerning making stops at different places along the way, doing some exploring, and then boarding the next train to continue our journey? Just how long approximately will the round trip take, and how much it will cost?"

Mr. Crawford shook his head. "No, I wanted to see what your thoughts were and then check with the train people to get that information. If all is good with them, what do you all think about the trip?"

Angelina raised her hand and excitedly shouted, "I move we accept the plan if it can be worked out with the train people and it is affordable."

Everyone raised their hands and shouted in unison, "I say yes." She paused. "I think that we should consider a backup plan in case making the trip by train is not practical or affordable. Have you considered the fact that if we go by airplane we will arrive at destination sites quicker and have more time to explore the territory around that site? I doubt that it would be any more expensive."

Guy shrugged. I really never considered that option, but it certainly has merit. It could shorten the amount of time we are away as well."

Gary nodded. "Well, I move that we check out both options and pick the most practical and least expensive."

The chorus of ayes indicated that a trip was in the offering. All that was left was to select the dates and the mode of transportation."

Chapter Nineteen

Goals and Accomplishments

A vacation trip to recover from a hectic but rewarding second year of college is a good time to start setting goals for the third year of college. Short term and long terms goal setting is important because once a more immediate goal is achieved it is important to have other goals to pursue. In setting goals make sure they are realistic and be prepared to alter the goals.

The idea of taking the train east died a painful but realistic death as it was decided that costs and time were not favorable for what they wanted to do. The airplane mode of travel with layovers in Chicago, New York, Boston, and Washington D.C., was the compromise that won out. It was decided that using those hubs they could explore them as a base of operation, visiting the many surrounding sites by car. Once the nucleus and surrounding areas of interest had been visited they would then move on to the next focal point.

By the time their journey had ended, a four week adventure, all agreed that traveling by plane and using a car to explore sites in surrounding the stopping point was an excellent compromise.

Gary's favorite stopover was New York City. Angelina, Greg, and Lance were also thrilled with the excitement they experienced in the Big Apple. Boston's Freedom Trail was a historical delight, and seeing the Nation's Capital was the Crawford's favorite stop. However, it was agreed that returning home was ever so nice as living out of a suitcase and staying in different hotels every night was tiring, expensive, and got a little old. They all agreed that there was nothing like sleeping in their own bed and eating a home cooked meal instead of a continuous menu of restaurant fare.

Soon after their return home, Greg began to get ready for the upcoming football season at OSU. He had quite a battle ahead of him if he was to see any playing time. It was explained to him that very few freshmen can count on making much of a contribution with red shirting the most logical option unless they can be at least second on the depth chart at their position. Lance headed off to attend one of the two basketball camps he had been advised by his coach to attend, and Gary and Angelina were content to spend their time in Lake Oswego visiting friends and relaxing from the long trip, the hectic activities of the 4th of July, and a strenuous sophomore school year. The Crawford's were content to visit with their family whenever the opportunity arose while preparing mentally for the upcoming school year. They were also wrapping their minds around the fact that they would soon have an empty nest to contend with after summer break ended.

Lying in bed on a warm August night after the excitement of the 4th of July festivities has come and gone and they had returned from their trip east, Gary turned towards Angelina and gently pulled her towards him. Offering no resistance she willingly sought the warm comfort of his welcoming body. She looked into his eyes and mummed, "I love you. I want to have your baby."

Gary kissed her tenderly. "I love you too. I want to have a baby with you too. Are we being too regimented with our plan to wait until a year from February to begin trying to get pregnant?"

She pursed her lips in contemplation of how to answer his question. "I would willingly begin tonight, but I know that waiting is best. Honey, the days, weeks, and months will pass quickly. If we don't wait, I'll not be able to finish my degree at CAL. I honestly believe that we would come to regret that decision."

"I know. It's just that I love you so much."

She giggled. "Well soldier, it isn't like I have cut you off. Unless I have been asleep the past few months, it seems that we do it almost every night."

He chuckled. "Yeah, and sometimes we do it more than once a day. I just like making love with you so much."

She smiled. "I will second that. Um, what do you want to do the rest of summer vacation? The Fourth of July celebrations and our trip east just about wore me out."

"Yeah, I know. That four week trip east has left me wanting to just veg out." He paused. "I don't know. What about enjoying family barbeques with your parents and our brothers, hanging out with friends, and maybe taking a short road trip?"

Angelina nodded her head in agreement. "So, where would you suggest we go if we decide to take a road trip?" She smiled as she started to stroke Gary in his most sensitive region. "Hmm, I think that my friend is starting to wake up. Do you think that he would like to pay me a visit?"

Gary moaned with excited pleasure. "Maybe we should talk about what we want to do the rest of the summer later. Right now I can't seem to concentrate."

The summer passed. Strangely, it seemed like only yesterday that he and Angelina were playing a game with each other in Gary's or Angelina's parent's home. Today is all that anyone really has, but given luck, good health and the blessing from The Source, today blends into many tomorrows. Today they were getting prepared to leave for college and begin their junior years. The tomorrow's that would follow would be memorable, but it was best to enjoy the todays. They only happen once.

Greg had taken off for college at OSU and football practice while Lance was getting ready to head in that direction two weeks later. The Crawford's were getting ready for another school year, and Gary and Angelina were packed and ready for their return to the Bay area and their junior year. It had been a long hot summer, a summer with many memorable moments spent with family and friends, but they were ready to return to continue their quest for their degrees.

A few days later a tearful send-off and the long trip to Oakland began. Of course the first stop was Shasta City. A day later two weary travelers checked in with their apartment manager.

"Well Treage, we're back for the next to the last lap."

"My God, you remembered. Congratulations, I was afraid that I would be reminding you forever." Treage winced. "I was hoping those words, the next to the last lap, would never be spoken, Gary."

Angelina chuckled. "Treage, you don't want to say never. It might come around to bite you."

Treage smiled and nodded his head. "Um, well kids, welcome back for the next to the last lap. Yes indeed, welcome back. Hope you kids have a fantastic year. Going to go for a repeat?"

"That's the plan. If you want, I think I might be able to get you free tickets again to some of our games."

"That would be nice. Maybe you could get one for one of the Stanford-CAL games? I think they play it at our place this year, um, CAL." He paused. "Um, I just thought I would give you a head's up about one of my new tenants. Your coach is quite the recruiter. He picked up a young man from Arizona, a catcher. He and his wife moved in and will have the apartment adjacent to yours. Amazingly, the misses is attending CAL like you are Angelina."

Gary smiled, nodding his head. "Is he a real prospect or just…"

Treage smiled. "He is the real deal. He has a rifle for an arm, hits with power, and is terrific behind the plate. With you, John and Bret, I think you'll have a fearsome foursome in the lineup this year. It could turn out to be the best middle of the lineup in all of college baseball."

Angelina chimed in excitedly, "Gary, this is so neat. With Bret, Cynthia, John, Betty and the new couple, we will have a nice group of friends to hang out with during our free moments." She smiled. "At the very least the gals will have somebody to hang out with while you boys are away on road trips." She paused. "By the way, Treage, what are their names, um, the new couple?"

Treage smiled and started to respond, "Um, their names are…" Before Treage could finish, Gary broke into the conversation,

"Honey, you should have told me. I wasn't aware of the hardship that you face when I'm on the road."

Angelina nodded. "Why would I choose to burden you with the loneliness I feel when you are gone. You have enough on your mind."

Gary nodded, turning to Treage. "I'm sorry for interrupting, Treage. Go ahead and tell us their names. We will make a point to make contact with the new people and make them feel welcome. Hopefully they will become our new friends so that Angelina has someone to hang out with while I'm on the road."

Treage nodded. "That's okay Gary. It is important to keep the little woman happy and understand what she goes through when you are gone on a road trip. By the way their name is Bordeaux, Cam and Susan Bordeaux."

Gary cocked his head, looking at Treage in awe. "Getting back to the tickets to the games, I don't quite get it. You are a CAL supporter and yet you also do nice things for the Stanford baseball players, at least me and now the Bordeaux's. What's that all about?"

Treage lowered his head, his eyes starting to get misty. "Um, I lost my son about three years ago. He was a terrific baseball player, a real prospect. I vowed that whenever the opportunity arose, I would do what I could to help out a struggling baseball player no matter what school they attended. I lean towards those that are married."

Angelina chimed in, "I can't wait to meet them, um, the Bordeaux's. It will be so nice to have a fellow student living nearby. I love Cynthia Pine to death, but she and Bret live in Palo Alto. I only see Cynthia at the home games and on the rare occasions that we have a couple get together."

Gary shrugged his shoulders, a sly smile slowly appearing on his face. "Well, I guess we'll just have to be more social this year."

Treage nodded. "Not a bad idea. All work and no play makes….."

Gary smiled. "I know Treage. Angelina reminds me of that all the time."

Angelina frowned, slowly beginning what she had probably held back for as long as she could, "Treage, you have never mentioned your wife. Um, do you care to share?"

Treage nodded. "Sally passed away about ten years ago. She had cancer. It isn't something that I choose to talk about, but since you asked…" He paused. "Sally was the love of my life. We only had the one son, Bobby. He was the center of our universe. I suppose that I put everything I had into him because he was headed towards accomplishing what I had failed to complete. As for Sally, she was a teacher. Damn, the kids just loved her." He paused. "Well, that is it for now. I am not going to give you my entire biography in one sitting. I'll just have to save some for later." He grinned.

"There is method to my madness. If I hold back, maybe you'll invite me to your place for dinner and conversation sometime."

Angelina smiled, nodding her head. "You can count on it Treage. I apologize for not asking you to dinner before. It has been…"

Treage nodded. "You don't owe me any excuses or apologies. I know how busy you two have been. Besides, I could have asked you to come to my place for dinner."

Gary chuckled. "Do you actually cook?"

Treage frowned. "You bet I cook. I like to eat. The last time I checked there wasn't anyone else at my place to do the cooking for me. Besides, I'm a pretty good cook if I do say so."

At their apartment, Angelina plopped into a chair after finishing her share of putting away the multitude of things they had brought with them from Lake Oswego. "I don't know about you, but I am pooped. What do you think about eating out tonight and waiting until tomorrow to stock up on groceries and what not?"

Gary nodded. "That is music to my ears. Um, we also have to check in with our schools tomorrow. After that we will actually have a few days to ourselves before classes begin. Strange, it seems like we've been here and done this before."

"You think?" Angelina smiled. "I plan to make every minute count too. I hope you are up to it, but I would like nothing better than to live in bed with you."

Gary shook his head, a grin slowly sweeping across his face. "I like your thoughts. I just hope that you will let me have a break from time to time."

"No problem, I just want to keep you close at hand."

Amazingly their junior year melted away with another national championship won. Bret went high in the draft, number three, ending up in San Francisco. Cam and Susan Bordeaux had become fast friends of Gary and Angelina, the Pines and Bordeaux's, spending many of their free hours hanging out together. Cam and Susan were also on the four year plan, and had decided to delay having a family until they had their degrees in hand. As far as the Bledsole's, John managed to get drafted in the tenth round by San Diego, a dream realized as he and his wife grew up there.

With finals behind them, the time had come again to head north to spend summer break in Lake Oswego. Saying goodbye to their friends was not easy and had to be accomplished separately. After saying their farewells to the Bledsole's and Bordeaux's Gary roamed about the Stanford campus to say goodbye to Brett. Cynthia was busy packing for the journey to where Brett would be located on the East Coast, and Angelina was wrapping up all of the last minute details she had to attend to on campus in addition to packing for the trip north to Lake Oswego.

Gary ran into Brett after his last final had been taken in the athletic complex. "I was wondering if we were going to say goodbye to each other or just act like two ships passing in the night."

Brett looked up from what he was doing as he continued to stuff gear into his baseball travel bag. "There isn't a chance that I wouldn't have looked you up to say goodbye." He paused. "Actually, this isn't going to be goodbye. You will be on campus next year leading the Cardinals to another national championship and hopefully I will be playing for the big club. We will have time to get together. You are my friend Gary and I don't plan to let our friendship end just because we might be a few miles apart."

Gary smiled at Brett as he watched him finish putting the last bit of his gear in his bag. "Stay in touch slugger and let me know how you like playing in Giants farm system. I doubt that you will be playing in the minors long. I wouldn't be at all surprised if the Giants bring you up to the big club towards the end of the season. Um, I hope to join you next year after we win another national title." He paused. "I'm sorry that Angelina wasn't able to be here to say goodbye."

Brett nodded. "Yeah, I think that Angelina and Cynthia have already said their goodbyes. Cynthia said something this morning about going to Berkley to see your wife." Brett paused as he proceeded to zip up this travel bag. "Yeah, Cynthia had a lot of stuff to accomplish before we take off, but there was no way that she would leave without saying goodbye to Angelina. So she decided to go to Berkley and pay your wife a visit to tell her goodbye." He paused. "You can count on it, um, you know, staying in touch. Please tell Angelina goodbye for me, will you?"

Gary nodded. "I will Brett. Angelina told me to tell you the same and send her regrets for not being able to see tell you in person. She is up to her ears with last minute stuff to do at school and with the packing for our trip home to Lake Oswego."

Brett nodded. "That sounds familiar. Just know that we will make it a point in the future to get together, the four of us and share war stories." He paused. "With you and Cam in the lineup I feel that the Cardinals have an excellent chance to take it all again. Let me know where you go in the draft. I'll be pulling for you to go number one. I'll also keep my fingers crossed that you get drafted by the Giants."

Gary nodded. "That would be nice, but I won't hold my breath. There are a lot of quality players out there. I thought you had a good chance to go number one." He shrugged. "I guess going out number three isn't too bad. It will get you lots of money when you get down to talking dollars and cents."

"I don't care about the money. I just want to play in the majors. I think that is the way you feel as well."

Gary nodded. "So, are you and Cynthia going to start a family?" Brett smiled. "We're already pregnant. The baby is due in February.

We didn't say anything about it before now because..."

Gary nodded. "I know. You and Cynthia wanted to make sure that it was going to take."

Brett nodded and stepped forward to give his buddy a hug. "Well, I have to shove off. Cynthia is waiting for me and knowing her she is getting more and more impatient with each passing minute. Stay in touch."

Gary nodded. "You know that I will. You go out there and show everyone that you belong in the majors. I have all the confidence in the world that you will be playing for the big club real soon."

Chapter Twenty

The Final Quest

What is a final quest? Is it better stated to say that whatever it is, it is merely a quest as final implies the end. What is the end? Maybe something ends and immediately something else begins. How can anything be final? Maybe everything is merely a transition from one thing another.

Another wonderful summer vacation was spent at home in Lake Oswego that involved a fantastic family excursion to Cabo. Mexico was an interesting, and pleasant departure from their previous vacations. There was something about the happy carefree attitude that the Mexican people exuded that really resonated with Gary and Angelina. They were mystified with the attitude that many people in the United State had with regard to the Mexican people. They were hard working, very family oriented, and they always seemed to have a smile on their faces. What was there not to like about the Mexican people?

After the months of June, July and most of August had passed on into history, again, as in the past three years, they found their way back to Oakland, paid Treage a visit to again get set up in their apartment, and then prepared to head out to their respective campuses to get their schedules solidified for their senior year. Gary was anxiously awaiting another year and a hoped for a high selection in the draft as well as being a part of another national championship team. He was also more than ready to embark on the journey to fatherhood.

The thought of playing with his buddy Brett at San Francisco would not have disappointed him, but he still had his heart set on playing for the Mariners. Angelina was anticipating another school performance, hopefully in the fall, and looking forward to motherhood. Beyond becoming a mother, she hoped to pursue her love of theater and performing in some musical productions with some spot appearances on stage. She secretly hoped it would be in Portland when a suitable musical performance arose, but she was fully aware that where she landed would be dependent upon where Gary ended up going once he had been drafted. A full time job was not on her bucket list as her first priority was the soon to be role as a mother and a wife of her beloved husband.

The next morning, after returning to Oakland for their senior years, they crawled into their cars and headed for their respective campuses. At 2:00 Gary returned home followed shortly by Angelina. Upon her entry into their apartment, Gary inquired, "Well, did you get all the classes you need for graduating this June?"

"Yep, I sure did. Just imagine a mommy to be will walk across that stage to get her degree."

"It is going to be a great day. I hope you know that I might be heading off to some far off place to begin my baseball career as soon as the Cardinal season winds down with hopefully another return to the college world series."

Nodding with a subdued, nearly blank expression on her face, she inquired, "Do you think that there is any chance that you will be assigned to some team that is close to Lake Oswego? Don't get me wrong. I will happily go where you go. I wouldn't even be disappointed if the Giants drafted you. That way we could continue to be close to Brett and Cynthia."

"If the Giants draft me we will also be able to be close to Cam and Susan. Yeah, and San Diego isn't too far away. We will be able to stay in touch with John and Betty." Gary shrugged. "I don't have a clue what is going to happen. If I am lucky enough to be drafted by Seattle I could end up playing in Tacoma."

"You don't think that they will bring you up to the big club?"

"I don't know, but I seriously doubt it. Most major league teams like to let their draft picks get some seasoning in the minors. I suppose that where I go and what my role will be will all depend on what the club that drafts me needs and how they feel about me. If I am hopefully drafted by Seattle and I were to guess, I would suspect that I'd at least start out at Tacoma. Of course they could farm me out to some other minor league club, but it would be in the northwest. Just keep your fingers crossed that I get drafted by the Mariners." He paused. "Have you run into Susan Bordeaux yet? I didn't see Cam. I sure hope they are coming back. Coach didn't say anything to the contrary. Without Cam, it could be a long or short season depending on how you view it."

"Honey, if they weren't coming back, I am sure that Treage would have said something." She grinned. "I am sure that we'll see them before classes begin. After all they do live next door."

Time seemed to fly as the fall merged into winter. Frequent visits with Cam and Susan made life in Oakland even more enjoyable. Brett had completed his first year in the San Francisco organization, finishing the season playing for the Giants and had returned to Palo Alto for the winter. With his return it again offered the opportunity for the Pines and them to get together with Cam and Susan. During the visits, Susan and Angelina hung on every word that Claudia had to say about her impending visit to the maternity ward.

Gary and Angelina were unable to spend Thanksgiving at home, opting to share the day with Cam, Susan, Brett, and Cynthia to enjoy a home away from home Thanksgiving dinner created by the culinary expertise of the female trio. Greg was the Beaver starting running back and had an appointment to playing in the "Civil War" game. Luckily Gary and Angelina were able to see the Beavers pull out an exciting victory on television, a call home soothing some of the disappointment in not being able to go home or have the family travel to them.

Christmas was no different as Lance was on the Beaver basketball squad, and Greg had an appointment in a bowl game. Gary and Angelina were wrapped up with the preparations for the sprint to the finish line to get their degrees while enjoying frequent visits with their friends.

At a New Year's gathering with Cam, Susan, Brett, Claudia, and some other friends from Stanford and Cal, Angelina cozied up to her husband in a secluded place at Cam and Susan's apartment in Berkley. "Do you realize that we only have to wait one more month?"

Gary leaned over and kissed her. "When are you going off the pill?" Angelina giggled excitedly. "I'm thinking that I will stop about the 25th of January. From that point on, mister, I plan to ravage your body every chance I get."

Gary chuckled. "You do know that you have to give me a break once in a while don't you? After all, I will be in the midst of another baseball season."

"Of course, that is a given. I have it penciled in all of your away games on the calendar. I figure that with careful planning and a willing partner we just might be able to pull off a miracle." She smiled. "A miracle, that is what I call having a baby. Bringing a new life into this world that is wanted and planned for in every detail is a miracle."

Gary nodded. "You know, I think that my parents have been introduced to the baby that we are going to have. Strangely, I feel that we were introduced before we were born. I know that mom and dad are close by. I can almost feel their presence. Maybe someday that mystery of life will be exposed or explained to us." He paused. "For now, all I can say with certainty is that I don't know."

Brett and Claudia interrupted their secretive discussion, "Hey, you guys it is time for you to rejoin the party."

Claudia chuckled. "All of that baby talk will just get you two into trouble. I should know because I went through it as you can see from my expanded tummy."

Brett reached over and rubbed her tummy, looking at Gary. "You know being a father is really starting to rev me up. It is too bad that the baby will be born during the beginning of the season." He paused. "We were thinking of relocating, um, buying a house, but I've heard some rumors that I might be traded." He sighed. "I just hope that something is finalized soon. Spring training is just around the corner and I would like to be settled before I have to report."

Gary grinned. "Just keep me in the loop Brett. For some reason I feel that what happens to you will have an impact on where I end up. Keep your fingers crossed for a reunion in Seattle."

Chapter Twenty-One

Cynthia

> Some say that life is two short. Others say that a person was taken before their time. What is your time? What is their time? What is anybody's time? Is it predetermined? Maybe it is best to say, "I don't know." Maybe it is best to take everything a day at a time and hope for a tomorrow."

January began on a positive note. The New Year's gathering that went into the wee hours of the morning introduced Brett, Cynthia, Cam, Susan, Angelina, and Gary to the New Year in a most positive manner. Brett was headed for spring training shortly while Cynthia was now in full bloom expecting their first child. The Bordeaux's were anxiously looking forward to another baseball season and hopefully another national championship and Gary and Angelina were counting the days until Angelina would go off the pill and they could begin frantic efforts to get pregnant. Everything seemed to be in place. Then it happened.

The phone rang in Gary and Angelina's apartment. It rang again and again. There was no answer. The message on the phone announced to the caller, "We are sorry to have missed your call. We are away from our phone for a short while, so leave a message and we will return your call.

The phone rang in Cam and Susan's adjacent apartment. It rang again and again. There was no answer. The message on the phone announced to the caller, "We are away, so leave a message and we will return your call."

The Wonderment of Life

The gathering at Treage's apartment was gathering steam as Treage's dinner offering of spaghetti was being relished by his four favorite tenants. The conversation was lively and the wine offering was being relished with a lively conversation about the upcoming season becoming louder and louder. Treage's loud, booming voice sounded with conviction, "I think that you guys are going to grab another national championship. Imagine, a three peat."

Gary frowned. "Don't count your chickens until them come home to roost, Treage. Without Brett and john in the lineup, we could be a little thin in the hitting department."

"Hogwash", Treage responded in a challenging voice. "Don't forget that you won your first national championship with just you and Brett and John in the lineup. Sure, John is gone, but you and Cam are still a very potent pair to draw to. Besides, your coach is a great recruiter. I'm sure that he will surprise you with some new and potent talent."

The sound of the phone, at first not heard, suddenly pierced the atmosphere of the gathering. Treage arose, excusing himself, "Um, I think that I heard the phone. I shall return. We're not done with this conversation."

For some reason the conversation ground to a halt as the foursome silently awaited Treage's return. Moments later Treage returned his face pale and drawn. His eyes glistened as tears began to trickle down his cheeks. He stopped upon entering the room, dropped his head, and stood there staring at the floor.

Gary was the first to speak. "Treage, what is it. Is there something wrong? My God man, you look as though you have seen a ghost."

Treage's voice cracked as he slowly began to speak, "That was Brett." Treage paused. "Um, oh God, what do I say?"

Angelina began to cry, pleading, "For God's sake, Treage let us know what is going on."

"Brett is going to need you guys more than ever. Cynthia, um, well, Cynthia is gone."

Susan screamed, "What do you mean? What do you mean by saying that Cynthia is gone?"

Treage's body began to shake as he walked towards Gary. "Cynthia was killed in an automobile accident earlier today. She was headed south on 101 to join Brett at his apartment in Arizona where the Giants are holding spring training. He left early to join the pitchers and catchers to get ready ahead of time."

Gary was stunned. Words seemed to be stuck in his throat as all he could do was get up and go to Treage and hold him in his arms. Finally he managed to sputter, "Damn it, damn it, damn it. Why, why, why? Treage, I don't understand. Everything was falling into place for Brett and Cynthia. Brett was going to be on the big club and Cynthia was due to deliver in a little over two months. Why?"

Everyone had risen and joined Treage and Gary forming a tight circle of clasped arms. Muffled sobs could be hears as Treage replied, "I don't know Gary. Who know why things like this happen. I guess it is all because of some plan. It is a time like this that you appreciate the treasure of life and come to appreciate each day that you get to spend on Earth. All I know is that Brett really needs us. He is beside himself."

Gary cleared his throat. "Excuse me. I have to call Coach Ralston. I think that he would like to know. I imagine that he is going to want to…" Gary's voice trailed off. Finally after a brief pause, he continued, "I wonder if we should go to Arizona to be with Brett or…"

Treage replied, "I think that you should call Brett. I have the number where he can be reached."

A few moments later Brett answered the phone. His voice was heavy with sorrow and hardly audible, "Hello, this is Brett speaking."

"Brett, this is Gary Mallon. Um, I don't really know what to say at a time like this other than to say that I am so terribly sorry. Angelina is devastated about your loss as Cynthia was one of her two best friends in the entire World. We both loved Cynthia very much."

Brett's deep breathing was most audible as he attempted to gather himself. Finally he replied, "Thanks Gary. I appreciate your condolences more than you can imagine." He paused. "Um, this is really a bad time for me. I feel completely lost. All I know is that I have to leave training camp after I receive her ashes from the crematorium and take her home. She asked me during one of her discussions to have her ashes spread over the waters of Lake Washington in Seattle. That was her home before she met me, you know."

"Do you have any idea when you will be coming north?"

"I plan go up to Seattle seven days from now. Her Family and I plan to have a celebration of life ceremony." He paused. "The Giants are allowing me to take all of this week and next off from camp without any repercussions in my quest to make the big club."

Gary nodded as he collected his thoughts. Finally after a moment's pause he replied, "Brett, just know that I am here for you and will do anything that I can to help you through all of this. It won't be easy, but you can make it buddy. You are strong and Cynthia would want you to continue. Please tell me what I can do for you."

Brett quickly replied, "Other than being there for me and giving me a shoulder to lean on, you know, being able to talk with you when I need someone to listen to me, I think that I would like for you to be the master of ceremonies for the celebration of life ceremony." He paused. "Um, her parents know that she wanted a celebration of life gathering rather than a funeral, so having you serve as the main speaker will be deeply appreciated."

"Brett, you honor me with your request and I will gladly serve in that capacity. Um, this isn't the time to talk about it, but within the next few days we will want to talk about the format of the ceremony. I assume that you will want an open microphone after the formalities are done."

"Yeah, that sounds good to me. Right now I am debating whether I want to speak or not. I will let you know when we talk about the format." Bret paused. Gary could hear him crying before he finally continued, "Gary, thanks so much for being here for me. We'll talk, but right now I just need to......"

"I understand partner. You sit down with a tall cool one and think about all of the wonderful times you spent with Cynthia. Whether you believe it or not, she is with you. "

Gary turned to all assembled at Treage's dinner party after hanging up the phone. "Damn, that was tough. That poor guy is really shaken. I have never seen or heard him cry before. If you don't mind I think that I want to go home. I'll share more with you later."

Angelina stood up and walked towards Gary, putting her arms around him. "Let's go my husband. All of a sudden I have lost my appetite and desire to be sociable."

The next few days were hectic. Attending classes, practicing with the baseball team, and working out the plans for Cynthia's celebration of life ceremony were draining. Coach Ralston had announced to the athletic director that Stanford would forfeit their first three games in the Hawaiian Tournament so that those on the Cardinal team that wanted to attend the celebration of life ceremony in Seattle could go. Coach Ralston even convinced the athletic director to allow those that wanted to attend to be flown on the Stanford charter plane to Seattle. It was going to be a team effort to honor Brett and his deceased wife Cynthia.

Ten days after Cynthia's death the celebration of life ceremony was held in the auditorium of the high school that Cynthia attended and graduated from. Prior to the beginning of the ceremony Gary was introduced to Cynthia's parents. "Mr. and Mrs. Kenton, I just want you to know how sorry I am for your loss. I will do everything in my power to make the ceremony a true celebration of Cynthia's life. Brett asked me, as you probably know, to be the master of ceremonies. He indicated that he will speak during the open microphone period after all of the formal stuff has concluded."

Mr. Kenton smiled and took Gary's hand. "I know how close you and Brett are and how close Cynthia was to you and your wife, Angelina. I know that somehow she will be honored that you will be speaking."

A short while later Gary walked to the center of the stage in the large auditorium of Emerson High School. Holding the microphone like it was a fragile flower he began, "My name is Gary Mallon. I am Brett Pine's friend and was Brett's teammate for three years at Stanford. I was also honored to know and be friends with Cynthia Pine, Brett's lovely wife. What am I supposed to say at a time like this? I haven't written a script. I think that I will just speak from the heart and let the words pour out of my mouth. I sincerely hope that what I have to say honors Cynthia as she so deserves to be honored. Maybe in doing so, I will also honor her parents, Mr. and Mrs. Kenton and her husband, Brett."

Gary stood there surveying the audience sitting before him. He knew that they were waiting for something special, a tribute to Cynthia. Slowly he began, "I got to know Cynthia Lovell Pine through her husband Brett. You see, Brett and I played on the same baseball team at Stanford. When I arrived, Brett was the center fielder. Somehow I managed to win that position, moving him to the designated hitter role. Maybe he was the designated hitter, but we all knew who the leader of our Cardinal team was. Brett was the man and Cynthia was his lady. She was the leader in their household, the glue of a very successful marriage. She was older than Brett, a graduate of this high school. She was a beauty. If you recall, she had beautiful blonde hair, blue eyes, and a fair complexion that was totally unmarred by imperfections. She looked like a model out of Vogue, but she was more than that. She was kind, considerate, a best friend of the love of my life, my wife, Angelina. Cynthia was beautiful inside. Her inner beauty emitted a glow that was noticeable to all. She captured your attention. She was smart, a good conversationalist and a loyal wife. She was also going to be a mother at the time of her untimely death, and what a wonderful mother she would have been."

Gary paused and looked around. He managed to see a few nods of approval. He began again, "Some of you would say that Cynthia was taken before her time. I would say what was her time? Some of you might wonder where she is going. I would say that I don't know, but I know that she will always be with Brett. She will be waiting for him in that distant place with The Source, and rest assured she doesn't feel cheated. She lived a good life, a full life. I will miss her. My wife will miss her. Brett and her parents will miss her as will you. But, know this. She doesn't want us to mourn. She wants us to remember what a great and full life she lived. So, I want you to all toast her today after this ceremony is done. Laugh, drink to her, and be thankful that you were fortunate enough to know her. I know that I will."

Gary paused. "I have been asked to tell you that it is now time for us to enjoy the open microphone session. You can come up and share your thoughts, you memories."

Later at a pub on the outskirts of Seattle, a huge gathering of friends, teammates of Gary and Brett, and family were adding the finishing touches to the celebration of Cynthia's life. Brett patted Gary on the back, leaned towards him and mumbled, "Thanks for all of the kind things that you said about Cynthia. I could never have pulled it off. Please don't be a stranger. You and I will play together again very soon."

Gary nodded. "Brett, you are the best. I know that this year is going to go very, very well for you. Save me a spot next to you in the outfield, will you?"

Brett chuckled. "Count on it. I am going to play right field, so there is room." He paused, a grin enveloping his face. "I'll tell our present center fielder that his spot is reserved for you."

Chapter Twenty-Two
Omaha Landing IV

    Coming to the end of a four year commitment to obtain a degree seems like the end of a long and tiring pursuit, but is it? Actually, isn't it just the beginning, the start of yet another chapter in one's life? Life after college is the beginning of a career. The dawn of a new chapter in life signals a continuation of life with no end in sight even though everyone knows that the end is inevitable. Or is it?

Other than two tragic notifications, the death of Gary's parents and the death of Cynthia Pine, February 20th would stand out as a most significant moment in Gary and Angelina's life. The memory would remain etched in their minds forever.

    Angelina burst into their apartment. "Hurry up and get naked. I am ovulating. This is the perfect time to conceive, and I don't want to miss it."

    Moments later they were in bed lying side by side kissing passionately and fondling each other's most sensitive regions. Angelina emitted a gasp of excitement. "I want you inside me. This is it. The time is right for me to get pregnant. I want you to give me a baby."

    Their love chamber suddenly was transformed into a compartment echoing sounds of the whining and creaking of their bed's resistance to their feverish movements and excited moans and gasps. Moments later all previous noises were extinguished by an excited scream and then another, punctuating the already noisy environment as Gary expelled a large rush of air and a loud groan indicating that he had reached an orgasm. Responding to his loud message, Angelina thrust her hips upward to accept every bit of his offering and the hot stream of semen that she felt surging into her love harbor. She screamed with excitement and then whimpered with exhausted excitement. Silence followed. Finally the announcement came, "You just made me a mommy. I love you so much. I just love you, love you, and love you!"

Gary, still attempting to catch his breath, managed a breathless response, "I love you too. Angelina, I love you so very much and I always will. You are everything to me."

Angelina pleaded, "Don't leave me. I want to feel you forever."

Gary kissed her passionately. "I won't, I promise that I will never leave you."

Giggling, Angelina teased, "You might want to revise that statement soldier. We would look kind of funny trying to walk around as we are now."

"You know what I meant."

"Yes silly. I was just kidding. Thank you for saying that though because I will never leave you either. You are my perfect lover, friend, partner, and everything. You always have been and always will be."

As pre-season passed, Stanford was having another good season thanks to fantastic recruiting by Coach Ralston. He had filled the necessary gaps. Although the team missed Bret Pine and John Bledsole, who with Gary and Cam had become a fearsome foursome, Gary and Cam were leading Stanford into league play and hopefully towards another return trip to the College World Series. Going into league play the Cardinals were 11-4. Weeks later the Cardinals had captured another league title and were again set to host the regionals. A victory there and they were assured of hosting the super regionals.

Gary had caught the eyes of all baseball scouts with his hitting stats and superior abilities in the outfield. His batting average hovered at or near .465 all season and his home run total had reached 32. Cam was only slightly less productive, but it was obvious that they really missed Bret's bat as their league record was less than usual, but still respectable at 25-8. Although the hitting production wasn't what it was when Brett was in the lineup, the pitching staff was stronger and had come to be relied upon to save many a close game.

On the eve of the beginning of regional play, Gary and Angelina hosted a small party attended by Cam Bordeaux and his wife Susan, and Treage. Susan, ever the gracious one gave Angelina a hug as she and Cam were greeted at the door of the Mallon apartment. "Thank you so much for inviting us."

Angelina nodded. "You are welcome. I don't know about you, but I have really missed Brett and Cynthia."

"Cam nodded. "Yes, I hear that he is back to playing right field. He talks all the time about how he hopes that he and Gary get to play in the majors together."

Treage chuckled. "Enjoy what is happening to you now and the success that Brett is having. Even if he and Gary don't get to play together, it will be a friendly rivalry."

Gary nodded. "Brett is a fine player. We really miss his bat. He paused, looking at Cam before continuing. "I don't know where we would be if you hadn't come on board. Cam, my man, you are having a great season. Just know that the guys are looking up to you and me for leadership. If we are going back to Omaha, we are going to have to produce and hope that our leadership can inspire the rest of the guys to come through."

Cam nodded. "Don't forget how well our pitching staff has done, Gary. Without their production I doubt that we would even be considering going back to Omaha."

Angelina shook her head. "Enough already, we have had enough baseball talk. I think that it is high time that we had a little mommy talk." She rubbed her tummy. "It won't be long before that blessed event comes our way."

Treage chuckled. "Just hope that he is healthy. You know. Just hope for ten toes and ten fingers."

Angelina frowned. "What if the baby turns out to be a girl?"

Um, well let's hope that she is healthy. I want to make a toast to Cam, Gary and the wonderful ladies that have their backs. Here's to Stanford going back to Omaha." He paused. "Have you heard the rumor?"

Gary frowned. "What rumor? Do you know something that you have failed to share Treage?"

The Wonderment of Life

Treage smiled. "I hear that the Giants are thinking about trading Brett to Seattle to get a couple of their young pitchers. I hear that Seattle might even throw in their center fielder. That of course is just a rumor."

Cam stepped into the exchange, "Where do you get your information, Treage?"

Treage smiled. "Oh, I don't know. I have a few contacts."

Gary pressed forward, "And who might they be and how reliable is the information?"

Treage chuckled. "Would a San Francisco front office friend of mine add some credibility?" He paused. "I understand that the Mariners really want you, Gary. I guess the deal is contingent on them getting you in the draft or having San Francisco trading to get you and then shipping you to them." He paused. "So my friend, you just might want to produce big time and get back to Omaha."

Gary nodded. "Well, I'll give it my best shot. I refuse to put myself above the good of the team. We have gotten this far as a team and we'll go as far as we can as a team."

Going into the regionals Gary appeared to be headed for a draft selection somewhere in the top three and as such could anticipate a lucrative contract. A sweep in the Sunken Diamond and the Cardinals were again set to host the super regionals.

On the eve of the championship game of the super regionals, Coach Ralston made his usual pitch. "We have one game left to play and we again get to go Omaha. I am not going to give you guys a pep talk because we are way, way beyond that. I am just going to say that if we play our game we will prevail. So, go out and do your thing."

It wasn't easy, but the Cardinals pulled out a squeaker, and after capturing the Super Regional title for the fourth straight year they were headed to the College World Series as the number four ranked team in the nation.

Graduation, to follow shortly after the trip to Omaha, was only a successful completion of finals away, and then the walk across the stage to accept a diploma. Angelina was nearly four months into her pregnancy and had finally agreed to let her parents and others know that she and Gary were expecting. As she prepared to board the plane for Omaha, she had the look of an exhausted warrior after having just completed her last final. She was going to hook up with her parents and brothers in a mere two hours for what she hoped would be another stroll to the championship and then life after college.

Stanford breezed through the competition, going undefeated with only an old nemesis, North Carolina, remaining before they could claim another championship. North Carolina had but one loss going into the championship round. So, it came down to what everyone hoped would be a one game run at destiny.

Coach Ralston gathered his squad together in the dressing room prior to what the Cardinals hoped would be their final game of the season, the championship game. "Gentlemen, today is make or break for us. If we win today, we will be crowned champions for the third straight year. Lose and we have to play those guys again tomorrow. You know how I hate losing, but somehow, win or lose; I can't look at this year as anything but being a success. Working with you gentlemen has been an honor. You are winners in more ways than what is shown on the scoreboard." He paused and lowered his head. "I love you guys. You have been so very special. Not only are you all great ball players, but you are so much more. You are good people and that is far more important than winning any game or any championship. So, let's go out there and give it our all and go home champions."

Gary rose and strode to the center of the dressing room. Coach, I think that it would be appropriate to dedicate this game to Brett Pine's deceased wife. Brett was a key component to our first two championships and his wife, Cynthia, was his motivating force."

Coach Ralston nodded. "I doubt that I could have said it any better, Gary. Yes, this one is for Cynthia Pine. I'm sure that Brett would approve."

The game was close. In the top of the ninth the score read 3-3 with the bases loaded and two outs. Gary strode to the plate with anticipation rising in the Stanford dugout. Surely, his teammates felt, he would come through again as he had all season.

The North Carolina pitcher wound up and delivered. Not to disappoint, Gary hit the pitch on the nose. Racing back, tracking the fly ball, the centerfielder from North Carolina leaped and at the last minute snatched a home run away with a fantastic athletic effort. The gloom in the dugout between innings should have forecast the final result. Moments later, the leadoff hitter ruined their chance to win their third straight national title, smashing a 2-2 pitch into the right field bleachers. Like it or not, the Cardinals had to play one more game if they wanted to be crowned champions for the third straight year.

The next day, the deciding game of The College world Series would decide whether they were national champions again or go home as a mere runner-up. Somehow the carefree attitude in the dugout prior to the game and during warmups forecast the final result. Somehow every Cardinal on the team knew that it was their destiny to win a third straight championship. They broadcast an air of confidence and an attitude that said, "Bring it on. Whatever you have to offer we will match and raise you one."

The game wasn't close. The Cardinal Pitcher was superb, spacing two hits throughout the game for a complete game shutout. The Cardinal hitters were all on their game with everyone contributing to the 14-0 blowout victory. They were National champions, having risen to the pinnacle of college baseball for the third straight year.

A day after taking his last final, Gary was called into coach's office. Coach Ralston sat there looking at some papers on his desk. Finally he looked up with misty eyes. "Other than telling you that I have loved coaching you the past four years, I want to share with you some news that I just learned. Gary, you went number one in the draft."

"Who drafted me?"

Coach shook his head. "It doesn't matter. As soon as the draft selection was made, Seattle and San Francisco pulled of a monstrous trade." He frowned as he struggled to make sense of the three way swap. "Well it is like this. It seems that Oakland drafted you with their number one pick. San Francisco then traded three pitchers and two outfielders for you and a couple of minor league hopefuls. San Francisco then traded you and Brett to Seattle for two pitchers and their center fielder. I guess that Seattle also threw in a utility infielder." He slapped his hand on his desk. "My man, you and Brett will be playing together again. How do you feel about that?"

"Well, I'll be damned. I guess that Treage knew what he was talking about after all." Gary pumped his fists, rose excitedly and navigated around the coach's desk to give his beloved coach a big hug. "Coach, I think that you know that I always hoped that I would end up playing with Brett again."

He looked upward. "I guess that someone up there really likes me and Brett. Who would have guessed?" He paused, tears welling up in his eyes. Finally he almost inaudibly whispered, "Coach, you are largely responsible for this day and I want you to know how much I appreciate you." Tears began streaming down his cheeks as he continued, "You have been like a father to me. I love you man."

Coach nodded. "I love you too. Thanks for a wonderful four years. He paused. "Before this mushy stuff gets completely out of hand I need to know if you have an agent yet."

"No, I am going to do what my dad did when he was in the majors. I am interested in playing with the right team, Seattle, and playing for the love of the game. I am sure that they will do right by me and that is all I really care about."

Coach nodded. "Playing for the love of the game is an admirable quality. If you love this game it will love you back."

Gary nodded. "That is the message my dad gave me. I have a wife and a baby on the way. As long as I make a decent salary, well, I just want to play for as long as I can for the right team. Seattle is the right team for me."

Coach smiled. "So, when is the blessed event going to happen, Gary?"

"Angelina is set to deliver sometime in November. Baseball season will be over, and I can be a full time father until spring training rolls around. I am so excited. I love that woman so much. With the baby coming, having completed the work for my degree, being around all of the Stanford players, having you as my Coach, and being married to the finest woman on the planet are more than special. I don't think that I could ask for more or be any luckier. I have been blessed. Someone upstairs must be smiling on me." He paused. "Coach, I hope that you know that the advice you gave me way back then saved my marriage. I want you to know that I am so grateful. Thank you. Just know that I thank you every day that I wake up beside her."

Coach nodded. "Well, treat her right and remember that you can be a good father and a successful ball player."

Gary attended Angelina's graduation ceremony and she attended his two days later. A visit to Treage after packing up their cars and they were off for home. Of course a stop at Shasta City was on the agenda.

Outside of Shasta City Gary's phone rang. "Hello, is that you my darling wife?"

"Yes my darling husband. I have a question."

"I will wager that I know what it is. Should I guess or just tell you what you want to know?"

"Okay, smart guy, lay it on me."

Gary chuckled. "The general manager wants me to come up to Seattle after we get settled back home to sign a contract. They are giving me a $1.5 million dollar signing bonus. Looks like the length and salary terms of the contract will be negotiable. Um, the fine points of the contract will be revealed when I meet with the GM."

"That is not what I wanted to know, but thank you for the information."

"Okay, what do you want to know? Do you want to know where I will be assigned to play?"

"The thought crossed my mind, and yes, where will you be assigned?"

"They are probably going to send me to Tacoma with the possibility that I will be called up to the big club at the end of the season. That is all dependent on my performance, where they are in the standings, and what their needs are, if any."

Angelina shrieked. "I am so excited. That means that I will get to see a lot of you except when you are on the road." She paused. "We can rent an apartment in the Tacoma area during the season, can't we?"

widow." "I wouldn't have it any other way. I don't want you to be a baseball The Mariners did not bring Gary up at the end of the year, opting to invite him to spring training. They felt that although his numbers were terrific that some more minor league seasoning would be better for his future. As they put it, there was no reason to get in a rush. Besides, Brett, who had been traded to Seattle, was putting up good numbers and playing center field. They were looking to make a trade or two that would put Gary in center field and move Bret right field and have one of the players that they traded for become their DH. The other one would hopefully be the utility outfielder since they were a little thin in the outfield.

Brett's trade to Seattle made it possible for a Pine and the Mallon reunion. Rekindling their friendship would be an instantaneous event. It was the best of all worlds. Everything was in place with the future looking very, very bright.

When Gary and Brett were not on the road, they were able to get together which allowed Gary to get some idea of what he would face when and if he went up to the big club. Gary's season at Tacoma was very good. Not only did he hit for a good average, .353, hit with power, but he played center field like a magician. Spring training beckoned and an opportunity to start in center field for the big club. Rejoining Brett was special. This time he would not be relegating Bret to the DH role, but he would be playing alongside of his buddy in the Mariner outfield. With all of the hurdles met and conquered, it was now time for him to focus on becoming a new father.

Chapter Twenty-Three

We Are a Family of Three

A new addition to a family is most always a blessed event. I say most always because most often planning for that blessed arrival insures that it will be loved and nurtured. Babies come into this world initially only want to be loved, fed, and have their diaper changed. Talk about change, when the new arrival hits the front door life changes forever.

November was always a special month for Angelina and Gary, but November 22 was a life changing date. At 11:00 pm, Angelina moaned. "Gary, wake up! My water just broke and I have started having contractions. I think we should go to the hospital."

Gary jerked to a state of alertness, quickly jumping out of bed and hurriedly put on his clothes as he continuously inquired, "Are you okay? What do you want me to do?"

Angelina chuckled. "Relax daddy, just finish putting on your clothes and then you can go into the bathroom and get me a wash rag and towel. I want to clean up a bit before I put on my clothes."

"Honey, forget the clothes. Let's just get you into a fresh nightgown. You'll be perfectly fine if you just slip into a bathrobe and slippers. That will be more than sufficient attire to go to the hospital in."

About an hour later Gary sat beside his wife's bed holding her hand. Angelina winced as another contraction commenced. "Damn, I wish the pain would go away." She gasped, "The contractions are about a minute apart. The nurse told me that they will deliver the baby right here in my room."

"I called your parents and they are on their way." Angelina moaned, "Oh God, please let this stop."

"Breathe honey, just take deep breaths and let the air out slowly. I'm here and everything is going to be just fine. I love you."

"Damn you, I love you too, but why did you have to do this to me?" Gary chuckled, "I thought it was your idea?"

Angelina giggled, "Can't you take a joke. All the movies I've ever seen the wife always complains about her husband doing this to her."

Just then the Crawford's came into the room. Sue excitedly asked, "Is everything okay?"

Gary nodded. "It won't be long now, Grandpa and Grandma. The contractions are now less than a minute apart. The doctor will be here in a minute. They are going to deliver the baby here. Angelina wants you to stay, don't you honey?"

Angelina nodded gritting her teeth. "Oh shit, it hurts so badly. God, please make it stop."

The doctor entered the room, took a brief look around, and commanded, "Grandma and Grandpa you will have to step aside. Dad, you can stay by your wife's side. Dad, be ready to catch your baby when I hand it off to you. It won't be long now." He grinned. "You can catch, can't you?"

A minute later, the doctor smiled as he handed the baby to Gary. "It's a boy, dad. You have a new son."

There is nothing like a birth cry. First, it announces the arrival of a new life. Second, it is a reassuring sound, a sound that signifies that all is okay. But it is that first view of the new life that is so overwhelming. Gary shook his head in awe as he thought, *"Yes, ten fingers and ten toes, and, oh my God, what a beautiful baby. My son, my son, oh my God, I love you so. Mom and Dad, if you are near, here is your first grandchild. It's a beautiful boy and he is perfect."* Then the dam broke as the tears came, tears streaming down his cheeks.

The nurse took the baby from Gary, chuckling. "All fathers do the same thing. I swear if I wasn't always anticipating what they are going to do I am certain they would let the poor little thing slip out of their arms or drown the baby with their tears." With the baby in tow, she walked to the side of Angelina's bed. "See mom, look what you have. It is a beautiful baby boy." She chuckled. "I thought I should let you have him before his father drowns him with his tears."

Angelina began to cry. "Can I hold him?"

"In just a moment after we clean him up and put some drops in his eyes." She walked over to the Crawford's. "See, you have a healthy grandson." Sue began to cry. "Oh, he is so beautiful. He is just perfect. Guy, please go get Greg and Lance. I think that it okay for them to be here now." She turned towards Gary and commented, "Gary, he looks just like your father."

Gary smiled. "I was waiting for that Sue, but I think that he looks just like himself. By the way, meet your grandson Louis Fredrick Mallon. Angelina and I decided that if it were a boy we would name him after his grandfathers. If we have a girl it will be named Susan Claudia Mallon."

With the arrival of January came the first snow. Snow, not a frequent visitor to the Willamette Valley decided to add icing to the cake with a thick layer of the white stuff. As Angelina nursed her son, Louis, she smiled at her husband. "I love you, you know."

"I know and I want you to know that I love you too. I've been thinking that we could…."

Angelina smiled. "If you are thinking that we could try to make another baby, I would agree completely. I think that February would be a good time to do it. We just might be able to get it done before you have to go to spring training."

"We haven't discussed this yet, but how many children do you want?"

She smiled devilishly. "If you promise not to stop making love to me frequently I would be completely satisfied if we stopped at two. What about you?"

"Two is a nice number. I think that when we know that the second child is healthy and doing well that it would be good for me to get a vasectomy. I don't want you to be on the pill any longer. I don't think that it is good for you."

Angelina nodded. "Thank you for that. I could have my tubes tied, but, well, thank you for that."

"I got a phone call from the front office. They traded the right fielder away for more pitching. It looks like they are going to give me a shot at center field and move Bret to right field. I suppose that everything will shake out during spring training. At least I am going to be given a shot at moving up to the big club."

"Wow! That is great news. So, they think that the Mariners can make a run for the pennant with you and Bret in the outfield and an improved pitching staff?"

Gary smiled. "Well, time will tell. We also have a pretty good prospect that will probably be our DH. If both Brett and I have a good spring camp, we very easily could be playing together in the Mariner outfield this year. Can you believe it? My dreams are coming true, all of them."

"What do you mean by all of them?"

"Angelina, I have never told you this before, but I wanted to marry you as soon as I knew what marriage was all about. I wanted to play baseball, to go to college, and I have always wanted to be a Mariner. Luckily, I got a bonus. We have Louis now and perhaps we will be lucky enough to have a Susan. Wouldn't it be nice to have a little boy and a little girl in our family?"

Angelina smiled as she removed Louis from her breast. "Poor little guy. He's all pooed out. Once he fills his tummy he's all done. After I burp him I am sure that he will go down until the 2:00 feeding." She paused and looked longingly into Gary's eyes. "Would you like to get naked? We should have plenty of time."

Chapter Twenty-Four

Life Goes On

Life goes on or as stated on Earth, time marches on. Yes, whatever time is, on Earth it just ticks away as seconds fade into minutes and then into hours, days, weeks, months, years, and more. On and on it marches forward. Will it ever stop? Maybe that is a topic too hard to understand much like where does the Universe end, or does it? Maybe time doesn't exist? What about the size of the Universe? What is infinity? What does all of this mean? I don't know, do you?

Gary was eighteen when he entered college, twenty-two when he graduated and began his first full season as a Mariner at the ripe old age of twenty-three. That first year, oh that first year, it was glorious. Brett Pine and the Mallon's were reunited as Gary and Brett began the season playing together in the Mariner outfield, Gary in center and Brett in right. As it was at Stanford, Gary hit in the number three hole of the batting order with Brett serving as cleanup.

Seattle was good. Their pitching staff was talented, young, and had great arms. The infield was sound and the outfield was the best that it had been in years. Catcher, well that was an issue as the veteran catcher Sammy Fielder was past his prime. He still handled the pitching staff well, but his arm was not what it used to be and his bat was lifeless. If the Mariners were going to be great they needed to add a quality catcher.

Gary nodded his head as he sat on the bench next to Brett. "We need a catcher partner. I love Sammy to death and know that he does a great job handling the pitchers, but his bat is dead. I have been watching what has been going on with Stanford. Cam is not putting up the numbers for the Cardinals that he did his first three years, so his stock has really fallen. He could be had by the Mariners if…"

"My thoughts exactly, Gary, do you think that the front office would be willing to take a chance on him? I know he has the stuff to make it big here. Wouldn't it be nice if he were to join us?"

"Our manager just might have something to say about that. I wonder what the Mariners would do if he was still undrafted when it came time for them to make a selection? Would they have to give up anything to draft him?" He paused. "Bret, do you think…?"

Brett nodded. "Do I think that he's ready to play in the majors? You were ahead of him at this point in his baseball evolution, and he…"

"Yeah, Cam is a catcher and it takes longer for them to get ready to play in the big show. A catcher's learning curve is a lot steeper than any other position other than being a big league pitcher."

Brett nodded. "I don't disagree. But in your gut you know as well as I do that he is ready, don't you Gary?" He isn't producing this year because there isn't anyone surrounding him to keep the opposing pitchers from pitching around him."

Gary nodded. "Yeah, he can hit and behind the plate he is exactly what we need. He has a rifle for an arm, he is accurate, and with a little help he will be able to manage the game like a veteran." He nodded his head. "Yeah, he might have to have some help from the bench in calling a game, but in all other aspects he is…"

The manager interrupted, "Are you going to share the scouting report with me or are you going to keep me guessing as to whom you are talking about?"

Brett grinned. "Skipper, if we can have a sit down with you after this game is over, Gary and I will share. I assure you that it will be worth hearing."

The manager, Scott Granger, nodded. "I respect you two and value your opinion. Just know that even if I agree with you it won't mean much because the front office runs the show."

Gary nodded. "Well, it wouldn't hurt to at least bring up the subject with them, would it? Who knows, they might listen and if they do we could just plug the only hole we have. Of course as a rookie I doubt that what I have to say is worth much."

"Are you kidding? I would go to war with you and Brett. Both of you plan on coming to my office after the game is over and you get showered and dressed." He grinned. "I don't much cotton to streakers or exhibitionists."

Brett shook his head. "Good one, Skipper, do you have plans to go on stage as a standup comic when you retire from this old game?"

On draft day, much to the surprise of Brett and Gary, Seattle landed Cam with the 200th pick in the draft. The trio was soon to be united. At a celebration party at Brett's lake house a week later, Gary greeted Cam with a firm handshake and a bear like hug. It is so good to have you with us, bro. Don't be disappointed about playing the rest of this year at Tacoma. I should know because it did me a world of good. If you pay attention and work on what they will try to teach you there is no way that you won't be with us next year at spring training. The rest will be up to you."

Brett chuckled. "I don't know who is happier, the girls or us. Look at them over there. You would think that they were meeting a long lost relative for the first time in years." He nodded. "Yep, this is going to be so good to have you with us on the big club."

Cam grinned. "Thanks guys, you don't know how excited I am. I feel so blessed that the Mariners took a chance on me."

Brett chuckled. "Cam, with the amount of your signing bonus, I think that it is the other way around. You are taking a chance on becoming a Mariner. How long is your contract, um, what are the terms of your contract?"

"They signed me for two years. I am going to get the minimum, but I really don't care. Just being with you guys and having a chance to play in the majors is a dream come true."

Brett cleared his throat with a moderately loud "Ahem". "Gentleman, and I use that term rather loosely, I think the time has come for me to share some news with you."

Gary grinned. "If you are talking about letting us know about that lovely lady that is approaching, I think the cat is out of the bag. What's her name?"

Brett's face reddened. "Her name is Eileen Rogers." He grinned. "No, she is not related to Roy Rogers and his wife Dale Evans."

Cam chuckled. "Well, congratulations if congratulations are in order. How did you meet her?"

"She's a real baseball fan. I met her at an after game party about a month ago. She was a guest of our manager. She and Scott's wife are pretty close." Brett paused. "Is it too soon? Um, you know. Is it too soon after Cynthia's passing to, um, you know?"

Gary smiled. "Only you know the answer to that question, Brett. As far as I am concerned I think that it is terrific. We were intended to be with someone and after the loss of someone, well, life moves on. Life is for the living and I think that you are entitled to live it to the fullest."

Cam nodded his head. "I second that. Brett, we just want you to be happy. So, I say go for it. If she makes you happy that is all that counts."

Gary whispered, "Before your lady gets here I just want to know how the Kenton's are reacting to your new lady?"

Brett shrugged. "They don't know. Strangely, since the celebration of life ceremony I haven't seen them once. I don't know what that is all about, but I guess that they just want to go in another direction."

Cam inquired, "Have you tried to make contact? After all it isn't like they live a long ways from you."

"Yes, I have tried a couple of times, but they seem very distant and vague. You know, I don't think that they were ever very pleased about Cynthia being with me. For some reason I think that they wanted something better."

Gary shook his head. "Brett, that couldn't be further from the truth. Cynthia couldn't have done any better. You go for it man. You are entitled."

Just then Eileen made her appearance. "Am I interrupting anything, Brett? You seem to be deeply engrossed in a conversation with your friends. By the way, my name is Eileen. You don't need to introduce yourselves because I know all about you. It is a pleasure to meet you."

Gary nodded. "Wow! You cut to the chase, don't you? Yes, it is a pleasure to meet you Eileen. A little later we'll introduce you to our wives. I am certain they will want to meet you as we hang out a lot with old Brett here." He grinned. "Besides, before we introduce you to our wives we feel obligated to share with you all of Brett's bad habits. It will be called full disclosure."

Gary momentarily left the conversation as he sized up Brett's new lady. *"Hmm, Brett certainly has an eye for the ladies. Eileen is not the beauty queen that Cynthia was, but she has a terrific personality, an athletically toned body, and catches your eye. I like the fact that she seems to be so comfortable talking to strangers. On second thought, she is no ugly child. Her long blond hair and those piercing blue eyes really capture your attention."*

The reuniting of the newly formed sextet went well. It seemed that life was truly moving on. It was a bright new day.

Chapter Twenty-Five

Retirement

All careers come to an end, retirement a reality, a sad reality that we don't go on forever without changing directions. Or is it? When a career comes to an end, an entire life's work and preparation comes to a fork in the road. As Yogi said, "When you come to a fork in the road, take it."

Seventeen years later and fifteen all-star seasons on record, Gary retired. During his illustrious career he had amassed a life time batting average of .343, hit six hundred sixty-four home runs, and had a life time fielding average of .998. He was named to the all-star team fourteen times, was on seven World Series championship teams and never was involved in a scandal for drinking, the use of drugs, or running afoul of the law. He was a role model that made baseball proud not to mention his family and friends. During his career he played for the love of the game never demanding a contract with a salary with a lot of zeros. Of course with performance bonuses and money made from World Series appearances, fourteen, he left baseball with a very nice investment account.

His son and daughter were in college when he retired, both attending Oregon State University. His son was taking the necessary undergraduate courses to allow him to become an astronaut. His daughter was very interested in space medicine, hoping to one day practice on some space outpost. Both knew that a bachelor's degree was just the starting point as there would be a need to go on to graduate school to attain their doctor's degrees.

Angelina's parents died when Gary was in his fifteenth season. They were killed in a plane crash on their way to Europe. There was suspicion that their plane was shot down over the Atlantic by a missile fired from North Korea. How do you justify, rationalize or even understand a senseless tragedy such as that? Perhaps you might suggest that bad luck or good luck occurs in pairs. Maybe you figure that there is a master plan. Then again, perhaps it is a test to see if someone or a group of people can rise above the tragedy and find a way to eliminate senseless and wanton disregard for the value of life.

Gary and Angelina were convinced that her parents had joined Gary's parents, revisiting The Source or wherever people go when they leave this life. No matter, both Gary and Angelina never felt alone. It seemed like their parents were always just around the corner looking for some way to be helpful, but always so very proud of their children and grandchildren.

Angelina balanced motherhood and being a devoted housewife with an illustrious career in music as an occasional guest singer/piano player at special events or acting in musicals in and about Portland. She was in demand, but always put her family ahead of her love of performing. Maybe that was one of the reasons she was in demand. Over exposure can sour the public's thirst for more, while holding back to stir their desires for more can whet their appetites with an unstatutable appetite for more.

As was Gary's parent's loss, the loss of the Crawford's was very difficult for all members of their family to rationalize. Good friends, loving family members and devoted lovers come along, but not often enough. Sadly they don't seem to stay long enough. Some say that those people leave before their time. What is their time? Maybe it was their time. That would be a lesson to be learned as the mystery of life unfolded and more experience and knowledge made the lesson come to be seen more clearly. At least that was the philosophy that Gary and Angelina elected to accept. They had a life to live. Their parents had lived their life. The reason for their departure would be known later they reasoned.

Greg decided to teach and coach football, opting to locate at Lake Oswego High School. Lance also joined the staff Lake Oswego as a teacher and the basketball coach. The Crawford and Mallon family remained close even after key members had been taken away.

At the news conference held to announce Gary's retirement from baseball, he was asked what his plans for the future were. Responding he announced, "I am only 40, going on 41 in a few days, but I feel that the time has come for me to hang up my spikes before someone tells me that it's time to quit and rips them off me. I have had a wonderful career, but I want to go out while I can still perform at a level that I deem acceptable." He paused. "However, it isn't time for me to stop contributing. As you know I have previously volunteered to support candidates that have run for the House of Representatives, the Senate, and the President of the United States. I now plan to run for office. I have been approached to run for the United States Senate to represent the state of Oregon." He smiled. "I suppose all of the off season political statements I have made about where our country is headed have put me into a position where it is time to put up or shut up. I have therefore decided to put up. So I will gratefully accept the invitation to run for the United States Senate and hope for the support of the people of Oregon."

One reporter inquired, "What party will you affiliate with when you officially announce your candidacy? Up to this point you have been all over the board, supporting candidates from both parties."

Gary smiled. "Isn't that what a person should do?" He paused. "Well, thanks to the common sense of the Oregon voters, I will run as an Independent. I have always, in good conscience, supported the person I felt was the best candidate. I hope the people of Oregon will feel that I am the best candidate and vote for me even though I am not running as a candidate from the Democratic or Republican parties."

Another reporter inquired, "Would you care to tell us what positon or issues you will run on?"

Gary nodded. "If elected, I will shed my political badge at the entrance to the Senate chamber and work for America and the people who elected me. Maybe you could say that my position is to put America, the people of America first and the people of Oregon next. I will represent Oregon with all of the energy that I can muster, but Oregon is only one of fifty states in the union. If I am lucky enough to serve, I will strive to narrow the chasm that now exists in America and try to achieve compromise and bi- partisan legislation. As I look across America today I see a long wide, very wide river. On opposite banks of the river I see the different parties. I hope to narrow the river so that the members of the parties can easily wade across to join forces for the good of the people of our great nation.

Another reporter raised his hand and inquired, "You and wife both lost your parents to suspected terrorist attacks. Do you have a plan to bring an end to terrorist activities?"

Gary nodded. "That is an excellent question. I am appalled at the terrorist activity that exists in our World. As you noted, I lost my parents and my wife lost hers because of suspected terrorist activity. Isn't it time that the peoples of the World stop fighting and begin to learn to love one another no matter what the color of their skin is, what language they speak, where they come from, what their sexual orientation is, or what their particular religious belief is or is not? I am running for America as a citizen of the World, the planet Earth." He paused. "I did not answer your question. It isn't because I am ignoring the question. Rather I would have to say that I need to work with other people to seek a solution. I know that we have to maintain a strong military and be very vigilant and aware of potential terrorist activity and planned attacks. I feel that we cannot do this alone. We have to forge alliances with other nations to root out those that would do us or others harm. Education, patience, vigilance, and remaining powerful are weapons that we can and should use. One thing that we shouldn't do is suggest that Christianity is the only path to achieving salvation."

The general manager of the Mariners held up his hands and announced, "Gary will take only one more question, so make it a good one."

One reporter eagerly waved her hand, catching Gary's eye. "Miss, I think that the men have dominated the questioning to this point. I think that it's time that your gender had their time in the sun."

She smiled. "My name is Tilly O'Keefe. That is a strange name to have and be a sport's reporter, but I am deeply interested in baseball and have been a student of the game all my life. So Mr. Mallon, um Gary, what do you think your chances are of being elected to the Hall of Fame?"

Gary's face immediately assumed a faint reddish hue as he dropped his head. "Miss or is it Mrs. O'Keefe, ah…"

"Pardon me for interrupting Gary, but you can just call me Tilly."

Gary grinned, nodding. "Okay Tilly, I think that I have always loved the game of baseball and played it for the love of the game. I am hoping that the game will love me back. A dear coach of mine years ago told me that if you love this magnificent game it will love you back." He paused. "You know,

I have loved my wife all my life. The thing that makes loving her so wonderful is that she has always loved me back. We love each other unconditionally as I have loved baseball. By the way, she is going to be in my corner for this run at winning the Senate seat."

Gary rose, smiled, and waved to the maze of reporters, retreating from the gathering. He smiled at Angelina as he approached her outside the interview room. "Well my dear, the campaign trail is long exhausting and bumpy. The task ahead of us is not going to be easy, but no matter the outcome it will be a wonderful experience. Can you believe all of the wonderful people we will have the opportunity to meet?"

Angelina squeezed his hand. Words did not come as the energy that she transmitted from her hand to his said it all.

Chapter Twenty-Six

Good Enough Isn't Enough

There once was a pretty good student who sat in a pretty good classroom in a pretty good school with a pretty good teacher. This pretty good student was taught by that pretty good teacher who always allowed pretty good to pass. This pretty good student wasn't a whiz bang at math or English, but for him a pretty good education was good enough to lead him down a pretty good path. This pretty good student didn't find school too exciting, but he wanted to do pretty good so he could get a pretty good job and have a pretty good life. He had some trouble with writing. His pretty good teachers in his pretty good schools had only taught him to spell pretty well and use pretty good grammar. When doing arithmetic problems pretty good was regarded as fine as five plus five didn't always have to add up to ten as a pretty good answer was nine because it was pretty close to being correct. In this pretty good classroom in this pretty good school where he sat he was surrounded by pretty good students of which he was not an exception. To the contrary, he was pretty much the rule. The first time that he knew what he lacked was when he looked for a pretty good job. When he sought a pretty good position he discovered that life could be pretty tough,

and soon he had a pretty good suspicion that pretty good might not be good enough.

In a broader sense, there once was great nation that gradually became a pretty good nation. The citizens of this pretty good nation were pretty proud of the greatness their country had achieved, learning much too late that if greatness is what is desired to be achieved that pretty good is, in fact, pretty bad or not good enough.

Gary was proud to be an American and of all that America had achieved. He did, however, have reservations about the direction the country was headed. Once the beacon of hope for the peoples across the World, the once bright light of hope was fading as greed, self-importance, and aggression appeared to be the direction America was headed. The greatest generation had come and gone. It had left its mark, a distinguishable mark to be proud of, but the mark was all but obscure. Gary was bothered by those of the collective many who spoke out of both sides of their mouth to justify what they once knew to be wrong. He was bothered by his fractured nation. Once a nation that achieved greatness by building things such as the transcontinental railroad and the interstate highway system, it had stopped building, allowing its infrastructure to slowly begin to crumble.

Also a bother to him was how people were elected to serve. It took a huge amount of money to run a campaign, to be able to present your case before the public so as to perhaps interest them in voting for you. It had reached a point where the money people, corporations, and special interest groups ponied up with the money for the person they felt was electable. However, that came with a price. The candidate was no longer his or her own person. They owed the huge contributors and organizations that got them elected. The result was often grid lock in Congress, rendering the President to be little more than a figure head. Sadly more and more, less was accomplished and that which was accomplished was not always good for the people. It was also sadly true that if a measure/law passed that was against a particular party's positon, they would spend an inordinate amount of time trying to repeal the measure/law. Many complained that their vote in an election didn't count. No wonder. The Electoral College turned a slight margin of victory in a state into an undivided vote for the marginal winner of that election.

One evening while talking with Angelina, Gary shook his head with a sadness that was vividly displayed in his eyes. "Have you ever thought that this country of ours is not the country that we were born into?"

Angelina nodded. "Sadly I have thought that ever so many times. What do you think has changed?"

Gary shrugged his shoulders and wrinkled up his nose. "Oh I don't know. Maybe it's like too many people don't obey laws. Maybe too many of our citizens have come to believe that "my rights" supersedes what the law states. Too many people do as they please, disregarding the laws. As an example, we have a cell phone law forbidding people from talking on the phone or texting while they are driving. How often do you see people driving down the street with that instrument of joy pressed to their ear as they pay little or no attention to what they are doing?" He paused. "Um, it goes without saying that our gun law, the right to bear arms, has come to mean that we have a right to own any sort of weapon to include military assault weapons. Too many people are killed in shooting rampages across our nation. I have to believe that the founding fathers never intended the right to bear arms to go to such extremes."

Angelina excitedly chimed in, "Or when you are standing in a cross walk and the cars continue to buzz on by with little or no regard to your desire and right to cross."

Gary nodded. "Yeah, and the people that ride bikes in congested areas with their heads down speeding through pedestrian walk ways with little or no regard for man, woman, child or pets. You would think that they were trying to emulate the racers in the Tour de France." He paused. "We used to work together to accomplish greatness. We used to build things. We used to be a sanctuary for the downtrodden, the poor, and those seeking a better life. We viewed education as the ladder we could climb to rise above our station in life and to achieve all that we can possibly be through hard work. Hell, kids today have problems even affording to go college because of the constantly rising costs. Sadly, if they do go to college they come out saddled with a debt that takes them forever to pay off. Honey, the middle class is disappearing. We are rapidly becoming a two-class society, those who have and those that don't."

Gary paused for a moment. "At the risk of sounding like a complete pessimist, I think that the upper class is hell bent on dumbing down the masses so as to create a two class society. The lower class, they might reason, will learn to be content to survive at a subsistence level as they grovel to the upper class for their pittance. An advanced education, the path to a better life, is becoming more and more difficult to obtain."

Angelina frowned. "I know how you feel about Washington D.C." She paused to allow her statement gain value and make a full impact. Finally continuing, she offered, "You feel that the government in D.C. is broken with both parties are so far apart that nothing gets done. Both of us are disgusted that the representatives have the nerve to point to the President or the other party as being the culprit. They no longer represent us, America. They represent big corporations and big money." Angelina paused reflectively. Finally she began again, "We used to be our brother's keeper. We pitched in to help the downtrodden, the disadvantaged. Now to show how far we have strayed all you have to do is look at the masses of homeless that clutter and litter our streets, loiter under bridges, or camp out wherever they find an open space to pitch a tent or a canvas covering. Do you really feel that you can make a difference, that your voice will be heard?"

"Honestly, I do not know. I just know that I have to try. I have to make my statement without coming across as an idealistic idiot that wants to give away the house, raise the white flag of surrender, and allow the bullies of the World to prevail. We have to become better students of history and then respond with purpose and respect for the rights of all peoples of this Earth. We have to once again lead with rightful causes."

Angelina nodded. "So, even though I think I know what you believe, please spell it out for me and tell me what you plan to do about it. Tell it to me as though you were standing in front of the voters you are trying to convince that they should support you. Tell me what you will say to earn their vote."

Gary frowned. His eyes narrowed with determination etched on his face as he began, "I doubt that I am going to win many friends when I say this, but here goes." He cleared his throat. "Well first off, for all too long the United States has been a selfish, self-centered bully. We have allowed money or the quest for wealth to define our policies at home and abroad.

We are no longer the nation that other nations look up to and respect. We no longer lead by example. We lead by force demanding that everything be done our way and that, in my opinion, is wrong. We need to stop being the World's policeman and let other nations solve their problems unless we are asked for assistance."

"Secondly, we have turned our heads away from the needs of our disadvantaged citizens." He paused for a reflective moment. "Third, we turn our heads as the Hispanics come to our country for a better life, to do the work that we no longer want to do and then complain because they are here. We do not demand that they register, obtain a work permit, or embark on the path to citizenship. Fourth, when we go to war it is often without a cause or an ultimate goal. Do you realize that we have not won a war since WWII? We have not gone into war with a win at all cost purpose or mind set like we had when we entered WWII. If we don't have that resolve, why should we go to war unless it is for personal national gain, um, to line the pockets of the industrial complex that makes money off of war?"

Gary paused again. "Within what I have already stated, I will specifically mention and offer solutions about universal health care, gun control, serving America as opposed to serving big money, the homeless, our tax code, the cost of education, fixing social security, leading as opposed to trying to force our way down other countries throats, and immigration." Gary smiled. "I will also mention a very unpopular idea. I believe that all citizens of this country should be expected to serve our country in some capacity. I would propose that we reinstate the draft, a requirement that all citizens upon graduation from high school serve for two years. They don't have to serve in the military, but they should serve our country in some capacity. With each year of service I would propose that they get a year of free education in college or a trade school." He paused. "Well, is that a laundry list or what?"

"Honey, I know that you are right and I love you so much for what you believe, but you might consider softening what you say just a bit." She paused. "Furthermore, I feel that too many issues might confuse the voters. Maybe you should settle on three or four issues that you think will resonate with the electorate and then pound on those issues over and over."

Gary nodded. "Angelina, do you know why I love you?"

Angelina smiled. "Well, other than my fantastic body and extraordinarily sharp mind, I don't have a clue." She chuckled. "Seriously, tell me what I don't already know.

"I know for a fact that I have never asked you why I love you before, and I also know that you have never asked me that I can recall."

She smiled, winking up her nose as she continued, "I suppose I've always felt that you loved me just for my brilliance, my fantastic personality, and my gorgeous sexy body."

Gary chuckled. "Well, beyond that, I love you because you serve as my moral weather vane. Before I have ever done anything of importance I have always sought your advice." He smiled. "So far, you are hitting for a fantastic average in guiding me along the right path."

"Well thank you my kind and wonderful husband. So, tell me what platform or message do you think that you could believe in and sell to the voters of Oregon?"

"Well, in addition to the aforementioned issues, of which I will whittle down to three or four issues, what do you think about the idea that, 'Good enough is not enough, that America is better than that and that we should strive again to raise the bar to be what the peoples of the World will again come to respect and admire? I want Oregonians to know that I will throw away my political badge and represent them and all Americans. I will vote not to go along with party politics, but to truly represent the people that have sent me to Washington to represent and to serve." He paused. "If I am to convince Oregonians that I will represent them, I have to take my campaign to them, all of them." He smiled. "In paring down the issues that I will address, I will listen and seek your advice on that point."

He grinned. "I have even been thinking about my campaign route."

Angelina sat up, focusing her attention on what Gary was about to add. "So, tell me your thoughts."

"Well, there is a lady, Lisa Teague, from Channel Two News that has suggested that I jump into the race as soon as possible. At the present time there are already a total of five candidates already in the race. There are two Democrats and three Republicans. I would be the sixth if I enter. If I am going to enter I have to do it now." Gary paused. "With my thoughts about taking my campaign to all of the people of Oregon I need to get started. Lisa has promised to give me all of the media help necessary to broadcast my campaign tour route."

"Hmm, so, you have already spoken with her about running for the senate and your campaign plans."

"Yes, we spoke shortly after I announced my retirement from baseball and broadcast my retirement plans."

Angelina frowned. "Hmm, this would be the first time that you have done something significant without discussing it with me. This Lisa gal must be something else to get you to have that discussion without conferring with me."

Gary nodded. "She is. Lisa is a dynamic voice, has the ear of the media, and she is very interested in supporting my candidacy. Other than that, to put your mind at ease, she is just a nice lady that I have met. She means nothing to me in a romantic sense. You are my lady, the love of my life, and the only person that catches my eye."

Angelina smiled. "Thank you for that. I have always trusted you, but I think you can see my concern considering that you…"

Gary nodded. "I know. I should have put you in the loop."

Angelina nodded. "Enough of this, Honey, I want to know the cities and towns your campaign tour will cover."

He grinned. "Right, you did ask. I guess I have to learn to be a better listener and learn to get to the point instead of dancing all over the countryside."

Angelina chuckled. "Slugger, if you pull that off you will be a very unique politician."

Gary smiled. "I think that I need to focus on hub cities, hoping to draw people from surrounding towns to that focal city or town to hear my message. I want to start and finish in Portland. Because Portland and the surrounding communities have such a huge population, I might begin on the west side of the Willamette River when the tour begins and hit the east side at the conclusion of the tour. That way the people in this area will have two shots at me. After hitting the west side I will move south to the Capitol, Salem. That will be my second hub, the place where I hope to draw the people from the surrounding towns to come to hear my message. I will then head south with hubs in Albany, Eugene, Roseburg, Medford and finally Grants Pass before heading west to the coast."

Angelina's eyes became bigger and bigger as she listened to Gary's plan. "So far that is a very ambitious goal, but I like what I am hearing."

Gary continued, "On the coast, my first hub will be Brookings. I will follow up as I head north to Bandon, Coos Bay, Newport, Lincoln City, Tillamook, Seaside and finally Astoria." He shook his head. "I will then head back towards Portland to hit the communities in Rainier, St. Helens, and Scappoose. After returning to Portland I will head east stopping in Hood River and The Dalles."

Angelina chuckled. "Slow down soldier. You are wearing me out."

Gary smiled. "We are just about half through as I will then head south with stops in Madras, Redmond, Bend, La Pine, and finally Klamath Falls."

Angelina held up her hands as though to indicate he needed to stop. "When we get to Bend can we take a side trip to Sisters? That beautiful town is very funky and the view of The Three Sisters is spectacular."

Gary nodded. "I don't see why not. Anyway, from Klamath Falls I will head to Lakeview and then head north to Burns, Ontario, and Baker City. I think that from there I would like to take another little side trip to Halfway."

Angelina frowned. "Halfway, are you kidding me? What is in Halfway and where in the hell did it get a name like that?"

Gary smiled. "There are people there and where the town got its name is a mystery to me. I just heard about it and figured that it would be an interesting place to visit."

Angelina shrugged her shoulders, doubt etched on her face. "Well, if you insist. So, what happens after Halfway?"

"We head back to Baker City and then continue on to La Grande, Joseph, and finally Pendleton. After Pendleton we head back towards Portland."

"Aren't there any towns to visit on the way back to Portland?"

"Right now I am considering Stanfield, Hermiston and Arlington. After that I think we will make a dash toward Portland stopping in Gresham."

Angelina nodded. "Let's go back to Halfway. Tell me a little about it and what intrigues you about that place."

"It is located east of Baker City. I am pretty sure that the population is comprised mainly of farmers and cattle ranchers." He grinned. "I have heard about that little berg and thought that going to halfway just might be the ticket. It will validate my claim that I am a citizen of Oregon and that I want to represent all of Oregon no matter where the people live."

Angelina chuckled again. "Well, nobody can say that you only went halfway into this campaign after visiting Halfway, Oregon."

Gary nodded. "I want to run my proposed route by Lisa to see what she thinks. She might have an idea or two." He paused, shrugging his shoulders. "I just know that if I am going to be true to my word, I need to show that my word has meaning, that the voters in all reaches of our state are as important as the heavily populated Willamette Valley."

Angelina nodded. "Honey, you just earned my vote. I would walk through cut glass and a mine field to support you."

Gary smiled. "Well it is going to take more than that. I have only one advantage and that is name recognition. I hope that I can get the kids and our brothers to stump for me."

"They will. All you have to do is ask."

Angelina looked at him intently. "Who do you think you'll name as your campaign manager."

"At my retirement interview I mentioned the thought that I would pick you. Will you do it? You know me better than anyone, you believe in me, and you are as smart as a whip." He grinned. "Besides, with you serving as my campaign manager we won't have to hire any musicians."

Suddenly Gary seemed to drift away into another world, looking at his lovely wife with love being broadcast so loud that it would drown out a stadium filled with rabid fans, yet so quiet and peaceful that all you could hear was the sound of his lovely wife breathing. He softly offered, "Honey, as you know one of us will leave the other first." He paused. "That is unless, God forbid that we would go as our parents did. I am not afraid of dying or whatever it really is when we leave this existence, and I am certain that you aren't either."

Angelina interrupted, "What are you trying to say? You are starting to scare me."

"I just want you to know that your beliefs are as important as or more so than mine. I know how you feel about supporting me, but I also know that you have such a love for music and care so much about the homeless people of our world. Please tell me that if I go first you will do your thing and not feel bound to carry on with my goals." He cleared this throat as he continued, "I love you more than life itself and can't imagine ever being with anyone else, but should I go first I want you to know that you deserve to be happy. You should feel that it is okay to find another man. We were put on Earth to love and be loved. We belong with someone. Men and women were created to be together. Um, people were meant to be with each other even if it is two men or two women living in a loving relationship."

"Don't you dare go there, Gary Mallon, I am married to you and will be as long as I continue to walk on this planet. You may choose to be with someone else if I leave first, but I won't. I refuse to be with anyone but you. You are my life." She frowned as her eyes misted and a tear started to escape from her eye. "Um if you want to be with someone else if I leave first I want you to know that it is okay. To love is to give, and I give you the freedom to move forward when I am gone."

Chapter Twenty-Seven

Campaigning

To get a campaign message out to the people traditionally takes money from avid supporters with deep pockets. Then again, perhaps a whistle stop tour of a state that a candidate hopes to represent can stir up the same amount of interest and support without being in debt to anyone, funding of that tour coming out of the campaigner's pocket.

Angelina's agreement to be Gary's campaign manager came with some concessions. First, their children Fredrick and Susan had to be an integral part of the campaign and travel about Oregon with them. She agreed that they could serve as an advance team, visiting the towns about the hub cities or towns a couple of days in advance of Gary's arrival. They would return to be with Gary and Angelina after they had spread the word through posting the posters announcing the time and place for Gary's speaking engagements. It was so helpful that the Portland media spearheaded by Lisa Teague had agreed to broadcast the progress of Gary's campaign tour, interviewing him along the way, and notifying cities or towns ahead that his campaign was coming.

Gary introduced Lisa to Angelina and his two children on the eve of their departure on the ambitious campaign trail. He made certain that Lisa understood and would mention that all of the funds for the posters, and travel expenses to include motel and restaurant expenses would be covered out of his pocket. Under no circumstances would he accept financial contributions to his campaign other than the hoped for free use of facilities where he would speak to the people along the trail. As to the cooperation of the Portland Media, well, it was considered a worthwhile news story, so the media was all too eager to broadcast his campaign progress.

The campaign was exhausting with little time to rest. Each stop was planned to last for a day with travel to the next stop set to begin after the visit of the last day at a hub city had concluded. It was a true whistle stop. By the time they had reached Eugene, fatigue was really starting to set in. Gary remarked after their visit in Eugene had concluded, "I am sure glad that we decided to focus on the cub cities and hope that the outlying town's people will travel to us to hear my message. Anything more extensive would be totally unrealistic."

Angelina nodded as she closed her eyes, too tired to response with anything more than mumbling, "Fredrick and Susan have been real troopers, branching out and hitting the surrounding towns. They must be doing quite a job because the crowds have been huge."

"I agree. They have been fantastic. I owe them big time." He paused. "It's also a blessing that the television stations in Portland took an interest in our "whistle stop" approach to campaigning. I owe Lisa big time."

By the time they had reached The Dalles the momentum of the campaign was rolling. The crowds were impressive and overflowing. The people of Oregon were starting to realize that Gary was serious about representing them and that no matter where they resided their vote mattered.

The trip through Central Oregon was glorious visiting Madras, Redmond, and Bend. After the stop in Bend was over they made a quick visit to Sisters and reveled in the beauty of the Three Sister's Mountains and its stark contrast to the flat sage brush and alfalfa adorned fields that were at their base.

South of Bend the campaign party visited La Pine and then it was off to Klamath Falls. From Klamath Falls they headed to Lakeview and wove their way through the eastern part of the state with a stop at Burns. From there, they headed towards Baker City. In Baker City, before taking the side trip to Halfway, Gary commented, "I am pleased with the reception we are getting. I am certain that not all people agree with everything I have to say, but at least they know that our motto of, "Vote for Oregon" is meaningful and heart felt. I feel that they are starting to accept me as one of their own even though I live in the dreaded valley." He smiled. "I suppose that in their eyes I am a flatlander." He chuckled. "At least I am an approachable flatlander that doesn't ignore the far reaches of the state."

Angelina nodded. "Yes, everything seems to be going well. I am looking forward to stopping in Halfway, Oregon. What a cool name. I wonder what the origin of the name comes from." She paused. "By the way, I have been meaning to tell you that I am impressed with the way you have been able to read the mood of the people you address at all of the different stops. You have cut your list of priorities down to at most three topics at each stop. So, what topic or topics will you address in Halfway?"

"I was thinking of talking about my view on gun control, tax reform, and my goals to represent all of Oregon without any particular party allegiance. What do you think?"

Suddenly a shiver raced up and down her spine. She frowned. *"I wonder why I feel this chill in my spine. It certainly isn't cold. In fact, it is flat out hot. Hmm, I wonder..."*

"Well, I would be careful when you address gun control. The people in this part of the state are pretty independent. I suspect that gun control is a sore subject for them."

Gary nodded. "I need to convince them that I don't favor abolishing the right to bear arms. I think that they will agree that assault weapons are an unnecessary evil that are used primarily to kill large numbers of people in a short span of time. An assault weapon should be reserved for use by the military or the police. They need to see that terrorists use assault weapons and the sale of them encourages the bad people to behave badly."

Hours later, Gary stood before a gathering in a reasonable sized structure along the main drag of Halfway. As he was concluding his speech, he turned to the assembled and offered, "I didn't come here to just present my ideas. I also came here to listen to you. So, if you have anything that you want to say or ask, I welcome your contribution." He paused. "I have told you that if I am fortunate enough to earn your vote that I will go back to Washington D.C. to represent you and all of Oregon. I am from the valley, but the people in the rest of the state whether it is in Southern Oregon, the coast, or out here in Eastern Oregon deserve to be heard and represented."

A man raised his hand and shouted, "How can you represent me if you plan to take away my guns?"

Gary nodded. "I don't have any intention of taking away your guns. I merely propose that we ban the sale of assault weapons that discharge close to thirty or more rounds of ammunition is a matter of seconds. Sir, I doubt that you own a weapon like I have just described, correct?"

The man nodded and then replied, "I don't hold that anyone should own such a weapon either, but the NRA suggests that passing such a restriction would be the first step in taking away our guns, taking away our right to bear arms."

Gary looked directly at him and slowly but emphatically responded, "Sir, I have no intention of standing for taking away our right to bear arms. I am a man of truth. To me deception and bending the truth is deplorable. So, when I say that all I want is to ban the sale of assault weapons that is exactly what I mean and nothing more. I will fight to the very end to protect your right to bear arms.

Just then a shadowy figure slipped by Angelina, Fredrick, and Susan. Dressed all in black the figure walked in a direct path towards Gary. Reaching Gary, he stopped and drew out a pistol, waved it in the air, and shouted, "I have something to say to you, you son of a bitch. You talk big and make it sound like we matter, but we all know different. You are just like all politicians. You're in this just for you and all of the fat cats of our society. So, take this and get a taste of the medicine that you deserve."

With that said the shadowy figure raised his gun, aimed it at Gary and fired. Four sickening sounds were heard. The first two were the reports of the two shots that the gunman fired, hitting Gary in the heart and the head. The third was the sickening sound of Gary's head hitting the wooden floor. The final sound was the muffled sound that the gun made when it was fired inside of the assassin's mouth.

Angelina stood frozen her eyes open wide in disbelief. All of the desire that she shared with her husband to represent and hear from all Oregonians whether they be from the valley, Eastern Oregon, Southern Oregon, or along the coast evaporated as she rushed to the side of her fallen husband. Even though she strongly believed and supported Gary's belief that all people's voice and vote mattered and was appreciated, at that moment only the man she loved mattered. She instantly realized that campaigning in the Willamette Valley could have possibly earned him a trip back to Washington D.C., would have been less exhausting, and so much safer. At that fleeting moment she recalled that she had pledged to help Gary to be true to his pledge, his word to represent the peoples of Oregon. Somehow it no longer mattered. The man she loved was gone, taken away by the bullets from the gun of a deranged human being that probably didn't even know why he shot and killed her husband. She recalled something she had heard when she saw the movie, Unforgiven, "When you kill a man you take away all that he is and all that he will ever be."

"Oh my God" she wailed. Why, why would anyone want to hurt you? You didn't do anything wrong. Oh my God, please help me to understand, to make some sense of this that has happened to the man that I love."

At that moment she regretted campaigning in Eastern Oregon. On the fateful day of a speech to the residents in Halfway, a community inhabited by farmers and ranchers, she felt anger and regret envelop her. All of a sudden she realized that that cold chill that had raced up and down her spine, the sky that had suddenly became dark and menacing with angry appearing clouds ever so distinctive and powerfully dominating, and the strange coloration of the sky that followed with its strange mixture of black, green, purple and even faint hints of yellow all had forecast something dreadful was about to happen. It was a sign and now she was forced to live with the result.

Kneeling beside her fallen husband, cradling his head in her lap, she knew that her life as she had known it up until then was over. She held the man she had loved for three months short of Forty-two years in her arms realizing that she would never again feel the love that she had known all of her life. The killer had extinguished the flame that had once burned so brightly.

Angelina learned later that the killer was a radical transplant from Northern Idaho, probably belonging to the White Supremes cult. She learned that he constantly spoke of, ranted and raved about liberal do-gooders that had nothing better to do than attempt to change the World order. He often screamed while standing on a lonely street corner somewhere in Halfway, "Why can't we just leave well enough alone. Change is not inevitable. Change is nothing more than the pipe dream of the Devil."

The campaign was over. It was now time for her, Fredrick, and Susan to go home. It was now time to try to pick up the pieces of their shattered lives and somehow find the courage to continue. After all, life is for the living. The departed will never be gone from their memory, but those left behind still have a life to live and contributions to make.

Chapter Twenty-Eight

Returning

Returning? Returning to where? Going home? Where is home? Is home here or there? Where is there? Who knows? Do you? Is going home merely awakening from a dream? Is it all real? Who knows? I can honestly say that I do not know. I just know that I believe that someday I will go home. Where home is, I don't know. From there, who knows?

Gary stood in the other place viewing the scene in awe. In the scene that unfolded before his eyes, Gary sadly noticed that Angelina was devastated. One moment she had been standing in the wings watching him begin his speech, and the next she was bent over him feeling his lifeless body. She screamed, "Why, why, why would someone do this? Oh God, why would anyone do this? Gary didn't hurt anyone." Her body continued to quiver with sobbing convulsions, her voice trembling as she continued, "I should have gone first. I loved him so."

Suddenly a clap of thunder and bolts of lightning dominated the environment just prior to a deluge of rain that began to pour down upon that remote village. The street in front of the hall, where just moments before Gary had stood delivering his message, was being pelted by the downpour. Everything as far as the eye could see was engulfed in rain. Water was everywhere as the rushing water, once a street, had become a raging stream of water, a small river. Residents would refer to it as a gully washer. No matter, it came suddenly and the results weren't pretty.

Gary mumbled to himself as he continued to watch the scene below, *"I don't get it. I was down there and now I'm up here watching everything that I experienced down there from up here in this other place."* He shook his head. *"I am down there, and yet I am up here and there hasn't been any lapse of time. It is almost like I'm here, but then I'm there. I guess The Source was right when it was mentioned that time does not exist. Strangely, I wonder about distance.*

How can I be here and there at the same time?"

The Source surrounded Gary as he viewed the scene in that distant world or other place. The pain he felt wasn't from the bullets that had pierced his head or entered his chest, passing through his heart. No, it was the pain that he felt for Angelina. "Why?" He turned about trying to find a focus point to direct his inquiry. "Why?"

"It is all a part of the plan, Gary. Your Earthly wife will experience what will seem to be unbearable pain. The people in Oregon will come to experience the same pain. The citizens of the United States will feel the pain because they have lost a hero. The value of the experience is when the people of the United States, the people of the World come to experience the pain, abhor what has happened and realize you weren't just a sport's hero. They will come to realize that the pain they feel is because you were more importantly a human being and that life matters. Life is precious."

The Source paused. "You have another journey to make." Gary frowned. "I do? Where am I headed now?"

"You will return to Angelina in what you might think of as a parallel existence. In your new state you will be able to see her, but she will not see you. You can't touch her and she can't touch you. You can't speak to her nor can she speak to you. However, you will be able to communicate with her, to console her, help her to pass beyond her grief, and help guide her to go on. It is up to you to find the way."

Gary frowned again, his eyebrows becoming deep furrows. "How will I be able to do that?"

The Source seemed to smile, nod its head as the message continued, "She will be influenced by you as though you were at her side. You will find a way. Look for the openings in that invisible wall that separates you from her. Find a way to go beyond your voice, your touch, and your visibility." The voice paused. "When your job is done you will again return to me."

Gary shook his head and frowned. "I don't understand. If she can't see me or hear me, how will I influence her, guide her, and console her?"

"There are ways that you will discover."

"Okay, I will try my best to do what you suggest, but I need to know if she will return. Will we be together if she returns?"

"Of course, she will return. I have already explained that to you. Don't you recall?"

Gary nodded. "I remember. I guess that I was just overcome by the newness of this adventure, the shock of seeing my Angelina suffering so much."

"That is understandable."

"Um, you didn't tell me if we would be together when she returns and when she will return."

"You will be together when she returns. When she will return is not important for you to know because it will almost seem as though you were never apart. Just remember that time means nothing here. The important issue here is the journey and how you and Angelina evolve."

"What about my parents, um and Angelina's parents, where are they? Did they return?"

"Yes Gary, everything, everyone returns to me. I have sent them on another journey."

"Will I ever see them again?"

"Yes, but it is not important to know how, or when, where or why. It will all be revealed when you are ready."

Gary nodded. "So, when do I return to her?"

His voice faded as though he had never spoken. Suddenly it was as though he had never left. At that moment he truly realized that time had no meaning. The true meaning was the journey or the distance traveled. At that moment, for the first time, he was starting to get a clue. *"It's all about distance."* He shrugged his shoulders. *"There she is. There is my beautiful Angelina. Now all I have to do is figure out how I can help her."*

Chapter Twenty-Nine

Courting Angelina

How do you get rid of a virus, cure a previously incurable disease or perhaps find a way to ease pain so that it doesn't influence how you continue on with your life? Is there always a scientific solution a medical cure, or is it possible that something else will work? A loss is a loss and it affects people differently. What is important is to somehow find a way to move on beyond the loss.

Sooner than Gary could blink an eye, he was standing beside Angelina. He reached out to touch her, and sure enough, he couldn't feel the touch of her soft smooth skin. She didn't respond to his attempt to touch her, nor did she react to his attempt to console her, whispering, "Honey, don't be sad, it's me. I will never leave you. I love you." There was neither a response nor any sort of reaction. It was as though he had never spoken. He was there, but then again, he was not.

Across the room sat their children. Louis began, "Mom, dad is gone. Susan and I are sad too. We miss him something awful, but he is gone. Life goes on. Let us know how we can help you."

Angelina smiled affectionately at her son. "Do you realize that your father has only been gone for a little over a week? Do you realize that I have hardly had time to catch my breath with all of the things that I have had to do?" Do you realize that I don't even feel as though I have had the time to truly honor your father? What can you possibly do?" She paused to collect her thoughts. "It is just enough for you to be here. I need you now more than ever. I have some decisions to make, and I will need your counsel, your advice." She paused. "Somehow with you both here I feel as though all is the same as it was before except for….."

Susan nodded her head observing the tears starting to flow down her mother's cheeks. "I know mom. Tomorrow at the celebration of his life we will have the opportunity to honor him. Greg, Lance, Louis and I will join you to honor him. All of his friends and admirers will have that same opportunity. Afterwards we will go out and hoist one for him and enjoy a nice meal. Hopefully we can laugh and enjoy talking about the joy he brought to our lives. He is gone but never forgotten."

Louis chimed in, "I am not much with words, but just know that Susan and I loved father more than words can do justice to our feelings. Our loss and yours is so hard to bear. I know that by being here we can face the future together and be strong together. We will move on together."

Angelina nodded. "On another subject, I just wish that those vultures that are after me to run for the Senate in your dad's place would stop bothering me. His body wasn't even cold before they started pressing me to continue on in his place." She paused. "As you know I supported your father in all that he was trying to do. I probably know better than anyone what he hoped to accomplish, but I don't think that I am the one to carry on. Somehow I feel that I have another mission. God, oh God how I wish your father were here so that he could…"

Louis slowly rose to his feet and approached his mom, kneeling before her. Slowly he took her hands in his. "Do you believe that what he was trying to accomplish is yours to carry on? If you have doubts about running for the Senate, I am sure that you have another mission that is just as important to pursue. You have Susan's and my complete support no matter what course you choose to take. Don't make a hasty decision. Take the time to make a decision."

"Thank you." She paused. "To a degree I do feel that I should carry on for Gary, to do what he had set out to accomplish. However, I think that I have a more important mission to accomplish. I really don't think that I'm the one to carry on in his place."

Louis shook his head. "Mom, you are so wrong and yet so right. Some would argue that you are the only person that can carry on in his place because you know best what he wanted to accomplish. I would argue that dad would want you to do your own thing and pursue what you believe is right for you. I feel the same way."

"Are you sure? Somehow I feel so conflicted. One part of me feels that he would want me to serve in his place while another part of me thinks that he wants me to address the homeless issue." She paused. Lowering her head she mumbled, "Once upon a time, not long ago, he told me that he wanted me to pursue my dreams if he were to be taken first."

Standing in full view of the proceedings, Gary nodded, and said, *"Atta girl, Angelina. Louis means well and is correct in telling you that I would want you to do your own thing, but he doesn't know what you really want to do. Only you know. All you have to do is dig deep into your soul and you will know. You need to know that whatever course you take I will be right there with you to support you."*

Susan offered, "Mom, I know that Louis and you both have good points. Personally, I think that you need to run. Oregon needs you and it is painfully evident that our country needs you. Run, please run and you will have all of the family's support. We have come this far. I feel it would be such a loss to quit now."

Gary felt defeated. He focused all of his thoughts trying to direct them as directly at his beautiful Angelina. *"Don't listen to Susan my darling. She means well, but she, they don't know what you really want to do. You have to do it your way by doing your own thing. I am gone from your life as you know it, but I am still with you. I love you. I love our children, but they don't know what is best for you. Only you know. Follow your heart. Do your own thing."*

Angelina frowned. "Strangely I feel his presence. What about you, Susan, are you getting the same feelings? What about you Louis? Do you feel his presence, your dad's presence?"

Susan nodded. "Yeah, I don't know how to explain what I am feeling. It is as though dad is talking around me. Somehow I feel a conflict of thoughts, of ideas."

Louis frowned. "I don't know what you are talking about. Dad is gone. How can you feel his presence?"

"Honey, you have in the past. You told me so." Angelina shook her head. "This is all too weird."

Gary smiled as he headed for Angelina's office, continuing to listen to the banter that was taking place. In the office he noticed that what was once his computer was on, but in the sleep mode. He reached out towards the idle computer and jerked back when his gesture of touching it seemed to cause the laptop to suddenly awaken, displaying on the screen an image of a pasture with horses in it. He smiled. *"Can you believe it? I am looking at what used to be my computer, and there is the icon that I used to touch to open up my email. Hmm, what if I hit the 'Google Chrome' icon? Nope, that doesn't do it. Focus Gary. Focus on the 'Google Chrome' icon."*

Momentarily the screen displayed a long narrow box. *"Hmm, focus on the 'G' key."* A moment later 'Sign In' was displayed. *"Focus on 'Sign In'.* Another moment passed and the 'Sign In' was displayed. "Hmm, focus on 'Sign In'."

"Wow! I'm in. Thank God I checked the box, remember me. Focus on 'Compose'. A moment passed and a place to type in an addressee was displayed at the top of the display. *"Focus on the 'A' key.* Angelina's name appeared. *"Focus on 'Angelina'."*

Gary was in. All he had to do was focus on a message to send to Angelina's computer. What would it be? How could he reach her without freaking her out?"

"I know what to say. Yeah, I will tell her to do her thing. Yeah, 'DO YOUR THING."

Moments later he was done. He had somehow caused, "DO YOUR THING" to appear. He focused on 'send'. He smiled noting that the message had been sent. Now he had to hope that she would open her computer and read the message. Would it freak her out? It was a risk he had to take. He had made contact, or at least he had opened the door.

In the living room Angelina acknowledged her children's prodding and the weird feelings that she was experiencing, "I have heard your suggestions. It is now time for me to process what you have said. I hope that I can make a decision that is best for me, best for you and best for everyone. If you don't mind, I would like to be alone. Come by tomorrow before the ceremony. If you like we can ride together to the Lake Oswego auditorium where your dad's celebration of life is to be held. I am not dismissing what you have said. I just need time to think. I just need some time to myself. I promise to give you an answer soon. I love you both more than words can say."

A few moments after her children had left she stepped into the office. She stood staring at Gary's computer for a moment and frowned. *"That is strange. His computer is, um, it looks as though someone has just used it. No, that can't be."*

She shrugged her shoulders. *"Why not, I'll check my emails and then shut the computers down and retire to the bedroom so that I can think about what I am going to do. Weird, everything has just been plain weird since he died. It is one thing to feel Gary's presence, but for Susan to feel it also? Am I losing my mind or am I just letting my sadness control my thoughts?"*

She noticed that she had two emails. The first one quickly found its way into the trash. The next email was strangely sent to her from Gary's address. *"What the fuck? What in the hell is going on here? I have an email from Gary?"* She nodded her head slowly as though she was processing all that was happening to her. *"That makes sense. Gary probably sent me an email before…"*

She opened the email and recoiled at the display that read -

DO YOUR THING.

She frowned, thinking to herself, *"Am I going crazy or…? Never in a hundred years will I be able to explain this. What's more, I'm not even going to try."* She reached for the delete button. *"I'm going to delete the message. If I don't, somebody will think that I've completely lost it. They'll think that I am now writing messages to myself from Gary's computer as though Gary is trying to contact me. Hmm, I wonder? On second thought, who gives a damn? Nobody is going to look at my computer. Hmm, maybe I should shut down Gary's computer."*

Standing by her, Gary recoiled in terror. *"Don't shut down my computer. Angelina, don't shut down my computer."* Quickly he focused on writing another message on his computer and then focused on sending it. While Angelina debated whether to shut down Gary's computer or not, she was alarmed to note that her computer displayed another message from Gary.

The message read-

DON'T

Gary had established contact with his beautiful Angelina. Would she be able to handle the weirdness of what was going on? He nodded as she shrugged her shoulders and mumbled, *"What the fuck. What is leaving his computer on going to hurt?"* She smiled. *"Maybe he is trying to make contact."* She frowned. *"Come on Angelina. You know that can't be. Gary is dead. There is no way that he can…"*

The next day, shortly after the celebration of life concluded, standing near the stage where all that wanted to speak had stood, Angelina motioned to her children. "I thought that I would tell you that I will listen to what the vultures have to say and offer. I have listened to your ideas, but as you know, I am an independent woman and will do what I think is best. I so appreciate your input and want you to know that I love you both so very, very much."

Louis and Susan nodded their approval. Louis offered, "The decision is yours to make. Please know that whatever you decide to do you have our complete support. Could I make a suggestion?"

Angelina smiled. "Of course you can. You always come up with the best ideas."

"Well, Susan and I feel that you should tell the vultures, as you put it, that you need just a little more time. Mention to them that you have a lot weighing on your mind and need just a little more time."

"That is wise advice. I know they are in a hurry with the election approaching, but what will another few day matter? They certainly don't want a reluctant candidate trying to win the Senate seat."

Just then a beautiful lady approached. "Angelina, Angelina Mallon, I am Lisa Teague."

Angelina recoiled. *"So this is the mysterious Lisa Teague, the news lady from Channel Two that helped give Gary's campaign tour news coverage. Shit, she is knockdown gorgeous. If I were a man I would be all over that. I wonder…"*

Lisa began, "I am the mystery lady that has been, was helping give coverage to Gary's campaign tour. Um, I have a few things to tell you if you have a moment."

Angelina nodded. "Sure, I have a few moments. Um, you are really quite attractive Lisa. I didn't know just how…"

Lisa smiled. "Thank you for the very nice compliment. Um, I want you to know that you were a very lucky woman. Your husband loved you more than words can say." She paused. "When I first met Gary I thought that he was just another sports hero that was trying to take a great sports career and turn it into personal gain. I was wrong." She nodded. "He was the real deal. He honestly believed that he could make a difference. More importantly, he was hell bent to go out there to walk the talk."

Angelina nodded. "Yes, he really did believe all that he said along the campaign trail." She paused. "Lisa, I guess I should tell you that when I heard about you from Gary I was a bit jealous. When I see you now, I know why."

Lisa smiled. "Angelina, excuse me for sounding harsh, but you don't have a clue. Your husband loved only one woman and that woman was you. I was merely someone that wanted to help him realize his dream and all I was to him was that helpful person that he could rely on. Can we move on and get to the point of why I approached you?"

"Sure, why not? I am open to listening and hearing what you have to say."

Lisa nodded. "Well, first of all, Gary mentioned to me several times that if something happened to him that I was to protect you from the wolves so as to allow you to do your own thing. If you wish to run for the senate I will do all that I can to help you. If you choose not to run I will do everything to ensure that the wolves leave you alone."

Angelina smiled. "That is very reassuring, Lisa. You don't know how much I appreciate what you have said. By the way, I think that I owe you an apology."

Lisa frowned. "For what, why do you feel that you owe me an apology?"

Angelina chuckled. "Come on Lisa. You are not an ugly child. I guess that I thought that there might have been something going on between you and my husband."

Lisa sternly replied, "Don't even go there, Angelina. Gary didn't even know that I existed. I was never more than a helper to make his campaign more viable. You were the love of his life."

"Thank you, Lisa. So, do you suppose that we can be friends?" "Definitely, I would like nothing more."

Angelina motioned with her head in the direction of two men apparently waiting for her conversation with Lisa to end. "Do you see those two guys over there, the ones in the Wall Street suits? Please stay with me. When they start to hit on me I am going to need your support and presence."

Lisa smiled. "So, I am going to be like a blocker for the runner in a football sweep. My role is to knock down all opposition, run interference, right? "

Angelina smiled. "That is the idea, but be gentle. I don't want anybody thinking that I am a brute." She paused as she noticed them approaching. She whispered, "I am going to tell them that I need a week to decide if my heart is in a campaign. I will tell them that I have to decide if Gary's name recognition is enough to carry me to the top and win the election. I have to have the time to decide if that is enough to cause me to run. More importantly I have to decide if I want to run."

Lisa smiled and patted Angelina on the back, whispering, "You go, girl. I've got your back."

Angelina nodded and then walked toward the men waiting to talk to her. "So, gentlemen, I have decided that I need some time, a week, to decide what I want to do. My husband has only been gone for a little over a week. Christ, his body is barely cold. I have to decide if I am a viable candidate. More importantly, I have to decide if I even want to run, if my heart is in this to give everything I have to give. Tell me what you think. Why do you feel that I am or can be a viable candidate?"

One of the men, John Chamberlin, offered, "I respect your wishes." He smiled. "I see that you have Lisa Teague serving as your bodyguard. She is tough and I know better than to tangle with her. We will give you the week that you have requested." He paused. "You asked why we think that you are a viable candidate. Well, we believe that you can be and are the right candidate to carry on in Gary's place because you and you alone know exactly what Gary wanted to do. I will add that if you do decide to run you must try to avoid trying to be something that you aren't. The public can spot a phony a mile away. If you speak as though you really believe what you are basing the campaign on, you'll do just fine. I will be with you as the assistant campaign manager. Since I see Lisa Teague, the anchor on KATU, with you I don't have to ask if you know her, but just a little information that you might want to process."

Angelina interrupted, "I just met her, but I certainly know who she is. She has been, was really helpful to my husband's cause, his campaign. I really like her style. She appears to be honest and forthright." She paused. "She advised my husband about how to run his whistle stop campaign tour and gave him excellent coverage. I fact, she got all of the Portland TV stations to help cover his campaign tour."

"Well, if you agree, she will be your campaign manager should you decide to run. She knows how to deal with the media, is savvy on the political issues, and will help guide you through the rough spots because she knows how to handle the press. I will just be happy to assist her in whatever manner I can."

Angelina inquired, "What about her job at KATU"

Lisa interrupted, "Well, she will take a temporary leave of absence if she thinks you have a chance to pull off the miracle of winning the Senate seat. She has set time aside for a meeting with you tomorrow if you are available." Lisa chuckled. "Pardon me for using the pronoun, she, but I really don't like to be a secondhand topic of conversation when I am present."

Angelina nodded. "I can be available, but as I said, I still need a week to process everything." She paused. "You know, I can't say that I know much about the political scene, who is good and who is not, but from what you have told me I am okay with you serving as my manager should I decide to run. John I am also okay with having you serve as her assistant if she agrees and if I run." She paused, glancing at her children who had stepped aside and remained completely silent. "Now if you will excuse me, my children and I have an engagement. We are going to lift a couple and have a nice meal in honor of my husband." She smiled. "It is an old Irish custom that I respect very much."

In the other dimension, Gary shook his fist. *"Atta girl, just be you. It was always better than good enough for me. Just do your thing."*

Angelina turned away from John and Lisa and began walking towards her children, stopped and turned back toward the two men and Lisa.

"One more thing, this campaign, if I run, is going to be all about the people. It was important to my husband and it is to me that all the people of Oregon feel as though they have been heard. If I'm in the race, I will campaign as hard in the far reaches of the state as I do in the population rich Willamette Valley."

John Chamberlin nodded. "Just know that the vote in the valley is crucial. You will win or lose the election here. I believe that it is important to saturate the valley just prior to the primaries."

"I don't doubt your wisdom for one minute, but you have to believe that if I am going to come across as authentic, the real deal, I have to try to appeal to everyone in this state. Just remember that a farmer in distant Oregon is going to be just as affected by what I do or don't do as the executive in downtown Portland. Every voter in this state counts and I will be going after every last one of them. No voter is more special than any other." She smiled. "If I run, that is the way it is going to be."

"What?" Reaching her children she noted a sly smile on Fredrick's face.

Fredrick chuckled. "Mom, Lisa is a real fox. Damn, her long brunette hair perfectly frames her beautiful face. Her big brown eyes reach out and grab you, and, oh what a fantastic body she has. I swear that she looks like a model, a centerfold out of Playboy. Of course she is wearing all of her clothing."

Angelina shook her head. "Fredrick, you are such a guy."

Susan quickly chimed in, "Mom, Fredrick is disgusting. All he thinks about, all men think about is how big a woman's boobs are, how good looking they are, and if they have a cute ass."

"Now, now, Susan, you wouldn't be pleased if men didn't look at you, would you?"

"I honestly don't know. I just know that I get tired of the whistles and the stares I get by some guys."

"Honey, your dad looked at me like that all of his life. The difference between his behavior and that of some men is that your dad did it out of love."

Susan frowned. "So, how do you know that their stares or whatever is out of love?"

Angelina paused reflecting upon her daughter's question. "Um, the best answer that I can give you is that you will know when it is an authentic look as opposed to a look from a predator. Men that show a definite interest in you for who you are and not just what you look like will always be a gentleman and treat you like a lady."

Chapter Thirty

Decisions, Decisions, Decisions

How do you get rid of a virus, cure a previously incurable disease? Is there always a scientific solution, or is it possible that something else will work, perhaps a different direction? How do you decide? Maybe you weigh all options making a Pro/Con list and go with the logical results.

The next day, Angelina was finishing her morning coffee and hurriedly gulping down the last of her toast and jelly when she heard a knock at the front door. Opening the door she nodded as she acknowledged her son and daughter's presence. She stood there for a moment looking at them. *"Fredrick is such a handsome young man. I think that he got the best of both his father and me. In no time at all the ladies will be swarming to try to put their brand on him. He is tall, has a well-toned, athletic body, and even white teeth. He is a hunk, a catch."*

She then turned her attention to Susan. *"Hmm, my daughter is a real looker. She complains about the guys ogling, but what can she expect. She is a beautiful young woman and quite well put together. Some man is going to enjoy her hopefully as much as her father enjoyed me. I just hope that she gets rid of her suspicious views of what men are looking for and allows them to get close enough for her to make a calculated decision that is well thought out and comes from her heart."*

Fredrick was the first to speak. "Well, are you just going to stand there and gawk at us?"

Angelina smiled. "Is it improper for a proud mother to study her handsome son and beautiful daughter? She stepped aside and allowed them to enter. "Um, I have to run in a few moments. I have an appointment to talk with Lisa Teague."

Fredrick smiled. "Lucky you, want me to stand in for you?"

Susan shook her head. "Fredrick you are such a guy. I swear that all you guys think with is the appendage that hangs between your legs."

Angelina raised her hands. "Stop it right now before this turns into a cat fight or a full blown spat. Actually, I am going down to tell her that I don't think that I am the person that should run for the senate."

Susan shook her head. "Mom, will you at least hear her out before you drop out?"

Angelina nodded. "I promise that is what I will do, but I am pretty sure that I want to go in a different direction. I have some ideas about solving the homeless issue and I want to see if Lisa can run interference for me.

Standing beside her, Gary pumped his fist. *"Atta girl, you do your own thing. You have always wanted to do something special with the homeless issue and this is the perfect time to broach the subject."*

It was the first of February and it was colder than a well digger's ass. There were other terms that could have been used to describe the white blanket that covered the ground and the chill that made it even more severe because of the 20 mile per hour wind, but most people didn't know about the Kea Bird and making reference to a Witch's anatomy just didn't see appropriate. The drive into Portland and up Sandy Boulevard was tricky at best, so when Angelina at last knocked on Lisa Teague's office door at Channel Two headquarters she was grateful that she didn't have to navigate the slick, icy streets any longer and could enjoy the comfort of her warm surroundings.

After the formalities of the greeting had concluded, Lisa got right down to business. "I have to warn you that the campaign trail is long and tiring. You have already experienced a huge portion of that, but there is much, much more to come because now the voters, if you run, have to switch gears and be open to your message. With that said, I want you to know that I respect you for considering a run, um, of attempting to carry on for Gary. Shit, I am so sorry." She frowned. "How else am I supposed to say it?"

"Gary died. Just call it what it is. He is my deceased husband." She paused and lowered her head. When she again looked up into Lisa's face, concern and caring were clearly present. "Lisa, just so you know, I miss him so much. I am still young, in good health and absolutely loved having sex with my husband. My breasts ache for his touch. The thoughts of having him make love to me are overwhelming. I often imagine that this is just a dream and that he will again walk through the front door of our home, but then I come to my senses as I realize that he isn't coming back to me. It is absolutely devastating."

Lisa nodded. "I understand, I think." She grinned. "I am not married, so I am not sure that I have ever felt the ache to have my breasts touched by anyone. He must have been very special."

Angelina nodded. "He was. If I agree to do this, run for the Senate, you have to know that running for the Senate was his dream. I was merely willing to support him and do all that I could do to help him realize that dream. I suppose that part of me wants to complete the job. Another part of me, well, I…." She paused, tears welling up in her eyes. "I don't know. I honestly don't know. I just wish that he were here to advise me."

"Angelina, if he were here we wouldn't be having his conversation." Lisa paused. "What do you really want to do?" Lisa reached across and took Angelina's hand. "Are you really sure that you are up to doing this? We are starting out so far behind. Essentially we are starting from scratch. The funds you have raised, none to my knowledge, won't even buy a two minute slot on one TV station."

Angelina nodded. "I know. It was Gary's dream to touch base with every possible place in Oregon, a road campaign tour of the state to win the vote by demonstrating that he wanted to represent all of the people. He wanted everyone to know that he didn't have his hand in anyone's pocket. He wanted to demonstrate that by voting for him the voters were voting for somebody without big money connections. He wanted people to know that he owed nobody except the people he would represent. He refused to be bought."

Lisa nodded. "That is an admirable goal and I can support that, but in reality it will not win you a spot in the November finals. The Republican and Democrat candidates will out spend you and make your run for office irrelevant. There won't be enough town hall opportunities or whatever to even come close to win let alone close the gap. People will consider voting for you a wasted vote." She paused and considered carefully what she was about to say. "Just so you know, I would have voted for Gary. Voting for you, well, that is another matter. You are a nice lady, but…."

"I know. I am not my husband. I would be viewed as a substitute, a second stringer." She paused. "So you think that I am wasting my time?"

Lisa nodded. "I agreed to meet with you, be your campaign manager because I was asked to by John Chamberlin. He is hoping that Gary's name appeal and recognition and lots of hard work could win the day and carry you on to the finals where your voice could truly be heard because the important money people would come to support you."

Angelina snarled, "That is not what I want. I don't need or want the big money people. If I can't win without them, well….." Angelina pursed her lips and nodded in recognition of the reality of the situation. "So, I am not only wasting my time, but I am wasting yours as well." She paused. "Again, I will say that I am not interested in the money people and neither was Gary. Maybe I have another mission that I need to pursue."

"Sadly, as I see it, that is about the size of it." "One question, when is the first debate?"

Lisa frowned. "Do you have in mind what I think you…?"

Insistent, Angelina again asked, "When is the first debate?"

"KATU is sponsoring a debate in two weeks." She frowned and then nodded her head as though a grand idea was being formed. "Well, I could get you on the panel of candidates for the debate and I could even argue the case that all candidates should be given equal time. We might even get more than an hour slot for the debate if I lobby hard enough."

"Would it be expensive?"

Lisa smiled. "No, if you are included in the debate it won't cost you a dime." She paused again appearing to be deep in thought. "Yes, I might be able to pull some strings." She paused. "We need to come up with a positon on some of the key issues."

Angelina frowned, "Enlighten me if you don't mind my show of ignorance."

"The old standbys would be the economy, jobs, tax reform, education, immigration, congress' ineffectiveness and inability to do America's work, and…"

Angelina interrupted, "I can speak to those issues, but I think that perhaps talking about the homeless issue could be a break through issue that the candidates might not be prepared to speak to."

Lisa smiled. "I like your enthusiasm and your creativity, but you have to understand that the moderator will have some issues to throw at the candidates for discussion with a definite time limit devoted to each issue. If we are lucky, we might be able to discuss four major issues. Sadly, the homeless issue would be so far down the list of priorities to bring into the discussion that it probably won't even see the light of day."

Angelina nodded her head. "I am afraid that you are right. It is a huge issue for Portland, for the rest of the country, and for me, but nobody really wants to even recognize that it is a problem until they have to wade through an encampment of the homeless with the liter that they indiscriminately deposit wherever they decide to drop it. I suppose it is called out of sight, out of mind or maybe even if I look the other way it doesn't exist."

Lisa smiled. "I have an idea. You have not made a public announcement about your plans to run for the Senate, right?"

"Does my husband's announcement prior to his death count?"

"No, as far as the public is concerned, you are just the grieving widow." She paused. "Sorry, I didn't mean to be cruel. I had to be honest."

"No apology is necessary. Please continue. I am all ears."

"First, I think that you should reconsider running for the Senate. Frankly, I don't think that you have a prayer." She paused. "The Governor is interested in doing some big things about the homeless issue that you are interested in. With the right person's help, he believes that he can get the financial support to construct a huge homeless facility in Portland as a starter. It would be a model to show mayors in the rest of the state that the homeless issue is solvable. His idea is to make it a non-profit venture. With the right person leading the way, he believes that he can shake the billionaire tree and come up with the funds to construct the facility, get the necessary donations to keep it going without having to impact the state budget, and get those poor homeless people off the streets. He wants it to be sustainable." Angelina nodded her head. "I have lots of ideas."

"Just know John Chamberlin is very interested in the homeless issue as well. I am certain that the Governor would be interested in listening to what you have to say."

Angelina cocked her head as if to say, "Are you serious?"

"Would John be a viable candidate for filling the position that the Governor is thinking about filling?"

"I don't know if John would be interested in leading the effort. That is something you might consider talking with him about." She paused. "Just for my information, what would you need for a salary if the Governor decides you are the one to head of the project, become the executive director?"

Angelina shrugged her shoulders. "I don't know. I really do not have any financial needs as Gary left me very well off and very secure. I would settle for a good insurance plan and travel expenses. I suppose I would have to pencil out if there are other expenses I might incur. One thing is certain. I would want and need to have an assistant and hope that he or she would be given a reasonable salary."

Lisa nodded. "So, it sounds like you are essentially volunteering your services."

Angelina smiled. "I suppose that would be an accurate assumption. So, it appears that you won't have to take that leave of absence with me backing out of the race. Will John be okay with my decision? He seemed to be quite eager to get me to run."

Lisa smiled. "What would your thoughts be about him being your salaried assistant? I am certain that he would jump at the idea if it were offered to him. By the way, just so you know, John aggressively pushed to get you to run for the Senate because he so believed in what your husband stood for and because he felt that you would be the ideal person to get his message before the voters. He will understand and support your decision to go a different direction whether you decide to hire him as you assistant or not." She paused. "Of course all of this is just informal conversation. At this point, we're just in the talking stages. You still have to be appointed by the Governor." She smiled. "I can get you an interview with the Governor if you are serious. I have his ear."

In that other dimension, Gary pumped his fist. *"Go for it girl. You will be terrific. You will be going so far beyond my dreams that..., I guess that I should write her a message to let her know that she is headed in the right direction."*

Angelina nodded emphatically. "Yes, oh yes, I am very, very interested. I have been preparing for this opportunity for a long, long time."

After the meeting with Lisa had ended and Angelina had returned home, she went into her office. *"I need to sit down and figure out what I anticipate my expenses to be and get prepared for the interview with the Governor. What I say to him has to be well organized or he will dismiss me as just another voice that has little or no credibility."*

Gary sitting beside her before what had been his computer once again, after mentally pushing the "compose" button, clicked on Angelina's email address in the address line of the new message display. He thought, *"This is so cool. Even though I can't make direct contact with Angelina, I can message her. I don't know how all this works, but I suppose that The Source knows and is somehow guiding me and helping me to get messages to her. I am confident this is what The Source meant when it was mentioned that I was being sent here to help Angelina move on with her life."*

After a few strokes on the keyboard, he was done. His message to Angelina was simple but direct.

Go for it girl. The homeless need you. You are the right person for the job.

Two days later, thanks to Lisa, Angelina sat in the Governor's office at his invitation. Waiting for him to enter, she allowed her thoughts to take liberties. *"Thanks to Lisa, it appears that I have an opportunity to realize a dream that I didn't really think was possible until now. I have been so focused on being a mother, a wife and doing all of my singing and piano gigs, that I.... Damn, I am absolutely certain that Gary approves. For some reason I think that I always knew that he would. The latest message on the computer that was waiting for me when I came home from my meeting with Lisa was just too weird. I wonder. Anyway, if you are listening, Gary, just know that I love you.*

You are the only man for me. I am yours for eternity. I am going to go for it. Keep your fingers crossed for me."

The Governor entered, walked to his desk, and turned to face Angelina. "Thank you for coming to Salem to meet with me. Lisa Teague had nothing but nice things to say about you. You come highly recommended. I want you to know that I respect Lisa's opinion." He paused as he lowered himself into his chair. "To be clear, is it true that you have no intentions of running for the United States senate?"

"No sir." Angelina's face reddened. "What I mean to say, Governor Hathaway is that I have no intentions of running for the senate. After my meeting with Lisa I discovered that the dream, my goal of what I really want to do may lie elsewhere, um, helping to solve the homeless issue. You are aware that I recently lost my husband?"

"Yes, and I want you to know how truly sorry I am. It was a tragic loss. I had high hopes that his quest to win the Senate seat would be successful."

"Thank you. For a while I was determined to carry on with his dream of going to Washington D.C. in an attempt to make a difference, but now I have another dream, an objective that I suppose I have had for many, many years. I share your vision about what to do with the homeless. I would like to see if you and I can come to an agreement as to how we can make strides to solve the homeless issue. That is what I really want to do, and I hope you will allow me to share with you some of my ideas."

The Governor smiled, clasped his hands together, leaning forward to place his elbows on his desk. "Well now, that is exactly what I was hoping to hear. Why don't you share with me what you have in mind? You have seen the plans for the building that I have proposed and hope to have constructed in Portland to house the homeless haven't you?"

"Yes, Lisa showed them to me. Um, I have studied them very carefully. Maybe that is where we should begin." Her mind wandered as she prepared to speak about the housing plan. *"Governor Hathaway isn't as old as he appears to be in the photographs I've seen in the newspaper. Other than graying hair, he could easily pass for a man of maybe fifty, fifty-five years of age at most. He isn't really handsome. He's just, um, impressive for a lack of a better word. Maybe his impressiveness comes from his height. Damn, he is one tall dude. I wonder if he played basketball. Hmm, I wonder how many other candidates he's interviewed or plans to interview. Maybe part of his attraction to the voting public is his seemingly acute interest in listening to what people have to say. He comes across as being a powerful man. He also seems to be open to ideas. That is very refreshing."*

The Governor nodded. "I agree. By all means let's start with how the building could be used most effectively. By the way, we don't have to be in a hurry. I opened up my schedule completely for you. The afternoon is yours. Please, let me hear your thoughts and how you might run with my idea if appointed to the position I am thinking of creating."

"Thank you. Well, to begin, I think I have this correct when I say that the building you want built or have remodeled to fit the plans I have seen will have twelve floors of dwellings to accommodate the homeless with an ability to expand upward. Each floor will have four apartments for families of three or more people with the other fourteen apartments suited for single or two person occupancy. At a minimum I believe that pencils out to accommodate a minimum of 612 homeless people. Am I correct in assuming that there is room for expansion if necessary?"

The Governor nodded. "That is essentially correct, but…"

"Excuse me for interrupting, Governor, but to continue, I suggest that the lobby floor could be used as the resident dining room and kitchen. It should also include a party room, and a lounge for the residents to get together or for social functions. Thus far my analysis of your plan indicates there would be thirteen floors."

Governor Hathaway smiled. *"This woman is very perceptive and has a strong sense of where this could go."* Nodding the governor suggested, "Please continue, Angelina. So far I really like what I am hearing."

Feeling a sense of reassurance, Angelina nodded and continued, "Let me see, there could be two floors located below the lobby floor. The first basement floor could be used to house the laundry service for the residents, a workout facility, and a place to store cleaning equipment and the necessary tools needed for maintenance and repairs. The second basement floor or the lowest level could be dedicated to the storage for food supplies, a walk-in cooler and freezer and the central heating and cooling system. I would suggest that the entire system be a central air heating/cooling system with a heat pump working in conjunction with an electric furnace." Angelina paused. "Are you with me so far?"

The governor smiled. "You are doing just fine. Please continue."

Nodding her head to display pleasure with his remark, she continued, "I have to say that the building you propose to house the homeless is one huge mother, a most impressive structure." She ducked her head, her cheeks taking on a crimson glow. "Pardon the expression, but the place will be really big. It appears that it will occupy a city block. The construction costs must be enormous?"

The governor nodded. "The costs are substantial, but it will come exclusively from donated money. When the building is completed and ready for occupancy, it will be completely paid for, and there will be a surplus of money available for at least a year's operation. All of this will not cost the State of Oregon a single penny."

"So, I take it that you have some donors lined up?"

"Actually, I have several. In fact, I think that we have enough donated financial support for at least a three year run before we have to come up with any new capital. After that, as a non-profit organization, the operational costs will be borne by fund raising. The only prayer I have of selling this to the legislature is that we won't have to tap into state resources to operate it." He frowned. "I suppose you realize that dealing with the homeless isn't exactly a popular concept. How does it go, "Out of sight, out of mind?"

Angelina nodded. "You hit the nail on the head and I want you to know that I am impressed Governor Hathaway, very impressed." She paused. "I don't want to get the cart before the horse, but I just want you to know that before I continue, I am very hopeful that I will be chosen to lead this program." She paused. "I think that I have to suggest that your building plan does not include one very important offering."

The governor frowned. "What would that be?"

"Many of the homeless are accustomed to living outside. A building represents confinement to them. As long as they have cover and are sheltered from wind and rain, they are perfectly content to continue living outside. I would suggest that in your proposed building that there will be provisions made for those people as well. Even though they may choose to live outside they can still take their meals inside and have the use of the bathroom facilities. Actually, that would be expected of them."

"Hmm, you say that some would live outside." He frowned. "Please explain how that would work."

"Well, there could be an extension to the building, cover of course. This extension would have a cement floor. It would be walled in with the walls being about three feet high. It would be open, but offer complete shelter from the rain and partial shelter from the wind. Those that choose to live there would have their own tent to live in." She paused. "It would be so important that adequate waste deposit cans or whatever be provided so that the residents would be able to keep the area clean. I wouldn't want us to just move the homeless and their litter to some place just to get them out of sight from the general public. I would want to encourage those people to develop a sense of pride in where they live."

The governor nodded. "I see you have really thought about this plan and how it can best accommodate the homeless. I am impressed."

"Thank you governor, I just feel that it is important to do one's homework."

As an act of protest, he held up is hands. "Please, in this informal gathering, why don't you just address me as, Tom?"

"Thank you Tom. Something that is worth mentioning when we talk about the site, um the location for the homeless' home is where it will be located."

"Do you have a recommendation?"

"I do." She paused. "You are familiar with the location of the Tilikum Bridge?"

He smiled. "I am. Yes indeed, I most certainly am."

"Well, there is more than ample room for the new building with more than adequate parking in the vacant lot that abuts the bridge. Um, that would be south of the bridge. It is close to OHSU, so it makes it very convenient for providing the necessary health care if we can get OHSU on board with the plan."

"That is a terrific idea. I confess that the idea crossed my mind, but to locate at the site you propose would have to be approved by the Mayor of Portland and the owner of the land." He smiled. Maybe that person, if the land is still in the hands of a private owner, will become one of our donors."

Angelina smiled, nodding her head. "Now, if you will, Tom, I would like to tell you how I view the day to day operation working and what the qualifications would be acceptable for a homeless person or family to be accepted and housed there."

The governor smiled. "Hmm, that is so very important if we are going to sell this concept to the legislature." He nodded. "Yes we should have expectations for the people we serve. This is what I am interested in. I have some thoughts, but I want to hear your ideas."

Angelina cocked her head. "Hmm, where should I begin?" She paused taking time to look at the expectant Governor. "Well, first of all, no drugs should be permitted. As you know, with the homeless there is a drug dependency issue. To be admitted a homeless person would have to promise to remain drug free with our assistance. If they can't remain clean, we will have to turn them away, evict them. We should not be viewed as a sponsor and supporter of drug usage. Otherwise the public will think that all we're doing is housing a bunch of drug addicts and encouraging them to continue with that pattern of life they experienced and practiced on the street. If we think that the homeless issue is volatile now, think what it would be if we didn't draw the line and refuse to allow drug usage to occur in the homeless facility."

The Governor nodded. "I totally agree. I suspect that one of the reasons that you are recommending the Tilikum site is because we can get help from the staff at OHSU to maintain a drug free environment." He paused. "You say evict them if they don't comply with our NO DRUG policy. What do you propose we do with them?"

Angelina frowned. "Quite frankly Governor, I have not allowed my thinking to go there to go that far. I guess I could say that I don't have a clue. I think that is an area where we need some help from other sources." She paused. "If we evict them because they violate our NO DRUG policy, without a backup plan we will just put them back on the street. That should not be an option."

The Governor nodded his head. "I like your honesty, and I agree that if we encounter that problem we should have a backup plan that has been thought out very carefully. I also agree that we need to consult other people to get their input."

"That is exactly how I feel!" Angelina smiled. "The old saying that two heads is better than one certainly applies in this case. Hmm, well, moving along, I stress that the homeless would have to agree to remain drug free. Although I have already covered that issue I feel that it is so important that it is worth mentioning again. Um, secondly, if a person comes to us with mental issues, they have to agree to take their prescribed medication. That will necessitate us working in cooperation with OHSU to get volunteer medical help to care for those poor souls. Right now they are the forgotten people, some of which are veterans."

"Bravo! You have struck a friendly chord with that idea. Please continue."

Angelina nodded, smiling. "Third, all people whether homeless or not should have access to a place where they can keep themselves clean and go to the bathroom. A part of keeping clean is having clean clothing to wear, and that is why I addressed the need for a laundry facility earlier. It is important that the resident's clothing can be washed and dried on a regular basis. By the way, I also feel that it is very important to have shower and lavatory facilities on each floor for men and women. They should be separated." She paused. "We aren't just providing the homeless with a shelter to get them off the street. We are providing them with a place where they can reclaim their dignity and feelings of self-worth."

The governor nodded. "I couldn't agree more."

"As I have said, and it can't be over stated, the people that would live in the facility would have an opportunity to reclaim their dignity, self-worth, and pride. A part of allowing them to reclaim their dignity is that they should be able to work and earn some money for the work they do. I feel very strongly that meaningful work is a pathway to elevating a person's feeling of self-worth." She paused. "Another part of my plan would be to provide them with an ability to govern themselves under the guidance of the executive director and his or her assistant."

"Let's stop right there. You have brought up two more issues. I suppose they would be provisions four and five under your plan. First, tell me about a resident having the ability to earn money."

Angelina chuckled. "I anticipated your response. That is a concern that I am certain will be scrutinized by the public as well. Well, there are things that have to be done around the facility such as preparing meals, cleaning the facility, doing simple maintenance, and doing the laundry. I am certain that there are more things, but... I would propose a salary somewhere near minimum wage be given to the residents that choose to and are selected to do these tasks. There would be other residents that would be capable of working outside the facility, but because of circumstances beyond their control they have been unable to get a job. No employer will even interview a prospective employee if they show up for an interview looking like they have slept on the streets, stink, and are dirty. We can help facilitate their reentry into society and the work force."

The governor nodded. "I doubt that if a person is homeless they can even have access to knowing about job openings. Angelina, I like what I am hearing. Please continue with your fifth issue, the governing of the people in the facility."

"I believe that part of restoring their dignity is allowing them to make decisions and to have viable input into the policies, activities, policing and supervision of their home. They are not animals that we just herd from one place to another. They need to rejoin society and have the means to reclaim the respect of the Portland community. I think that could be accomplished by having floor captains that would in turn be a member of a governing body, two members of which serve in an advisory capacity, um, that means that the executive director and the assistant would be a part of that governing body."

"Would they, the executive director and the assistant chair the governing body?"

"No, I feel that their role would be as advisors."

"Well, that sounds good, but some would say that you are letting the inmates run the show and in time the place would become a slum not too different from being on the street except that they would be fed and have shelter."

Angelina nodded. "I would agree that the wrong person or persons hired as the executive director and the assistant might allow that to occur. That is why I feel that you have to weigh very carefully who you hire." She paused with a convincing smile spreading across her face. "You can't go wrong by selecting me to fill the role as the executive director. I have the knowledge and the desire. I honestly cannot conceive of our plan failing."

The governor smiled. "You say our plan. That supposes that you should and will get the job?"

"I do. Let me ask you a question. Do you really think that there is anyone out there more qualified or ambitions to make our plan work than me?"

He smiled. "Talk to me about salary. If you were appointed to be the executive director what compensation would you expect?"

"I would want full dental and medical coverage in addition to expenses to cover my travel expenses should I be called away from the facility to attend meetings or conferences."

He frowned, raising his eyebrows. "Is that all?" Angelina nodded.

"That would make you almost the same as a volunteer."

Angelina smiled, shrugging her shoulders. "That is exactly what I would be, but I would be a volunteer with a commitment. I would work eight or more hours a day, five days a week, more if necessary. I would be under contract."

The governor smiled. "I guess that you don't need the money or you are just plain crazy."

Angelina smiled. "I think that you know that I am not crazy. Yes, I am very well situated financially as my husband, well, just let me say that we invested wisely during his playing career and now I don't need a supplemental income." She paused, lowered her head as if preparing to lead a charge through a barrier. When she again raised her head her eyes were narrowed and her jaw set with an air of determination. "Governor this is going to be a nonprofit operation. As such the public needs to see that the executive director is not just another political figure getting an outrageous salary."

"What are your thoughts about the salary of the assistant?"

"You and the legislature are the boss. He or she would have to negotiate their salary with you. However, the person that gets the job should not expect to earn a salary that is offensive to the general public. What is the going rate for a fully tenured teacher with fifteen years of experience these days in a school district such as Portland Public or a person holding an administrative assistant position in the district?"

The Governor nodded. "I suspect that it would be in the neighborhood of $60,000 -$120,000."

Angelina coughed, cleared her throat and then protested, "You suggest a salary range that is too broad. I would suggest that the range should be between sixty and seventy-five thousand."

The governor nodded. "Yes, yes indeed, you have really thought this out. Quite frankly Angelina, I have to say that I am impressed." He leaned back in his chair and closed his eyes. Momentarily he opened his eyes and looked directly into Angelina's eyes. "When I leave this meeting with you today, I am going to take at most a week to arrive at a decision. With that said I hope you know that I feel it prudent for you to go before the legislature to explain to them what I have heard today and get their approval for my recommendation."

Angelina offered, "I would expect that would be the case as we want the operation to be completely transparent. The person you hire should be able to pass a litmus test, so to speak, so that there is no hint of impropriety."

She paused. "Does that mean that you will be recommending me for the position?"

"I think that it is only fitting that you have input as to who the assistant will be."

Angelina cocked her head and frowned. "So what are you saying?"

"Do you want the job, because if you do, you are hired. Um, that of course is with legislative approval which I fully expect to obtain."

Gary, who had been present in the parallel universe, pumped his fist. *"Yes, yes by God Angelina, you are going to recover nicely. I sincerely doubt that you'll need me anymore, but I wouldn't object if I were allowed to stick around. I think that I will go to my computer and write you a message."*

Moments later Gary had finished writing his message.

You did good girl. Congratulations and know that I love you.

Sooner than the time it takes for an electron to move from one orbit to another inside the nucleus of an atom Gary was home. The Source greeted him as he returned with a cheery greeting, "Welcome back, Gary. Relax and observe. Before you know it I will be sending you on another journey."

"I am going somewhere?"

"Yes, that is according to the plan." The Source paused. "Gary, I have already explained that time has no meaning to me, but to you, you do have a bit of a wait. You have to wait for Angelina because she is going with you."

"How long will I have to wait?"

"That was a poor choice of words. Time, as you will recall, doesn't exist. I suppose you had too much exposure to that word on Earth."

Gary frowned. "I don't know how else to express it. Let me just say that I miss Angelina and hope she will be here soon."

The Source seemed to smile. "That's close enough. Just know that she will be here before you know it. Relax and enjoy the view." The Source paused. "I will tell you where you are going next when Angelina returns and she is with you." There was a long pause. Finally The Source began again. "I suppose that this is when I can revel to you about Angelina's return. Please know that she is but a short distance from you. As an electron in an atom changes orbits with no noticeable lapse in, your word, time, she will be here. You see, since I am everything she is at my fingertips, so to speak. Well, I'll reveal more about that later."

Gary nodded displaying apparent understanding even though his thoughts betrayed his outward display. *"I still don't get this absence of time and total reliance on distance. Relating Angelina's distance from me and the amount of time it will take her to rejoin me to the movement of electrons in an atom just doesn't make any sense. I suppose I have a lot of learning to do."*

The Source gruffly scolded, "Gary, Gary, Gary, you have so little faith. As I have told you the time, a poor choice of words, will come when what I have told you will make complete sense. Just be patient, observe and enjoy what you are about to experience."

Chapter Thirty-One
Who Are We

Who are we? Do you really know? Is all that we are displayed through the human body or is there more. What about the inner self? What is the soul or the spirit? Is it real? Are we real or are we just a dream. Maybe we are just the puppets that play on God's stage performing for the pleasure of The Source. Maybe we are just a reflection of The Source. Who know? I know that I don't. Do You?

Who was Angelina Crawford? Who was Angelina Mallon? Who was Gary Mallon? Who were Guy and Sue Crawford? What about Lance Crawford or Greg Mallon? Who were Fredrick and Claudia Mallon? Let us not forget Fredrick and Susan Mallon, Gary and Angelina's children. Was Angelina just the daughter of Guy and Sue Crawford? Maybe she was just the wife of Gary Mallon or perhaps merely the mother of Louis Fredrick and Susan Claudia Crawford. Sometimes people are so devoted to a single purpose, a single idea that they never expose the real "them" or consider their real "person" until they are alone on center stage and have the opportunity to do a solo.

It was a fact that Angelina loved Gary Mallon almost from their births. She loved him all of his life and pretty much was willing to take a back seat to his successes, placing on the back burner her goals. She also loved her children dearly, being devoted to their successes and not passing judgment on their failings. She was a real beauty, a lady that captured your attention whether she walked into a room for a close up view or was seen from a distance. Her blue eyes were the portholes to her soul and expressed deep meaning, love, devotion, and understanding. Her blonde hair never seemed to gray and highlighted her beautifully sculpted face. Her body was the envy of all women that met her and the focus of many a man's attention. She was loyal and loving. She was also talented. She loved to sing. She produced a sound that warmed a person's heart and soothed a person's nerves with her melodic voice, a voice that was so beautiful that at times it made a person want to cry when they heard it and then applaud until she responded to the demand for an encore when she had concluded. It was as though her audience was listening to a nightingale. She also played the piano. She didn't just play that instrument. She let her fingers waltz across the ivories to produce music that not only entertained her but all that were in her presence when she played. She was the real deal choosing to operate in the shadows like an undercover agent. Some might say that she was dependent. Many might even say that she was totally willing to cater to Gary's every need without question or objection. However, she was independent. Oh good Lord was she independent. Gary knew it and so did everyone who really knew her.

After Gary was killed she considered running for the Senate, but that thought gave way to her real ambition. She wanted to make a difference and she felt that the ideal starting place was to reach out to help the homeless. Thankfully she was introduced to a supportive Governor and later was able make a huge national impact with her humanistic, idealist, but realistic ideals and ideas.

Chapter Thirty-Two

Angelina's Story

Sometimes a person's story is not really told until they are gone and even perhaps those that were around them are gone. It takes time to gather and compile all of the information about their life. Those revelations used to be told via tales. Now the story of a person's life is told by biographies scripted by those who really knew them and by public records. Someone who was thought to be less than successful in life might be celebrated and honored as the truth about their life is known.

When Angelina and John Chamberlin took the reins of Humanity House, the plight of the homeless in Portland and too many places in the United States was deplorable, almost seemingly hopeless. They did not view the challenge they faced that way. To her and John, anything was possible if a workable strategy and adequate financial backing was in place. It also took undying energy and a commitment to that purpose.

To set the wheels in motion after being appointed to the position of executive director, Angelina hired John with the endorsement of the Governor and the legislature. In her notification meeting with the Governor, her appointment by the Governor and confirmed by the legislature as the executive director to head up the homeless program, she came armed with a proposal for a strategy of what to do if a homeless person did not conform to the requirements for admission to the homeless shelter.

After exchanging words of greeting to each other, Angelina began, "Thank you, thank you very much for trusting me to head up the homeless program. I am very excited and welcome the challenge. I am also very pleased that my selection of John Chamberlin to be my assistant was approved." She paused. "Sir, John and I have a name for the dwelling that the homeless will occupy. We think that it should be called Humanity House."

The Governor smiled and nodded. "I think that is a most appropriate name."

She continued, "Governor, I also have an idea as to what to do with the homeless residents who do not conform to the requirements for admission and continued living in Humanity House."

The Governor nodded. "Well, go on. Don't keep me in suspense. I have been pondering this issue. I have an idea, but I want to hear yours."

Angelina slowly began, "Well, we can't just throw out the homeless that violate our simple guidelines for admission and continued living in Harmony House because they would just return to the streets. In no time at all the public would see our program as a failure as the numbers of homeless returning to the streets increases as I am certain that it would. So, I propose that the homeless that we serve know right off the bat that failure to comply with our regulations will give us cause to remove them and place them in an encampment located on the Central Oregon Desert somewhere east of Bend. It would be a confined area that could be monitored. This would require gaining permission for the location of such an encampment. It would also require an enforcement team to ensure that the homeless do not destroy or trash the environment. That would involve not only some enforcement officers but an enclosure to that the homeless do not roam all over the Central Oregon desert and find their way into locations such as Bend, La Pine, Redmond, etc."

The governor nodded. "Playing devil's advocate I suppose I need to know how you propose that they would be fed and kept clean."

Angelina smiled. "There are agencies such as the Salvation Army in Portland that would provide the food from donations. It should be food that requires little or no cooking. It would be nutritious, but not require refrigeration. We would transport the food to them." She paused. "As for keeping them clean, I think that we would have to locate the encampment facility near a water source. I would need some help in this area." She paused. "I honestly believe that anyone that views the difference between living in Humanity House and being transported to the Oregon Desert would opt to stay at Humanity House and comply with our regulations. Governor, nobody, but nobody would remain on the streets of Portland boundaries. The homeless of Portland would choose to either live in Humanity House or the Oregon Desert."

The Governor nodded. "Again playing devil's advocate, I would ask what would prevent a homeless person that did not choose to comply with the regulations of Humanity House and did not want to go to the Oregon Desert from just stepping across the border into Gresham, Lake Oswego, Tigard, Wilsonville or other nearby communities."

"That is a good question. My answer is that we need to work with the city governments that border Portland to ensure that they will round up the homeless that gravitate to their area, offer them the opportunity to come to Humanity House, or transport them to the Central Oregon Desert. Eventually I believe that we will by example convince them to join our efforts and establish their own program that would be completely patterned after ours. We, I believe, have a goal of removing all homeless people from the streets of the communities in Oregon."

The Governor nodded. "Yes, I can see how it would work. I will endorse your plan and go to the legislature to apprise them of and petition them for approval to the alternative of living in Humanity House or like facilities that are instituted in Oregon. I honestly believe that this could be a win, win solution." He paused. "You have my blessing and support."

After her meeting with the Governor, she sought and received the support of Portland's Mayor, John Keeler and the Portland City Council. With their aid and the Governors persuasive persistence, she was able to obtain the property south and adjacent to the Tilikum Bridge as a donation. Finally, after the new building for the homeless had been completed, she convinced Mayor Keeler to use police personnel to round up the homeless located within the boundaries of the city and transport them to the Moda Center for a inaugural gathering that Angelina and John hoped would be a huge step towards transforming the lives of the homeless from street people to contributing citizens.

Just prior to the inaugural gathering of the homeless, Gary petitioned The Source with a very convincing proposal, "Source, I should like to return to Angelina. I believe that she needs a vote of confidence to move forward with her idea in a convincing manner."

The Source seemed to smile. After a brief pause, the voice directed, "Blink your eyes twice and you will be there. Blink once and you will return to me unless I feel you have overstayed your visit and have nothing more to do."

Gary blinked, and then he blinked again. Suddenly he was sitting in what used to be his and Angelina's office and at what used to be his desk in front of his computer. Angelina sat beside him seemingly in a quandary. He looked at her and then at his computer. *"Well, I'll be darned. I was there and now I am here. Time really doesn't matter. Now if I could only figure out the ability for me to be here and there as if I was always here or there. No matter, that will be a subject I will bring up at a later time with The Source."*

Gary activated the computer as he had done before and began to draft a message to Angelina. Moments later the message was sent.

Angelina reacted somewhat startled by the notification that she had a message. *"I wonder. No, it couldn't possibly be true. Oh well, I'll open the message and see what it is all about."*

The message read – You have the right idea about what to do with the homeless that do not adhere to the standards you have set for Humanity House. I believe in you, so go for it girl.

Angelina was completely confused and at a loss as to how the message had come to appear and from whence it had come. *"Could it be? No, that is impossible. Gary is dead. There is no way that he could be writing to me. Oh well, the message does confirm what I believe so I will go forward and make it work."*

After Humanity House was up and running she recalled that first gathering vividly. Facing the multitudes of homeless people surrounding her on the floor of the Moda Center where the Trailblazers played, the sight she saw was beyond horrific. The gathered mass of humanity wore clothing that was ragged and filthy. Men's faces were adorned with shaggy unkempt growths that resembled a patch of weeds. The women were only a bit more tidy but still unsightly. The state of their person was depressing as was the odor their bodies emitted. Most, if not all, had probably not had a bath for days and days and days. Their teeth, well, what was left of them were stained with gaps between them, the missing probably rotted from improper dental care.

It was a tough crowd. She could sense resistance and an attitude of, "So what are you going to try to force me to do now? What in the hell are we doing here? Why did the police round us up like cattle and bring us to this place?" She turned to John and muttered, "I believe that we have a real uphill battle facing us. They don't seem to want to be here. If the police weren't here I have no doubt that they would bolt and run for whence they came." She paused. "By the way, I have forgotten before now to set in motion another idea that I have to help these poor souls find a way back into society as a contributing member."

John nodded. "So, what is your idea? I hope that you do not plan to unveil it today."

Angelina shook her head. "No, I think that I have to get my idea cleared with Governor Hathaway first. However, just to keep you up to speed, I think the piece that we are missing is offering the people that come to us an opportunity to advance their education. I would imagine that some of these people need some more education to even be considered for a job."

John nodded. "Good idea, yes that is a good idea that we can discuss in detail at a later time." He paused and smiled. "Getting back to your apprehension about communicating effectively with these people, let me assure you that if anyone can convince these people that we are here to offer them an opportunity to reclaim their humanity and dignity, it would be you. Go give them hell."

Angelina smiled. "That is an interesting choice of words. I wonder if they haven't already experienced hell." She pleaded, "Please feel free to jump in any time. I hope that I don't stray off message and don't lose them before I get to the heart of the matter. By the way, when I am done I want you to address the issue of what they will experience should they choose not to adhere to our standards for admission and continued living at Humanity House."

John frowned. "Has the Governor given his approval?"

Angelina smiled, nodding. "Yes, he called me last night and gave me the go ahead, the green light. Apparently the legislature is completely behind the idea."

John nodded. "In that case, you can count on it. I will be glad to address that issue." He smiled. "Is there a reason that you are asking me to address that issue instead of tackling it yourself? Too many voices might confuse them."

Angelina nodded. "Yes, you are a man and can be viewed as an authority figure. If you tell them it will carry more punch than if I tell them." She smiled. "I think what we are going to do is play good cop, bad cop." She smiled. "I am sorry to put you in the position of playing bad cop."

John chuckled, catching the humor of her statement. "Angelina, just relax and put that lovely smile on your face. You will do just fine. I have your back and will do as you have asked."

Standing in the middle of the floor on the logo of the Blazers flanked by John Chamberlain, she looked all about her as she made a complete three hundred sixty degree turn to survey the crowd. Holding a sound powered phone that transported her soft, but determined melodic voice to the ears of the assembled, Angelina began, "You may ask why you are here. I can understand your confusion and perhaps even your disgust. You might feel somewhat threatened by the fact that the police gathered you up like livestock and brought you here and continue to stand guard. I suppose that if I were in your shoes I would feel the same way." She paused. "Well, let me assure you that you are not in trouble and you will not be asked to do anything that you don't want to do." She smiled, trying to assure the assembled that what she had to say was authentic. "Before I begin, if anyone that is here wants to leave now, please feel free to get up and leave. Nobody will stop you. In fact, someone will even give you a ride to where you came from if you decide to leave. However, if you do decide to leave you will come to regret it because we are offering you hope and a chance for a better life."

She stepped back letting her hand holding the microphone drop to her side and waited, again surveying the crowd as she made another complete revolution. Not a soul stirred other than to look around to see if anyone was about to take Angelina up on her offer. Finally a voice from somewhere in the gathering shouted, "Why would we leave before we hear what you have to say? So, get on with it. We don't have all day and quite frankly, my butt is getting tired of sitting on this hard floor."

Smiling, she again stepped forward and held the microphone near her mouth. Continuing, she replied, "Thank you for that, whoever you are. By the way, my name is Angelina Mallon." She smiled. Chuckling as she continued, "I guess I am a bit nervous. I should have introduced myself first. Oh well, if that is the only mistake I make while addressing you, it will be a miracle." She again paused. "We are offering you an opportunity to reclaim your humanity and dignity by offering you a place to live, a home if you will, with food to eat, an opportunity to wear clean clothing, and provide you a place to keep yourselves clean. If you choose to accept our offer, you will live in a place where you will have your own room that will afford you privacy and an ability to be alone if you so choose. If you don't want to live inside, there are provisions for you to live outside in a sheltered area with the same opportunities as those that choose to live inside." She paused. "Does anyone wish to leave now?" Again she stepped back, allowing her hand holding the microphone to drop to her side and waited while she again surveyed the audience. Nobody stirred.

"Well now", she said as she again stepped forward to speak. "You might ask what you have to do for this to happen to me, for me." She paused again. "The requirements are simple. You will be allowed to become a part of this new community, your community if you pledge to enter with the promise to make a commitment to not use drugs, agree to keep yourself clean and presentable, and to take part in governing yourself." She smiled nervously. "Damn, I am really nervous. Would you believe that I almost forgot to mention that if you are supposed to be on medication prescribed by a doctor, you must agree to stay on that medication?" She paused again. "I again ask if anyone wants to leave. If you do, please feel free to get up and go. I must remind you that if you do choose to leave you will regret it." Nobody stirred.

She glanced at John who smiled, nodding his approval.

"Now is the time for me to explain how the program works." She paused and looked around. "First of all we offer a facility that is huge and ideally located near the Tillicum Bridge on the waterfront. The place you will come to call home has fifteen floors. The lowest floor is what I will refer to as the food storage area, refrigeration area, and the place where your home's heating and cooling equipment is located. The next floor up is the laundry area and the equipment area where we keep the tools needed for repairs and the cleaning of your building. It also has a workout area for you to exercise. The next floor up, the ground floor will be where you will have your dining area, kitchen, our offices, and can be a meeting area, a lounging area, or a place for a social gathering for you and your friends or family. It is an area where you can greet people that you might know, that you want to invite for a visit, people that you not have had contact with for a long time." She paused and looked around the arena to observe the reaction of those assembled. What she saw were looks of disbelief with some of the gathered wiping away tears.

Angelina also wiped away a tear as she continued, "Here is the deal. On each of the next twelve floors there will be four apartments to house a family of three or more people. The other fourteen apartments will house one to two people. There will be a bathroom and shower facility for men and women on each of the top twelve floors that are separate so that you all can retain your modesty."

She stepped back, again letting her hand holding the microphone drop to her side. It was her ploy to set the tone for what she would say next. Then with an emphatic gesture she stepped forward and pledged, "I will not be your boss." Turning towards John and extending her arm towards him, she said, "Mr. Chamberlin will not be your boss. With our guidance and I stress guidance you will govern and supervise yourself. Each floor will have a floor captain that will be part of a governing committee. Mr. Chamberlin and I will serve as advisors to that committee. You will learn more about that later."

She turned towards John and inquired, "Do you have anything to add to what I have said so far?"

John shook his head, responding, "No, go ahead. You are doing just fine."

She stepped forward and in a less emphatic tone continued, "There will be opportunities for you to earn money by applying for and being accepted to do a variety of jobs such as kitchen work, waiting on tables, doing clean up, and doing laundry work. Those of you with the skill can secure a job to do maintenance or repair work. We will pay minimum wages for those jobs." She took a deep breath and then continued, "Let me tell you that the goal is to allow you to return to society as an employed and contributing member of the Portland community. Not all of you will return, but some of you will because you will be given the opportunity to do so if you have the desire and the ability to do so. Are there any question?"

A woman in the middle of the gathering stood. Angelina acknowledged her asking, "Please wait a moment and allow me to come to you with this microphone so that all of those gathered here can hear your question."

A moment later the lady asked, "Where do I sign up?"

Angelina laughed and gave the lady a huge hug. When she released the lady from her grip, she took the microphone and responded, "You all can sign up here and now. We will want to know your name, your social security number if you have one and your medical history if you have one. You will be given an identification card eventually, but you can begin to move in today as soon as you have been registered. By the way, all of your belongings that you want to bring with you can be transported with you to your new home. Obviously we cannot accept shopping carts, tarps, or items deemed to be junk by you and the people transporting you to your new home."

A man stood, waving his arms above his head. Angelina approached him with the microphone. He inquired, "What about my dog? Is he considered junk? Am I able to bring my dog with me?"

Angelina frowned. Taking back the mike from him, she turned towards John and said, "John that is something that we did not consider. What are your thoughts?"

A murmur arose from the assembled. Several voices were heard to say, "Here we go again. It will be just like always. We won't have any rights."

John waved his arms frantically as Angelina approached him with the microphone. After securing the microphone he began, "Please, please let me comment. Can I have your attention?" He held up his arms to encourage a return to order. When it was finally quiet, John continued, "Mrs. Mallon and I did not think about that when we developed the plan. The question just asked caught us a little bit off guard as we were more focused on considering what living in Humanity House would be like, how to make it your home."

The man spoke out again. "Right now the street is my home and my dog lives where I live."

Voices were heard to murmur, "Right on, who wants to go to that fancy place if I can't take my dog."

John turned towards Angelina and inquired, "Do you see a reason why they can't bring a pet such as a dog or cat with them?"

Angelina shook her head responding, "I think that would be fine as long as we are talking about one pet and those that bring the pet with them are willing to be completely responsible for the pet by cleaning up after it and making sure that it does not disrupt the community."

John nodded and offered, "You heard her. It is okay to bring one pet with you. Feeding your pet does bring up an issue we did not consider. I think that this might be one of the first things that the governing council can discuss after you are all moved in and the floor captains have been chosen by the members of your floor." John paused. "There is one more very important thing that you need to know. If you do not adhere to, follow our policies as stated here today, you will be turned out of Humanity House and sent to an encampment in Central Oregon. You will not be allowed to return to the streets of Portland. The communities surrounding Portland will not allow you to live on their streets either."

There was complete silence at first followed by a faint murmur of the assembled. Finally a man rose, raising his hand. John approached him and handed the microphone to him. The man began, "My name is John. Most of you here know me or have heard of me. You know me to be a straight shooter. I don't bull shit around. I think that what I have heard today is awesome. I honestly feel that anyone that doesn't agree to the terms set forth by, um, whatever their names is just plain crazy. I plan to stay. All those assembled nodded their head in approval and began to clap. Soon, the applause turned to cheers. At that moment, Angelina and John had won them over. They were on their way.

Chapter Thirty-Three

Wearing Another Hat

In the world of work we all wear a hat. The hat might be that of a laborer or it could be the hat of a supervisor. Trying to wear more than one hat is difficult if not impossible if you want to be efficient and effective.

Gary was so proud watching Angelina tame an uneasy crowd, completely winning them over. Before returning to the other place he sent her another message. It read – You did good girl. You are on you way.

Gary blinked. Now he was home and was most curious about how he was able to move from place to place as though he had always been at the new place even though he wasn't at the place but where he had been. Questioning The Source, he asked, "I am not certain that I know how I get from here to there as though I have always been there even though I have been here."

The Source replied, "Do you realize how you used the computer to communicate with Angelina?"

"Yes, I focused all of my thoughts on making the keys on the computer do what I wanted them to do. My mind or directed thoughts acted as my fingers used to when I used the computer."

The Source replied, "Very good Gary. You are starting to get the idea, but realize that even before it was your mind that made your fingers do the work. Mind is everything. Perhaps you are starting to realize that I am the universal mind."

Gary frowned. "You mean that I move from place to place by just letting my mind serve as my vehicle of transportation?"

The Source seemed to smile. "Now is the time to return to watching Angelina."

Transitioning the homeless from their street environment, establishing the government and the supervision of their living environment went very smoothly, surprisingly so. There were many success stories. Families that had been forced to the streets by the loss of a job and subsequent inability to make rent or mortgage payments were able to clean up and find jobs. After a while on their new jobs, they were able to leave Humanity House and return to society as a contributing member with the ability to afford their own home off the street. The city of Portland helped with the transition by offering affordable low cost housing to those ready to leave Humanity House.

An important piece of successfully transitioning some of the residents back into society was an educational offering. Thanks to Portland State University's educational department, they offered those desiring to expand their education or complete high school course work to earn a diploma some courses that were offered at Humanity House. The teachers were students at PSU who were working towards being certified teachers. This program supplemented their student teaching experience. The requirement for the PSU students to enter the program was to commit to a full year's teaching assignment. PSU called the program Intern Teaching an option to serving a term of student teaching.

The word spread. Soon, Angelina was in constant demand to speak to groups in other communities and other states about the success of Humanity House, how it worked, and how it came into being. Gradually she was forced to spend more and more time away from the now financially self-sustainable facility for the homeless to speak to interested groups. She was forced to place more and more of the daily routine on John's plate. No longer was he merely her assistant. He was, in all practicality, in charge and forced to wear two hats.

The phone rang in Angelina's office. Picking up the phone she answered, "Hello?"

A familiar voice, the newly elected Governor Sandra Johnson, said, "Angelina, this is Sandra Johnson."

"Hello Governor Johnson. What can I do for you?"

"Maybe it isn't what you can do for me, but what I can do for you. Would you have a free moment to come to Salem to meet with me?"

"I always have time for you Sandra. What will we be discussing?" "Let us just say that the topic will be Humanity House and so much more. Maybe a more accurate topic would be hats. Would tomorrow at 1:00 work for you?"

"Yes, that will work just fine for me, Sandra. I will see you tomorrow."

After hanging up the telephone, Angelina sat at her desk reflecting on what she had just heard. *"I have known Sandra since she became the Governor a little over two years ago and have always known her to be a straight shooter. She is as honest as the day is long and very, very short on bull shit."* She smiled. *"If I were a man I would be chasing her all over the country. She is knockdown gorgeous and has a fantastic body. I wonder why she is still single."* She chuckled. *"Come on Angelina, the only thing that matters here is what she has to talk to me about. You don't suppose…."*

She got up from her desk and strode into John's office. "John, I have to be in Salem tomorrow to meet with the Governor. I think that something really big is coming down the pike. I would just like to make you aware that you might be changing titles and roles and looking for an assistant." She smiled. "This might just be what I had hoped for years ago when we started Humanity House. I will call you after the meeting with the Governor has concluded."

In the Governor Johnson's office, Sandra began, "Angelina, you are probably aware that right now you and your program for the homeless are gaining more and more national recognition and support each passing day. In fact, it is becoming so popular that, well, the President of the United States wants to meet with you."

Angelina's excitement could not be contained. Clapping her hands together in an overt display of excitement she shouted, "Yes, yes, yes! This is the best! This is the news I have been hoping for and waiting to hear since, well, since Humanity House came into existence or even maybe before when I was formulating ideas as to how I could help the homeless. At the national level we can do so much that is just starting to gain momentum in Portland and across the state. We have established strong roots in Portland,

Salem, Lincoln City, Bend, and Medford as you well know. Many other towns and cities across Oregon are buying into the concept."

The Governor smiled. "Yes that you have. Humanity House is becoming a household word at those sites." She nodded. "Ah yes, yes it could, um, make a national impact as it already has the attention of the governors of many other states. I think that we have to consider what might happen should you get an offer that you can't refuse." She chuckled at the reference to "The Godfather". If what happens occurs as I believe it will, who would you recommend to replace you?"

"Is there even a doubt in your mind? John Chamberlin has been wearing two hats all too long. It is time that he be given the reigns and have an assistant. It is time that Humanity House has leadership that is there all the time. In my opinion, John is the only person to be considered to replace me. Um, of course that is if I am offered the position by the President."

The Governor smiled. "Nothing is certain in this life, but the President indicated to me that it was all but a done deal." Sandra paused. "How long have you been the head of Humanity House?"

"Since its beginning, um, it's been fifteen years come next month." "How old are you?"

Angelina frowned. "Don't you know that you aren't supposed to ask a lady how old she is?" She smiled. "I am 58 and still single." She paused, dropping her head. "I plan to stay that way. I have an appointment to keep. Someone very, very special is waiting for me."

The Governor frowned. "I don't think that I need to ask you for a clarification. I probably wouldn't understand." She hesitated, and then continued. "So, the President will contact you. We are going to miss you."

Time on earth passes quickly, but where Gary was it didn't exist. A blink of the eye could represent a century, a little less or more on Earth. How is a lifetime measured? Certainly the important thing is not how long, but the accomplishments and the impact made.

Angelina made that impact. Humanity House, a name used for all of the homeless homes established across the nation was being received with enthusiasm. Cities impacted with homeless issues were starting to realize that homelessness was an issue that could not be ignored. It could be resolved.

When the unfortunate were reintroduced to an opportunity to again rejoin society in a positive manner it was in reality a win, win solution.

Gary so enjoyed watching Angelina's efforts take root and prosper. He missed her, but for a reason that he did not fully comprehend her absence from his life was similar to the blink of an eye.

During one of those blinks of an eye, he was able to observe the meeting that took place between Angelina and the President of the United States. Once it had been agreed that she would receive the appointment to head up the Humanity House homeless program, the discussion moved on to where Angelina would have her headquarters.

President Andale peered over the top of her glasses, folded her hands and began, "I assume that you will be okay with setting up shop, um, locating your headquarters here in Washington D.C."

Angelia frowned. "Actually Madam President, I was thinking about locating my headquarters in Oregon, specifically at or near Portland, Oregon."

The President's mouth opened as if to say, "Are you kidding me?" After a significant pause, President Johnson asked, "This is a bit of a surprise. Would you care to share your reasoning?"

Observing the President's momentary state of shock, Angelina's mind framed an image of the stately lady sitting in front of her. *"The President appears to be a very powerful lady. When she looks at me over the top of her glasses it sort of reminds me of my seventh grade teacher, Miss Peacock. Holy crap, she was a monster. You didn't dare cross her for fear of receiving one of those menacing looks that gave students when they were even a little bit out of order. The President is going to be a tough nut to crack."*

Angelina nodded. "Well, I know that my thoughts might be or seem odd, but I think that it is important to consider the following. Some might ask where is home? I would say that home is where the heart is. A person's heart, my heart isn't always located in a specific geographical location as the place where a person resides is merely an address. The heart might be somewhere else."

The President frowned. "Could you be a little more specific? I'm not certain that you have answered my question. Then again, perhaps I just don't understand fully what you are saying."

Angelina smiled. "President Andale, I am not a politician. Washington D.C. for me would be a place where I just would have an address, a location. My heart would still be in Oregon. As such, I am not certain that my efforts would be totally directed or completely focused on promoting Harmony House throughout the country. I might fall short of your expectations."

"Go on, you have my ear."

"Well, it is like this. I was born and raised in Oregon. Other than going to college in California and spending time in Seattle during my late husband's baseball seasons, my heart was in Oregon. My children live in Oregon. My friends live in Oregon. Have you ever been to Oregon?"

"No, I can't say that I have. My home is in Florida." Angelina smiled. "Where is your heart?"

President Andale nodded. "My heart is in Florida. I miss it so."

"That is exactly how I feel! Because of the job that you were elected to, you are forced to live in Washington D.C. I am not being elected to a positon. My position because of its newness and lack of tradition really has no permanent address. Actually, the headquarters for Harmony House could be anywhere. When my time with Harmony House passes, the headquarters could easily be located elsewhere. After all, where it is located is just an address. This place needs a heart at that address."

"Please continue."

"Well, let me tell you why I love Oregon and want to locate the headquarters there. Oregon is very diverse. We have the coast people, the valley people, the Eastern Oregon People, and the Southern Oregon People. All of those different cultures are different and yet they are all contained within the boundaries of a small state. We have the desert, the Pacific Ocean, the Cascade Mountains, the high lakes, the lushness of the valley, and, well, in my opinion we have it all. Have you ever seen a picture of Mt. Hood, Mt. St. Helens or Mt. Jefferson?"

"Of course, but what has that to do with the price of cottage cheese?"

"Well, those mountains are completely different, but they are so incredibly beautiful, beautiful in different ways. Looking at them brings me such joy. Watching the Columbia River rush towards the sea inspires me. Seeing all of the beautiful bridges in Portland enthralls me. Living in Lake Oswego allows me to live near a large city, but it also allows me to live in the quiet solitude of a town void of the constant hub bub of a big city. It is home. It is my home, and that is where I want the headquarters to be located. That is where my heart is."

The President nodded. "You present an interesting case in support of your proposal. What if I said that you had to locate the headquarters in Washington D.C.?"

Angelina's eyes started to gloss over, tears welling up, preparing to leak down her cheeks. "I have wanted the position you have offered me most of my life. As badly as I want to serve and head Harmony House nationally, I would have to respectfully decline and remain in Oregon as the head of Harmony House for the State of Oregon."

The President grinned. "You are tough Angelina. You are one tough lady. You would be an excellent poker player. I can now see why Harmony House has been so successful." She paused. If you promise to call me Teresa from now on when we talk, I will submit to your demand. The national headquarters of Harmony House will be located in Portland, or is it Lake Oswego where you want to hang your shingle?"

Madam President, um, Teresa, I am perfectly okay to have the national headquarters located in Portland." She shrugged. "It is only a few minutes' drive from Portland to Lake Oswego."

"Okay then, your next task is to prepare a budget for this positon which I assume will be the cost of the headquarters, staff, your salary, medical benefits, and your travel expenses. You know that you will be doing a lot of traveling, don't you?"

"Teresa, I am fully aware that I will be on the road or in the air a lot. By the way, I will not be asking for a salary. This is a non-profit organization and as such I will not want or require a salary. What you have asked me to prepare in the budget other than a salary, will take care of my needs."

"Nonsense, your salary will be set at $100,000 and that is my final offer."

Chapter Thirty-Four

Going Home

Going home can be an exhilarating experience, something to really look forward to as you prepare to return. The reunion with loved ones is exciting, fun, and long anticipated. What happens when going home as it relates to human kind is unexpected and certainly not planned for as you would plan for a get together with friends, for a family reunion, for a visit to your parent's home, or for a visit you your children's home after they have left the nest. As far as our reality knows what is going home all about? Is it the end or the time to take another journey?

Gary's conversation with The Source prior to returning to help Angelina was very revealing. As it was explained to him by The Source, his return was akin to having never left because as he was of The Source and in reality he was a part of The Source. As such, even though he had been on Earth, he really had never been away from The Source because The Source was everywhere and encompassed everything.

The Source, in its usual form asked Gary to tell how far it was from one place in the vastness of everything to another. Specifically the Source asked Gary to tell how far it was from one designated point to another based on what was pointed out for him to consider. Gary pondered the question for moment and then replied, "I suppose that since you are everything, undefined, and never ending the distance would be very hard for me to estimate. I suppose my best answer would be, I don't know."

"Very good, Gary, you are starting to get the idea. Now watch very carefully."

The two points that The Source had pointed out suddenly closed so that they were as one.

"Now how far apart are the points I have pointed out?"

Gary nodded his head in contemplation. "Well, they appear to not be any distance apart at all."

The Source continued, "Now think of your experience on Earth. The distance between the Moon and Earth was thousands of miles as you came to know it, correct?"

Gary nodded.

"In your mind, the distance between the two celestial bodies just observed was very close as though they were touching. Distance is relative. To me, it is as close or as far as I want it to be. Since everything is of me then what might be, in the terms you learned of on Earth, celestial bodies could be thousands and thousands of light years apart. However, as I have pointed out to you they could also be next to each other, touching. That is because everything is of me and I can make things as big or small as I choose. I can transport you from one place to another as though you have always been at the place where you are going."

Gary nodded. "So, what has this to do with what is coming next?" "Good question. You and Angelina, when she returns, are going to a place that by definition on Earth is very, very far away. However, as I brought the two points together that I pointed out to you that will be how you will experience your travels to your new home. As you fold a piece of paper on Earth and poke a hole in the folded paper with a pin, that is how I can enable you to go from one celestial body to another. It will be as though, in your words, no time as elapsed." The source paused. "Gary, on Earth time is something that is used to measure how long it takes to go from one place to another. Perhaps it is best if I say that since everything is of me, and just as I can show you that two distinct points located in space can become one, so too can that be the way things, in what you call the Universe or all of the many Galaxies, be reached. You describe the distance between far off objects in terms of light years. As you will learn as your travels continue, although distance is relevant, it can become insignificant by employing one of my many tricks. So, all of the many celestial bodies are in a sense very close and can be thought of as relatives or they can be considered to be very far apart and not related at all. It is all a matter of how the mind perceives it. I am giving you the gift of being able to perceive the mysteries of life and what I have created."

Gary inquired, "When will Angelina return?"

"She will be here before you can snap your fingers or blink an eye." The Source paused. "Gary I want you to observe what is about to happen and I believe that you will better understand what I have been trying to explain."

Gary nodded, watching a scene on Earth unfold. He blinked.

Two events occurred as though they occurred simultaneously. First, he noticed Angelina's arrival at one of the Humanity House sites, a site located in Dallas, Texas. Inside the building she was greeted by the executive director of the Dallas, Texas Humanity House. As their hands met in an introductory greeting a huge ball of fire enveloped the entire scene. He shook his head in disbelief as he saw Angelina shaking the hand of the executive director of Humanity House in Dallas, Texas one moment and at that very moment she was standing beside him.

He was afraid to blink again. He didn't want Angelina to leave.

Chapter Thirty-Five

Another Journey

A trip, a journey or a visit usually begins and comes to an end. But does it? Maybe it is only a part of a continuum that never ends. Perhaps until we really come to know The Source by becoming a part The Source of everything, all we will know is there appears to be a beginning and an end. You might ask, "Is there really and end? Is there really a beginning? Maybe those questions will be answered when we come to know The Source and become a part of The Source.

Gary was stunned. Angelina was beside him as though she had never left.

At Angelina's first sight of Gary, she frowned, displaying confusion. "Gary, oh my God, is it really you?" Not waiting for a response she rushed towards him, falling into his arms. "Oh how I have missed you. I love you so much."

Gary chuckled. "It is me, and I have missed you too. I love you. I never stopped loving you." He smiled. "Have I changed much?"

"No, you look the same since…, um, have I?? She frowned. "Where am I? What is going on? Would you please tell me what has happened? Am I…?"

Gary smiled. "You have not changed a bit. You are still as beautiful as when I left you." He paused before beginning again. "You want to know if I really left you." He waited for her mind to catch up. "You have returned to The Source. I have been waiting for you. I guess you might say that you are in a place that the people on Earth call Heaven. Personally, I like to think of it as a station where we get passes to go onward to different places. As they say on Earth, I died and left you. Now you have died and have rejoined me. We have returned to The Source as promised." He smiled. "You don't have the perspective that I do, but just know that for you and me it is though we have never left The Source. We were there and now we are here and it all occurred in the blink of an eye." He paused, looking at her affectionately as he kissed her on the forehead. "I love you. I have always loved you and I always will. You might say that I have loved you since and until the twelfth of never, and that is a long, long journey." He grinned. "Um, remember, time does not matter or exist here."

Angelina looked up longingly into his eyes. "I don't understand."

Gary smiled. "You will or at least you will have a clearer understanding of what has happened. The Source will explain it all to you."

Angelina nodded. "Am I still your wife?"

"Yes, my darling, forever and ever if that is what you want and how you feel."

She nodded her head. "I do, oh, Gary, I do. I have missed you so much. By the way, I didn't remarry. I was always faithful to you. There was never anyone but you."

Gary nodded. "I know. I have been watching your life unfold."

Her eyes twinkled. "So, it was you. You were with me when I needed you the most."

Gary nodded. "I don't know how, but, yes, I was with you." He paused. "For what it's worth, you did good Angelina. No, you did better than good. You made a difference and I am so proud of you." He placed his hands on her shoulders and looked into her eyes. "So, are you ready?"

"Am I ready for what?"

"The Source wants to talk to us."

While the reunion was taking place, The Source had surrounded them, evident, but not noticed because of the emotional reunion. Suddenly, a strong powerful voice boomed, "Welcome home, Angelina. You have been missed, and you did very well on your first journey. Just know that even though your dream differed a bit from Gary's, what you did made a difference. The United States is similar to a child going through the "terrible two's". That nation, though powerful, abused its power and became selfish, self- centered and at times unruly. What you did was to begin a process of self-awareness that will lead them to realize that they must take care of their own, be helpful to others, but not expect that they can always have their own way. They must realize that their way isn't the best way for all the peoples on Earth. The program you established for the homeless is a giant step forward in that direction. Others that follow you will need to continue to lead by example. Your efforts will eventually spread to the rest of the world you left on Earth."

Angelina nodded. "What has happened to me?

The Source seemed to smile although the form surrounding Gary and Angelina had no distinctive shape or form. "I will explain it to you as I did to Gary when he returned." There was a pause. "If you recall, scientists on Earth discovered that when they looked at an atom they were able to notice electrons orbiting inside the atom. They also noticed that the electrons changed orbits with no time, your word on Earth, elapsing as the electrons moved from one orbit to another. It was as though they were there and then here. It was though they had always occupied their original orbit or their new orbit. That is what happened to you."

"You mean that I was on Earth and then here as though I never left this place?"

"You have the idea. Now let me demonstrate."

Suddenly Angelina was able to see herself entering Humanity House in Dallas, Texas, being greeted by the executive director, shaking hands with him, and then observing a huge ball of fire enveloping the entire scene. All the while she was standing beside Gary in the presence of The Source.

"Wow! That or this is amazing." She paused. "So, what is next?"

A rumbling sound suddenly enveloped them, not dissimilar to the massive thunder storms they had experienced on Earth. There was a powerful rush of wind, seemingly propelling them through space. As they moved forward their bodies gradually changed from a mature adult form to that of a teenager and then gradually into a young boy and young girl. In the distance, or so it seemed, they heard the volume of the booming voice gradually fade as it said, "Now is the time for you to begin another journey, a voyage to a different place. Your parents are waiting for you."

In unison Gary and Angelina asked, "Where are we going?"

The indescribable shape that had surrounded them seemed to point in a direction ahead of the direction they appeared to going. "In terms of Earth's location it is out there, far, far away from Earth, but still with and of me. Where you are going you will still be of me, but you will have another life to live. Your new lives will be on a planet that is exactly like your first home, Earth." The Source paused. It was almost as if The Source was sensing that what had been said was not being understood. Continuing, the Source explained, "Your new home is located in a solar system in another galaxy. It is in a sense a reflection of Earth. Earthlings could never reach that place in their lifetime, a poor choice of words, with the technology they now possess. To get there would be much like thinking about how a pin might pass through a piece of folded paper. In the blink of an eye you will pass through one galaxy into another. That is the beauty of my creation. It has no limits, no barriers. There is only infinite space filled with an infinite number of galaxies, solar systems, suns, planets, comets and moons. You see, I am the way, the path to everything."

Gary shook his head displaying confusion. "I suppose I get it, but..." "Not to worry Gary. As you experience journey after journey, it will become clearer, more understandable."

Angelina nodded inquiring, "Does that mean that Gary and I will be a reflection of who we were when we were on Earth or who we are now? Will we still be together?"

"That is close enough, and yes. Just know that you will continue to grow in your ability to love and form great relationships. Your knowledge will expand as you continue to learn. You might say that you have only begun your total life's voyage that will never end. You might think of what you have experienced as being similar to being in Preschool or Kindergarten. You have many grades to conquer and pass through." The Source paused. "As with your last journey, you will again return to me as you are of me. Eventually you will become me even though you already are me in a sense me." The source paused. "Think of it this way. All matter is made up of atoms which are part of molecules. Think of yourselves as an atom, a part of a molecule which is a part of me."

Angelina nodded and then inquired, "What about our parents? You say that they are waiting for us?"

The Source responded, "Yes, you will be with them again. They have missed you as you have them. However, their feelings of missing you are more like the joy of experiencing the formation of a new life. That experience will be the joy they will experience with your births."

As Gary and Angelina looked towards where The Source seemed to point, the volume of The Source's voice began to fade away. A faint voice, neither masculine nor feminine said, "Farewell for now my children. I will always be with you. I will see you again when you return to me. Enjoy your journey."

Suddenly there was the familiar sound of a newborn, the familiar birth cry. Adjacent to that hospital room where the first birth cry was heard another familiar sound was heard as another birth cry was heard. The time had come for Gary and Angelina to rejoin their parents. Their lives were about to begin anew.

The End

Epilogue

The reality we know or have known is based upon what we experienced at that moment or this moment. The beginning of life has its onset at conception. Within the comfort of the womb the soon to be newborn experiences stimulus while probably recalling nothing. The birth cry I suppose is a bit traumatic to the newborn but joyful to the expectant parents. I ask, is that where it all began or was there really a beginning elsewhere in a place that none of us have experienced as we can recall or know at this time. Was a course of our lives set in motion with only self-determination and our ability to think directing the path we will travel or was there a pre- determination of that final destination?

I am not a religious man, rather a man of faith and beliefs. Call me spiritual. What are my beliefs? To that question, I might respond, "What is religion other than a man-made concept or idea?" It is not good or bad. Rather it is an ongoing force that has been responsible for many conflicts, yet so many wonderful occurrences. People describe themselves as atheists, agnostics, Christians, Buddhists, people of the Islamic faith, Catholics, Methodists, people of the Jewish faith, Mormons and too many other ideologies to mention here. The important thing is that everyone believes in something and is to a certain degree tolerant of the beliefs of others as long as those beliefs are not a radical belief that is intended to inflict harm onto others. Even an atheist, a believer in science or "this is all there is" person believes in something.

I continue to question and ask questions about who I am, where I came from and where I am going. Have I been living a dream, or is life as simple as that portrayed by the different religions? Does life cease when we move from the existence we are now experiencing in this life or does it continue? Does it ever end? What is life all about? Are we real or just an illusion? Is there one God, one Source? What is the meaning of what we experience? How much more is there to learn? Are we ready for more of the mystery of life to be revealed to us? Is there one son of God? Maybe we are all sons or daughters of God? Maybe the difference between Jesus and you and me is that we are not devine.

We are bound by tradition, by myth, superstition, and knowledge passed down by word of mouth that has evolved into a written form. This written form has been translated many times. Some written works have disappeared or been deleted while still others find their way into our possession. The Dead Sea Scrolls are a prime example.

Is loving, forming wonderful relationships, and continuing to learn enough or is there more? Is there ever an end to this wondrous mystery we call life? Who am I and who are you? Where am I from and where am I going? Do you have the answer? Do you think that you know, or are you willing to admit that you just do not know?

I am content to say that I don't know, but in a parallel breath I choose to indicate that not knowing is not good enough. I shall continue to question and to wonder, but I will never stop believing that this is not all that there is. I will keep wondering and searching. I believe that there is more. It might occur in a place called Heaven, but maybe it will be more than that as we move towards becoming completely united with God or The Source. I just have to take solace in believing that I will experience more and know that I will rejoice in experiencing that which is beyond and never ending.

I have questioned the meaning of life since I was old enough to wonder. Before I began to wonder, to question, I was influence by the teachings that I experienced in Sunday school. When those teachings appeared to always point to two extremes, good and evil as portrayed by going to Heaven or going to Hell, I began to wonder. Is there really a place called Heaven? What about Hell? If it exists, where is it? If it exists, where is Heaven?

I used to lie on the driveway of my home somewhere around the time I was preparing to go to college. On a wonderful, warm summer night, I reveled in the beauty that I saw as I looked upward into the heavens. All of those twinkling lights that appeared were so abundant, so far away, yet so real. "What is out there", I asked? "Is there more? Does it ever end? Who or what is responsible for all of this wonderment? Will we ever be allowed to know the truth, the real meaning of all of this?"

Have I asked fair questions or do you feel that I have lost my way and am a man of no faith, no beliefs or perhaps distorted beliefs?

I have asked the questions posed previously, and here is my answer. I believe. I believe there is more. I don't know what the God figure is about, but whatever it is, it is so powerful, so loving, so meaningful, and so infinite that I don't have adequate words to describe it. I am not content to just read a book that many deem holy. I am not content to merely follow the herd in a direction that leads to a place that nobody really knows any more about than I do. I believe in love. I believe in forming good and lasting relationships. I believe in the need to continue to learn. What do you believe?

My book is a connection of spirituality, political thoughts, and coming of life as a young man and woman experience life in this world with the promise that there is more, a return to The Source. This man experiences an athletic endeavor and gradually seeks a life of service in politics. The woman dedicates her life to loving her husband, her family, and then giving back to the homeless issue. This book is about the Wonderment of Life.

www.ingramcontent.com/pod-product-compliance
Lightning Source LLC
Chambersburg PA
CBHW060454030426
42337CB00015B/1590